GENDER AND SEXUALITY IN THE EUROPEAN MEDIA

This edited collection brings together original empirical and theoretical insights into the complex set of relations which exist between age, gender, sexualities and the media in Europe.

This book investigates how engagements with media reflect people's constructions and understandings of gender in society, as well as articulations of age in relation to gender and sexuality. The chapters also explore the ways in which negotiations of gender and sexuality inform people's practices with media, and not least how mediated representations may reinforce or challenge social hierarchies based on differences of gender, sexual orientation and age. In doing so, the book showcases new and innovative research at the forefront of media and communication practice and theory. Including contributions from both established and early career scholars across Europe, it engages with a wide range of hotly debated topics within the context of gender, sexuality and the media, informing academic, public and policy agendas.

This collection will be of interest to students and researchers in gender studies, media studies, film and television, cultural studies, sexuality, ageing, sociology and education.

Cosimo Marco Scarcelli is Assistant Professor at FISPPA, University of Padua. His research interests deal with digital media with a focus on young people, intimacy, gender, sexuality, digital literacy and media education. He is chair of the Gender and Communication section of ECREA.

Despina Chronaki is Adjunct Lecturer at the National and Kapodistrian University of Athens and the Hellenic Open University (MA in Journalism Studies). Her research focuses on audiences of popular culture, children's experiences with media, ethics and porn studies.

Sara De Vuyst is Postdoctoral Researcher in the Department of Languages and Cultures at Ghent University. Her research interests are feminist media studies, issues of gender, sexuality and ageing, and gender inequality in journalism. She is vice-chair of the ECREA Gender and Communication section.

Sergio Villanueva Baselga is Assistant Professor at the University of Barcelona. His research focuses on the relationship between media and health identities, stigma and resilience, considering that media, film and culture are part of the social determinants of health. He is vice-chair of the Film Studies section of ECREA.

ROUTLEDGE STUDIES IN EUROPEAN COMMUNICATION RESEARCH AND EDUCATION

Edited by Ilija Tomanić Trivundža
University of Ljubljana, Slovenia
Christina Holtz-Bacha
Friedrich-Alexander University Erlangen-Nurnberg, Germany
Galina Miazhevich
Cardiff University, UK

Series Advisory Board: Nico Carpentier, François Heinderyckx,
Robert Picard and Jan Servaes

https://www.routledge.com/Routledge-Studies-in-European-Communication-Research-and-Education/book-series/ECREA

Published in association with the European Communication Research and Education Association – ECREA (www.ecrea.eu), books in the series make a major contribution to the theory, research, practice and/or policy literature. They are European in scope and represent a diversity of perspectives. Book proposals are refereed.

For a full list of titles in this series, please visit www.routledge.com.

13. (Mis)Understanding Political Participation
Digital Practices, New Forms of Participation and the Renewal of Democracy
Edited by Jeffrey Wimmer, Cornelia Wallner, Rainer Winter, and Karoline Oelsner

14. Radio Audiences and Participation in the Age of Network Society
Edited by Tiziano Bonini and Belén Monclús

15. Media Accountability in the Era of Post-Truth Politics
European Challenges and Perspectives
Edited by Tobias Eberwein, Susanne Fengler and Matthias Karmasin

16. Gender and Sexuality in the European Media
Exploring Different Contexts Through Conceptualisations of Age
Edited by Cosimo Marco Scarcelli, Despina Chronaki, Sara De Vuyst and Sergio Villanueva Baselga

GENDER AND SEXUALITY IN THE EUROPEAN MEDIA

Exploring Different Contexts Through Conceptualisations of Age

Edited by Cosimo Marco Scarcelli, Despina Chronaki, Sara De Vuyst and Sergio Villanueva Baselga

Routledge
Taylor & Francis Group

LONDON AND NEW YORK

ecrea | European Communication Research and Education Association

First published 2021
by Routledge
2 Park Square, Milton Park, Abingdon, Oxon OX14 4RN

and by Routledge
52 Vanderbilt Avenue, New York, NY 10017

Routledge is an imprint of the Taylor & Francis Group, an informa business

British Library Cataloguing-in-Publication Data
A catalogue record for this book is available from the British Library

Library of Congress Cataloging-in-Publication Data
Names: Scarcelli, Cosimo Marco, editor. | Chronaki, Despina, editor. |
De Vuyst, Sara, editor. | Villanueva Baselga, Sergio, editor.
Title: Gender and sexuality in the European media : exploring different contexts through conceptualisations of age / edited by Cosimo Marco Scarcelli, Despina Chronaki, Sara De Vuyst & Sergio Villanueva Baselga.
Description: Abingdon, Oxon ; New York : Routledge, 2021. |
Series: Routledge studies in European communication research
and education; 16 | Includes bibliographical references and index.
Identifiers: LCCN 2020050305 (print) | LCCN 2020050306 (ebook) |
ISBN 9780367407322 (hardback) | ISBN 9780367407346 (paperback) |
ISBN 9780367808792 (ebook)
Subjects: LCSH: Sex role in mass media.--Europe. |
Sex in mass media--Europe. | Gender identity in mass media--Europe. |
Older people in mass media.--Europe.
Classification: LCC P96.S52 E97 2021 (print) | LCC P96.S52 (ebook) |
DDC 302.230538--dc23
LC record available at https://lccn.loc.gov/2020050305
LC ebook record available at https://lccn.loc.gov/2020050306

ISBN: 978-0-367-40732-2 (hbk)
ISBN: 978-0-367-40734-6 (pbk)
ISBN: 978-0-367-80879-2 (ebk)

Typeset in Bembo
by Taylor & Francis Books

CONTENTS

List of illustrations   *vii*

List of contributors   *viii*

Editors' introduction   1
Sara De Vuyst, Despina Chronaki, Cosimo Marco Scarcelli and
Sergio Villanueva Baselga

PART I
Young people, sexuality and gender performance: Texts
and audiences   **9**

1 Feminist YouTubers in Spain: A public space for building
  resistance   11
  Núria Araüna, Iolanda Tortajada and Cilia Willem

2 Un/fit for young viewers: LGBT+ representation in Flemish
  and Irish children's television   24
  Florian Vanlee and Páraic Kerrigan

3 Breaking the silence: Young people, sex information and the
  internet in Italy and Portugal   41
  Daniel Cardoso and Cosimo Marco Scarcelli

4 COVID-19 pandemic and discourses of anxiety about
  childhood sexuality in digital spaces   58
  Despina Chronaki

PART II
Adults, sexuality, gender and the media in research perspective 73

5 HIV-related stigma in the European cinema: Conflictive representations of a cultural trauma 75
Sergio Villanueva Baselga

6 Build it and they will come: Sex toys, heteronormativity and age 86
Paul G. Nixon and Anja Selmer

7 Fuelling hate: Hate speech towards women in online news websites in Albania 100
Emiljano Kaziaj

8 'Tell me how old I am': Cinema, pedagogy, adults and underage trans folks 119
Magalí Daniela Pérez Riedel and Pablo Ariel Scharagrodsky

PART III
Elderly have a voice(?): Sexuality, gender and the media across texts and audiences 133

9 Invisible aged femininities in popular culture: Representational strategies deconstructed 135
Sofie Van Bauwel

10 'Old dirty pops and young hot chicks': Age differences in pornographic fantasies 146
Susanna Paasonen

11 Hustling and ageism in the films *Eastern Boys* and *Brüder der Nacht* 161
Antonio A. Caballero-Gálvez and María Porras Sánchez

12 Ageing women on screen: Disgust, disdain and the Time's Up pushback 175
Karen Ross

13 No Country for Old Men?: Representations of the ageing body in contemporary pornography 190
Federico Zecca

Index 203

ILLUSTRATIONS

Figures

7.1 Percentage of news items with hate speech content based on topic   106

7.2 Percentage breakdown of groups targeted for hate speech   108

7.3 Age groups targeted for hate speech, showing gender (number of news items)   111

7.4 Topics of articles with hate speech, based on gender of news subjects (number of news items)   112

7.5 Articles containing hate speech/discriminatory language: is there a photo?   113

7.6 Subjects of photos by group   113

7.7 A deeper understanding of the use of photos   114

Tables

2.1 LGBT+ characters in Flemish domestic youth fiction programming since 1999 (N=25)   32

2.2 LGBT+ characters in youth fiction programming broadcast in Ireland since 1992 (domestic and imported programming aimed at youths) (domestic, N=1; imported youth programming, N= 23)   35

CONTRIBUTORS

Núria Araüna is a lecturer and researcher at Rovira i Virgili University (Spain) and a member of the Asterisc Communication Research Group. She holds a Media Studies BA degree, an Anthropology BA degree, a master's degree in Creative Documentary, and her PhD dissertation on gender representations and love relationships in Spanish music videos was awarded by the Catalan Audiovisual Council. Her current research focuses on adolescents' audiovisual produsage on social networking sites, gender relationships and popular feminism online. She is also working on feminist documentaries and the representation of Spanish feminism since the Transition.

Antonio A. Caballero-Gálvez holds a PhD in Audiovisual Communication and Advertising and a master's degree in Cultural Management. He is an adjunct professor in the Department of Communication Studies at the Universitat Rovira i Virgili, an adviser for the master's degree programme in Cultural Management and the master's degree programme in Social Media at the Universitat Oberta de Catalunya, and a member of the editorial team of the *Catalan Journal of Communication & Cultural Studies*. His research work focuses on the representations of masculinities in contemporary audiovisual media, queer theory and the visual representation of gender identities. He carried out pre-doctoral research at the Humboldt Universität zu Berlin and post-doctoral research at the Universidad Mayor de San Andrés (Bolivia) as part of the Santander JPI scholarship programme. He has worked as a researcher at Andalucía's Observatory of gender-based violence in audiovisual media (Universidad de Málaga) and attended the inter-disciplinary research seminar on Gender, Aesthetics and Audiovisual Culture (GECA-UCM).

Daniel Cardoso (MSCFA Research Fellow) holds a PhD in Communication Sciences from the NOVA University and is a research fellow in the Department of Sociology at Manchester Metropolitan University, UK, and a member of RCASS and its Gender and Sexuality Research Group. He remains associated with LUSOFONA University, Lisbon, where he taught for ten years. His main areas of research are consensual non-monogamies, BDSM, gender and sexualities, young and new media, and cybercultures. His work and activism can be found at www.da nielscardoso.net

Despina Chronaki (PhD, Loughborough University, UK) is an adjunct lecturer at the National and Kapodistrian University of Athens and the Hellenic Open University. Her research focuses on audiences of popular culture, media ethics, porn studies, sexuality and children's experiences with media. Her interests also include cultural approaches to audiences of horror, drag culture and fantasy audiences. Most of her publications focus on audiences' constructions of popular culture, including children's experiences as audiences of sexual content, media literacy and ethics. Her recent publications include *Discourses of Anxiety over Childhood and Youth Across Cultures* (eds) (Palgrave-MacMillan). Since 2007 she has been collaborating with media scholars from around the world in a number of EU-funded European, national (Greek) and international projects and invited to present her work in domestic, European and international conferences and meetings (https://en-uoa-gr.academia. edu/DespinaChronaki for a detailed record).

Sara De Vuyst is a postdoctoral researcher in the Department of Languages and Cultures at Ghent University in Belgium. She is working on the ERC project 'Later-in-Life Intimacy: Women's Unruly Practices, Places and Representations'. Her research interests are feminist media studies, older queer women's media experiences, representations of women's later-in-life sexuality, and gender issues and technology in journalism. Sara De Vuyst is vice-chair of the ECREA Gender and Communication section and author of *Hacking Gender and Technology in Journalism* (in the Routledge series, Disruptions: Studies in Digital Journalism).

Emiljano Kaziaj (PhD) currently works as Media Team Leader for USAID's 'Justice for All' project in Albania. In this capacity, Emiljano is leading and supporting several university and media-related activities, including: establishing the first MA programme in Investigative Journalism at the University of Tirana, Department of Journalism; mentoring the leading fact-checking service in Albania (Faktoje.al); and supporting an array of capacity-building activities for students of journalism. Previously, Emiljano worked as a full-time lecturer at New York University in Tirana, where he taught in courses in media and communication and carried out research on media and human rights. In 2016/17 he served as adviser to the Minister of Social Welfare and Youth, pushing for improvements to the mechanisms around child rights and protection in media by advocating for an updated Code of Broadcast for Albanian media. Emiljano holds a PhD in Communication from Ghent University, Belgium, and studied public relations for his master's degree and journalism for his bachelor's degree at the University of Tirana. He is a Council of Europe-certified trainer on human rights and has contributed to the implementation of several development projects on human rights and media carried out by INGOs in Albania. Emiljano has a passion for writing. Besides a number of academic articles published in high-ranked international journals and some book chapters, he regularly publishes opinion pieces on the role of media in society in leading news outlets in Albania.

Páraic Kerrigan (Dr) is a teaching fellow with the School of Information and Communication Studies at University College Dublin. His research pertains to the dynamics of diversity in the media industry and its production cultures, specifically centred around Ireland's LGBT community. This research forms the foundation for his first book, *LGBTQ Visibility, Media and Sexuality in Ireland* (Routledge 2020). He has also published a number of articles on media work and workers in the creative industry and has written about how social media technologies have responded to contemporary identity politics.

Paul G. Nixon is a principal lecturer in Political Science and the Strategic Partnerships Co-ordinator at The Hague University of Applied Sciences. He is Visiting Professor at Masaryk University, Brno, Czech Republic. His work is situated at the interface between technology and society. He has contributed chapters to many edited collections on the use of ICTs, particularly in the fields of political parties, electronic democracy and social welfare. He has co-edited nine collections, the most recent being *Sex in the Digital Age* (with I.K. Dusterhoft, 2018) and *Digital Media Use Across the Lifecourse* (with Rajash Rawal and Andreas Funk, 2016).

Susanna Paasonen is Professor of Media Studies at the University of Turku, Finland. With an interest in studies of sexuality, networked media and affect, she is the PI of the Academy of Finland research project, 'Sexuality and Play in Media Culture' and the Strategic Research Council-funded consortium, 'Intimacy in Data-Driven Culture'. She is most recently the author of *Dependent, Distracted, Bored: Affective Formations in Networked Media* (MITP 2021), *Who's Laughing Now? Feminist Tactics in Social Media* (MITP 2020, with Jenny Sundén), *Objectification: On the Difference Between Sex and Sexism* (Routledge 2020, with Feona Attwood, Alan McKee, John Mercer and Clarissa Smith), *NSFW: Sex, Humor and Risk in Social Media* (MITP 2019, with Kylie Jarrett and Ben Light) and *Many Splendored Things: Thinking Sex and Play* (Goldsmiths Press 2018).

Magalí Daniela Pérez Riedel received her PhD in Communication from the Universidad Nacional de La Plata, Argentina. Her areas of study are digital communication, discrimination, queer studies and representations of LGBTQ people. Magalí is the author of *Gender and sexual diversity in the blog Boquitas Pintadas* (2014) [original title: *Género y diversidad sexual en el blog Boquitas Pintadas*] and the editor of *Trans, Out, and in the Public Eye: Representations of Transgender People on Television and Film* (working title) (Peter Lang). She is the author of 'Homo y transfobia en la web: testimonios de activistas LGBT' (in *Género y TIC*, ECOSUR 2018, edited by

Esperanza Tuñón and Abraham Mena Farrera) and co-author with Pablo A. Scharagrodsky of 'Educational trajectories of the female trans students of the Mocha Celis Secondary School in Argentina' (in *Antagonizing White Feminism: Intersectionality's Critique of Women's Studies and the Academy*, Lexington Books 2020, edited by Noelle Chaddock and Beth Hinderliter). Magalí was formerly co-director of the outreach project 'Prácticas de comunicación y educación por la desobediencia sexo-genérica' (Universidad Nacional de Quilmes), directed by Pablo A. Scharagrodsky.

Karen Ross (PhD) is Professor of Gender and Media in the School of Arts and Cultures, Newcastle University, UK. Her teaching and research are focused on issues of gender, media and society including aspects of social media and political communication, and she has published widely on these topics. Her most recent monograph *Gender, Politics and News* was published in 2017 (Wiley Blackwell). She is editor-in-chief of a major new reference work, the *International Encyclopaedia of Gender, Media and Communication*, which was published by Wiley Blackwell in June 2020, and is the UK and European coordinator of the Global Media Monitoring Project.

María Porras Sánchez holds a PhD in Cultural and Literary Studies in English. She is an assistant professor in the Department of English Studies, Universidad Complutense de Madrid, Spain, and she also collaborates at Universitat Oberta de Catalunya. She has formerly taught at Aberystwyth University (Wales, UK). Her research interests include cultural studies, comic studies and postcolonial literatures. She combines her teaching and research with her work as a literary translator for publishing houses such as Editorial Siruela and HarperCollins. She has co-edited, with E. Sánchez-Pardo and R. Burillo, *Women Poets and Myth in the 20th and 21st Centuries: On Sappho's Website* (Cambridge Scholars 2018). Her latest work to date is a critical edition and translation of *Headscarves and Hymens: Why the Middle East Needs a Sexual Revolution* (2018), by Mona Eltahawy.

Cosimo Marco Scarcelli, PhD in Social Sciences, is Assistant Professor in the Department of Philosophy, Sociology, Education and Applied Psychology at the University of Padua, where he teaches Sociology of Digital Media and Digital Culture and Society. His research interests deal with digital media, with a focus on identities, young people, intimacy, gender, sexuality, digital literacy and media education. Since 2018 he has chaired the Gender and Communication section of ECREA. He has been associate editor of 'The International Encyclopedia of Gender, Media and Communication' edited by K. Ross (Wiley 2020).

His recent publications include: 'Sexuality, gender, media: Identity articulations in the contemporary media landscape' in *Information, Communication and Society* (with T. Krijnen and P. Nixon, 2020), 'The mediated erotic lover: Young heterosexuals and the role of pornography in their negotiation of gender roles and desire' in *Journal of Gender Studies* (with R. Stella, 2020), 'Teenage perspectives on sexting and pleasure in Italy: Going beyond the concept of moral panic' in

Discourses of Anxiety about Childhood and Youth across Cultures edited by L. Tsaliki and D. Chronaki (2020). His work and updates can be foud at www.cosimomarcoscarcelli.com

Pablo Ariel Scharagrodsky holds a PhD in Social and Human Sciences. He is a researcher and professor at the Universidad Nacional de La Plata and Universidad Nacional de Quilmes. His research interests focus on history of education and physical education and sports from a gender perspective. He has published more than ninety articles in national and international journals. His latest publications include 'Educational trajectories of the female trans students of the Mocha Celis Secondary School in Argentina' (in *Antagonizing White Feminism: Intersectionality's Critique of Women's Studies and the Academy*, Lexington Books 2020, edited by Noelle Chaddock and Beth Hinderliter; co-author with Magalí Pérez Riedel); 'Trans-formando el espacio educativo y deportivo: El caso de la comunidad trans en la capital argentina', in *Revista Investiga+*, 2(2), 2019; and *El rostro cambiante del deporte. Perspectivas historiográficas angloparlantes (1970–2010)* (Editorial Prometeo 2019; co-editor with César Torres). He is also editor of *Mujeres en movimiento: Deporte, cultura física y feminidades. Argentina, 1870–1980* (Prometeo Libros 2016).

Anja Selmer is a research student at the University of Oxford, UK. Her research interests lie in feminist science and technology studies. Specific areas of interest include human–machine interaction, digital sexual practices, heteronormativity and the sexualisation of self. She has recently completed a research project that focuses on sexual behaviour and sex toy usage, based on qualitative interviews conducted with respondents from the United States and Europe. She has previously studied at the University of Oslo and the University of Maastricht.

Iolanda Tortajada is a senior lecturer in Communication Studies at the Rovira i Virgili University (Tarragona, Spain) and member of the Asterisc Communication Research Group. Her research primarily deals with the changing depiction of different types of femininity, gender and sexual identity mediatisation, the relationship between the media and gender violence, alternative masculinities, and minorities' media and technology appropriation. She is currently coordinating a four-year research project on sexual identities and social networking sites funded by Spain's Ministry of Economy, Industry and Competitiveness. She is also coordinating the Audience and Reception Studies section of the Spanish Association for Communication Research and vice-chairing the Commission for Audiovisual Diversity of the Catalan Audiovisual Council.

Sofie Van Bauwel is Associate Professor in the Department of Communication Studies at Ghent University and currently also Head of Department. She is a member of the research group Centre for Cinema and Media Studies (CIMS) and her research centres on gender and media. She is involved in several projects with a focus on the media as signifying articulations in visual popular culture. Her research activities cover gender, sexuality and media, on which she has published – for example, a book with Tonny Krijnen, *Gender and Media: Representing, Producing, Consuming* (Routledge 2015).

Florian Vanlee (Dr) conducted a FWO-funded PhD research project titled 'Sexual Diversity on the Small Screen: A qualitative research into the representation of and public debate about LGBTs in Flemish television fiction series' at Ghent University. Using a multi-methodological approach, his research analysed how sexual and gender diversity are constructed in Flemish television fiction, how LGBT+ characters and narratives are negotiated by television professionals and how queer television theory relates to smaller national contexts. After obtaining his doctorate, he started working as a postdoctoral researcher for ECOOM-VUB, with a focus on artistic research and its evaluation in the Flemish higher education context.

Sergio Villanueva Baselga (PhD) works as an assistant professor at the University of Barcelona. His research focuses on the relationship between media and health. His research departs from the premise that the media and culture are part of the social determinants of health defined by WHO. In this way, he critically examines the media and the cinema as articulators, creators and structural constituents of the narratives that make up different health stigmas and, in general, collective identities. He has been visiting researcher at the University of Rostock (Germany), the Aristotle University of Thessaloniki (Greece), the Carlos III University of Madrid (Spain), the University of Chicago (US) and the University of Exeter (UK). In addition, he has worked as postdoctoral researcher at the La Caixa Foundation, at the BigVan Science company and at the Barcelona Institute for Global Health (ISGlobal).

Cilia Willem is Associate Professor at the Rovira i Virgili University (URV), where she teaches media and communication. She is a member of the Asterisc Research Group at URV, where she leads a research tier on technology and media appropriation of disadvantaged groups such as sexual, gender and ethnic minorities and young people. She has published several book chapters and peer-reviewed articles in academic journals on topics of media, popular culture and gender. Willem has been the main editor of the *Catalan Journal of Communication & Cultural Studies* since 2014.

Federico Zecca is Associate Professor at the University of Bari 'Aldo Moro' (Italy). He is part of the editorial staff of the journal *L'Avventura: International Journal of Italian Cinema and Media Landscapes*; co-editor of the journals *Cinéma & Cie: International Film Studies* and *Cinergie: Il cinema e le altre arti*; and member of the editorial board of the journal *Porn Studies*. He is a member of the scientific committee of the Udine/Gorizia FilmForum and one of the coordinators of the Porn Studies Section of the MAGIS – Gorizia International Film Studies Spring School. He has published widely on intertextuality, intermediality, media convergence,

Italian popular cinema and US pornography. Among his books: *Gli estremi dell'hard: Due saggi sul porno contemporaneo* (2013, with Stephen Maddison); *Cinema e intermedialità. Modelli di traduzione* (2013); and *Porn after Porn: Contemporary Alternative Pornographies* (2014, co-edited with Enrico Biasin and Giovanna Maina). He has more recently co-edited 'Inside Gonzo Porn', a special issue of *Porn Studies* (2016, with Enrico Biasin), and 'Reinventing Mao: Maoisms and National Cinemas', a special issue of *Cinéma & Cie* (2018, with Marco Dalla Gassa and Corrado Neri).

EDITORS' INTRODUCTION

*Sara De Vuyst, Despina Chronaki, Cosimo Marco Scarcelli
and Sergio Villanueva Baselga*

Media are a key site for the construction, negotiation and opposition of gender, sexual identities and performances at a social and cultural level (Krijnen & Van Bauwel 2015, Ross 2011). In this respect, the relationship between gender, sexuality and the media has been studied from different theoretical and research perspectives, including the areas of anthropology, psychoanalysis and feminist and cultural studies. Media studies scholars, drawing on diverse epistemological and methodological approaches to gender and sexuality, have offered insights into a wide range of topics related to media representation, audiences and production. For example, there is a significant body of scholarly work on the presence and portrayal of women and sexual minorities in various types of media content and workplaces (Edström 2018, De Vuyst 2020, Krainitzki 2016, Lemish & Mulbauer 2012, Montiel 2014, Ross & Padovani 2017), on the engagement of audiences with mediated sexual content (e.g. Chronaki 2013, Scarcelli 2015, Smith, Attwood & Barker 2015) and the articulation of sexual identities through the use of media (e.g. Andreassen, Petersen, Harrison & Raun 2018). The *Handbook of Gender, Sex, and Media* edited by Karen Ross (2011) can be seen as exemplary of this research tradition and brings together studies on gender, sex, sexualities and the media. This collection provides a rich set of chapters about different ways in which gender is performed in media contexts across the globe and focuses on diverse expressions of sexuality in media reception, production and representation.

While previous academic work has elaborated extensively on gender, media and sexuality, looking closely at either gender and media or sexuality and media, an emerging gap concerns the more systematic collection of research that approaches these interactions from the perspective of age. We believe that age and ageing must be taken into account since they are inherent elements that play a mediating role in how gender and sexuality are shaped and media messages are constructed, produced and interpreted by audiences. For example, studies have shown that older women tend to be invisible in popular media content and represented in a way that confirms rigid ideas about gender, sexuality and ageist assumptions (Dolan & Ticknell 2012, Montemurro & Chewning 2018, Tortajada, Dhaenens & Willem 2018). Just like gender and sexuality, age and ageing are not static, fixed categories but rather social and cultural constructions that are constantly changing and being renegotiated at both the level of public discourse and the level of individual perceptions (Krekula, Nikanda & Wilińska 2018, Sandberg 2008).

The aim of this edited volume is to explore how engagements with the media reflect people's constructions and understandings of gender in society, how age is articulated in relation to gender and sexuality and how negotiations of gender and sexuality inform people's media practices. This book offers original empirical and theoretical insights into the complex relationship between age, gender, sexualities and the media. In doing so, it showcases new and innovative research that is at the forefront of media and communication practice and theory. This collection covers a diverse array of topics such as gender performances in different media and contexts, sexuality and gender representations in digital and traditional media, expressions of age in relation to pornography and the portrayal and perception of gendered and ageing bodies on screen. The chapters explore, on the one hand, aspects of the changing social and sexual landscape; and on the other hand, how media construct gender and age through censorious or polarised perspectives. Our underlying goal is to inform academic, public and policy agendas by uncovering the subtle ways in which gender, age and sexuality can reinforce or weaken each other as systems of privilege and oppression in the media.

Since this publication is situated at the intersection between cultural studies, gender studies, feminist media studies and sexuality studies, it moves beyond an understanding of gender and sexuality within the man/woman bipolar. Instead, it considers the social, historical and cultural trajectories running through the relationship between gender, sexuality and age. In order to explore gender, sexuality and age as social and cultural constructions, we draw on the concept of intersectionality that identifies a mode of analysis integral to feminist, gender and sexuality studies based on the idea that ethnicity, class, gender, sexuality, age and other identity markers are mutually constitutive (Crenshaw 1991, Lykke 2010). We believe that it is of utmost importance to understand how the notion of age defines and redefines the connection between gender and sexuality to offer a full understanding of how dynamics of difference and sameness shape media landscapes.

In line with the cultural studies perspective, the contributions in this edited volume take into account the complex interactions between media representation, reception and production in processes of meaning-making (Buckingham 2008, Livingstone 1998). This means that the chapters not only represent a wide variety of studies on different types of media texts and genres (television, cinema, digital spaces), but also include the voices of media producers and audiences to gain insights into how media messages are socially constructed and interpreted. It is important to note that our understanding of how people in different age groups and parts of Europe perform, understand and consume media, especially in relation to gender and sexuality, is continuously changing with the proliferation of online media (Attwood 2012). That is why the chapters focus on the more traditional media forms as well as take into account the complexity of the transmedial, convergent and participatory nature of popular culture and media today.

Finally, it is essential to note that the book highlights the potential of media to both reinforce as well as challenge systems of oppression and social hierarchies based on differences of gender, sexual orientation and age. This is why we explore the nuances of contemporary sex and gender scripts across different ages by looking both at normative interpretations of gender and sexuality and those that challenge and move beyond the heteronormative and homonormative, fixed categories of gender and stereotypical accounts of age and ageing.

Contents of the edited volume

The added value of this volume can be derived both from the choice of topics and authors. The contributions have been selected to reflect a wide range of case studies in various national contexts. The authors of the chapters are working in different countries such as Italy, Greece, Spain, Ireland, Albania, the United Kingdom, the Netherlands, Finland, Portugal, Argentina and Belgium. They present different theoretical and analytical perspectives on gender, sexuality and age. The combination of research that covers different national and cultural contexts as well as academic cultures that spread across Europe is one of the most important contributions of this book to current debates on age, gender and sexuality. Considering that previous collections on the topic of gender and media mostly include work from specific national contexts or different parts of the world (e.g. Ross 2011), we believe that a strong focus on the European dimension within the contributors' discussions is necessary to explore the specificities of the European context. This also allows for a comparative perspective that can offer new insights into similarities and differences between European countries.

Furthermore, by bringing together scholars working on gender, sexuality, age and media across Europe, this edited volume links up with the rationale of the ECREA book series to create a space for media and communication research focusing on Europe and stimulate collaborations among researchers. In addition to geographical diversity, we have strived for diversity among the authors in terms of age and academic positions. The collection brings together research from early-career and established scholars who engage in an interesting epistemological dialogue with each other about gender, sexuality and age in people's practices with the media.

Last but not least, the edited volume builds bridges between different ECREA sections. Through the cross-sectional collaboration between the Gender and Communication and the Film Studies section, it was possible to embrace more epistemological approaches on the topic and contribute further to creating shared spaces for cross-sectional academic dialogues. This objective is also reflected in the composition of the list of authors who come from a wide range of ECREA sections and working groups such as Gender and Communication, Film Studies, Children, Youth and Media, Digital Culture, and Audience and Reception Studies. As a result, the contributions reflect a diversity in theoretical perspectives related to the fields of feminist media studies, post-structuralism, sociology, media and cultural studies, through which researchers explore the tropes, definitions, and understandings of age, gender, sex and sexuality that are played out in mainstream and digital media. The chapters employ a variety of methodological approaches and present a wide range of empirical cases such as qualitative interviews, textual analysis, surveys and multi-method research.

To connect all these chapters and angles, we have decided to choose a structure that is cross-cut by age, dividing the book into three Parts: children and young people, adults and adulthood, and elderly people. In this way, we want to ensure that voices from different generations are represented in the book, as well as their specific challenges and experiences in relation to media. Some of the chapters can be considered a hinge between different Parts in the edited volume because they make references that go beyond age groups. The chapter outline will be further discussed below.

Chapter outline

The book is structured as follows: it starts in Part I: Young People, Sexuality and Gender Performance: Texts and Audiences, with contributions that focus on young people. These chapters address the topic in relation to media texts (representation) and audiences (consumption).

More specifically, Iolanda Tortajada, Núria Araüna and Cilia Willem's chapter 'Feminist YouTubers in Spain: A public space for building resistance addresses gender and sexual violence in the context of feminist activism in Spain (Chapter 1). In light of the #MeToo campaigns at a national and global level, the authors process Spanish feminist YouTubers' contributions to the creation of a digital public space for resistance and solidarity. Their argumentation draws on the effectiveness of digital spaces as vehicles of political and social mobilisation, especially in matters related to gender and feminist politics.

Moving forward to issues of representation, Florian Vanlee's and Páraic Kerrigan's chapter 'Un/fit for young viewers: LGBT+ representation in Flemish and Irish children's television' comparatively explores youth television programming in public service broadcasting (PSB) in Ireland and Flanders (Chapter 2). It highlights the (in) visibility of queer sexualities in children's television. Their main argument draws on the fact that queer televisibility was not part of the programming in Ireland or Flanders until the 1990s. According to the authors, it is the increasingly globalised nature of children's television from the noughties onwards that led to a subsequent increase in LGBT+ televisibility in both countries. Their research provides a comparative account of the two media cultures, highlighting the different ways in which LGBT+ voices and representations made their appearance in the national television programmes. By acknowledging the cultural and social differences between the two cases, the authors highlight the shared discursive ways in relation to sexual and gender diversity that are embedded in PSB children's programming.

In Chapter 3, 'Breaking the silence: Young people, sex information and the internet in Italy and Portugal', Daniel Cardoso and Cosimo Marco Scarcelli provide a comparative account of Italy and Portugal on the issue of adolescents' search for sex-related information online. By employing this approach to qualitative interviews about sex-related topics, they illustrate adolescents' shared discursive patterns in talking about learning or just being informed about sex through online sources. They want to establish a cross-cultural research dialogue addressing the complexity through which adolescents negotiate online information about sex, and thereby broaden the scope of research in cultural contexts that are still silencing issues of non-heteronormative sexualities. The significance of 'gender' in their analysis about adolescents' fears and expectations and their redefinitions of what constitutes information about sexual issues is remarkable.

In Chapter 4, 'COVID-19 pandemic and discourses of anxiety about childhood sexuality in digital spaces', Despina Chronaki discusses anxieties about children's sexuality in the context of the COVID-19 pandemic. Her study is based on an illustrative sample of press news online across Europe with a focus on items discussing popular topics in relation to children and mediated sexual content amidst lockdowns. Topics such as children's experiences with pornography, zoombombing incidents, fears about online sexual abuse during quarantine and Pornhub's provision of premium accounts in COVID-19-affected areas are just a few of those regenerating heated policy, public and academic discussions about childhood regulation and anxieties of children's leisure. This chapter highlights how technologies of sexuality serve as platforms of regulation and self-regulation, especially in turbulent times.

The second Part of this edited volume, Adults, Sexuality, Gender and the Media in Research Perspective, includes chapters addressing adult sexualities and how those are performed and represented in popular contexts. In Chapter 5, 'HIV-related stigma in the European cinema: Conflictive representations of a cultural trauma', Sergio Villanueva Baselga conducts a textual analysis of popular films addressing issues of people living with HIV and shows how normative constructions of stigma still apply to representations of people living with HIV. By analysing the films *Drôle de Félix* (2000), *Pride* (2014), *Theo et Hugo dans le même bateau* (2016) and *Bohemian Rhapsody* (2018), Villanueva Baselga looks at how 1980s HIV discourses – defined and understood in terms of cultural trauma – still underpin such popular texts. The study indicates that UNAIDS 90–90–90 achievements in the diagnosis and treatment of HIV that have enhanced peoples' with HIV lifestyles have not been broadly embraced by film creators.

In Chapter 6, 'Build it and they will come: Sex toys, heteronormativity and age', Paul Nixon and Anja Selmer engage in a much-needed discussion on the sociocultural construction of sex toys. They provide a critical account of how the sex toy market seems to be moving towards heteronormative formulations of the products, followed by an empirical approach to users' perceptions. By combining qualitative and quantitative research methods, the authors explore people's constructions of the sex toy products and markets through perspectives of age, gender and sexual preferences. Their approach draws on the socio-historical development and perception of sex toys and is an excellent example of how important it is to approach sexual cultures from a cultural perspective.

Chapter 7, 'Fuelling hate: Hate speech towards women in online news websites in Albania', written by Emiljano Kaziaj, returns to the issue of representation by investigating the contested and increasingly popular topic of hate speech against women in four major Albanian online news websites. His discussion focuses on young adult women, 19–25 years old, who are a group targeted through hate speech practices in terms of gender and age. Kaziaj employs both qualitative and quantitative analytical strategies to map the discursive patterns through which women 19–25 are framed in online news media discourse in Albania. His policy-oriented work provides insights about how online media professionals could work towards less censorious – if not biased – media coverage of gender-related issues in the country.

Chapter 8, 'Tell me how old I am': Cinema, pedagogy, adults and underage trans folks', stays within issues related to representation. Magalí Daniela Pérez Riedel and Pablo Ariel Scharagrodsky examine the representations of transgender children in media across Europe and the USA in the *3 Generations* (2015), *They* (2017) and *Girl* (2018) films. Their discussion revolves around the scrutinisation of the young transgender body and identity from parents, relatives and doctors, as well as its ethical perception. Looking at the topic through how transgender minors experience their relationships with adults, the authors explore the cinematic representations of transgender youth through established adult notions of teenage life as a hormonal and social transition. Although discourses about how to 'correct' the non-acceptable body are reiterated in the films according to the authors' analysis, they argue that the films give room to broader discussions about the rights and needs of transgender minors in a context that fails to recognise their bodily integrity and personal autonomy.

The final Part of this edited volume addresses the topic of later-in-life sexualities. Most contributions in Part III, Elderly have a Voice(?): Sexuality, Gender and the Media across Texts and Audiences, discuss issues of representation of elderly bodies and later-in-life sexuality in particular. In Chapter 9, 'Invisible aged femininities in popular culture: Representational strategies deconstructed', Sofie Van Bauwel explores the representation of ageing women in popular television fiction. She highlights the contradictory nature of ageing womanhood being mostly absent and ubiquitous at the same time by arguing that whenever present, ageing femininity is overstated and sometimes manifested excessively. By embracing approaches that discuss ageing in popular television in celebratory terms as well as those that are more critical towards industry's intentions in constructing the ageing body discursively, she uncovers representational strategies applied to ageing femininities in popular media content.

In Chapter 10, '"Old dirty pops and young hot chicks": Age differences in pornographic fantasies', Susanna Paasonen engages with Finnish audiences' preferences in pornography and discursive constructions of the ageing body. Her analysis based on survey data explores female audiences' preferences and dislikes in pornography through the lens of age. She is particularly interested in investigating the ageing male body as an ambivalent, simultaneously attractive and repulsive pornographic fantasy figure. In exploring how discourses of control and submission come into play during porn consumption, Paasonen unpacks the ways in which ageing bodies signify excessiveness and authenticity. In the process, participants' negotiation of sexual fantasies also experiments with the appeal of older male bodies as sites of disgust and taboo transgression to be enjoyed from a distance.

In Chapter 11, 'Hustling and ageism in the films *Eastern Boys* and *Brüder der Nacht*', Antonio Caballero-Gálvez and María Porras Sánchez present the results of the analysis of two films, *Eastern Boys* (Robin Campillo, 2013) and *Brüder der Nacht* (Patric Chiha, 2016), to understand the discursive construction of gay prostitution. By drawing on critical approaches to the gay sexual body in terms of health/fitness and hyper-muscularity, they mainly focus on elderly gay bodies compared and contrasted with Eastern European male bodies as represented in the films analysed. By engaging with a psychoanalytic approach to the film narrative, the authors highlight the responsibility of gay media in the creation of an unreachable ideal of youth.

Karen Ross' chapter 'Ageing women on screen: Disgust, disdain and the *Time's Up* pushback' continues with the topic of representation and revisits feminist debates about women's invisibility in popular culture to provide an analytical account of the absence – or rare appearance – of older women in popular culture. Following a socio-historical approach to the topic, Ross explores the tropes of older womanhood as manifest across a range of popular mainstream media. In this process, she revisits established notions about ageing when it comes to gender, both when it comes to older women's representation and older women as audiences depicted in texts. The author concludes her discussion, considering what she calls 'a pushback' by industry agents (women actors and directors) who work towards putting older women at the centre of their narratives, thereby offering space for manifestations of the ageing female body in popular culture.

The last chapter of this Part, which is also the final contribution to this edited volume, 'No Country for Old Men: Representation of the ageing body in contemporary pornography' (Chapter 13) addresses ageing male bodies in pornography. Federico Zecca explores the discursive construction of the ageing body in pornography amidst the proliferation of digital technologies that have increased visibility of such representations. His study contributes to filling a gap in research, given the lack of analytical approaches to the ageing body in pornography. Based on textual analysis, Zecca offers a mapping of the available discourses about the ageing body in contemporary pornography. To do so, he draws on the socio-economic angle of the sex industry and an epistemic dynamic related to the formation of the pornographic subject. For his analysis, he combines ageing studies with media studies and unpacks the codes and conventions through which pornography (re)presents the ageing body.

References

Andreassen, R., Petersen, M., Harrison, K. and Raun, T. (2018). *Mediated intimacies: Connectivities, relationalities and proximities*. London: Routledge.

Attwood, F. (2012). Sex and the media. In K. Ross (ed.), *The handbook of gender, sex, and media* (pp. 457–469). London: John Wiley & Sons.

Buckingham, D. (2008). Children and media: A cultural studies approach. In K. Drotner and S. Livingstone (eds), *The international handbook of children, media and culture* (pp. 219–236). London: Sage.

Chronaki, D. (2013). Young people's accounts of experiences with sexual content during childhood and teenage life, *Communication Review*, 16(1–2), 61–69.

Crenshaw, K. (1991). Mapping the margins: Intersectionality, identity politics, and violence against women of color. *Stanford Law Review*, 43(6), 1241–1299.

De Vuyst, S. (2020). *Hacking gender and technology in journalism*. New York: Routledge.

Dolan, J. and Ticknell, E. (2012). *Aging femininities: Troubling representations*. Newcastle: Cambridge Scholars.

Edström, M. (2018). Visibility patterns of gendered ageism in the media buzz: A study of the representation of gender and age over three decades. *Feminist Media Studies*, 18(1), 77–93.

Krainitzki, E. (2016). 'Older-wiser-lesbians' and 'baby-dykes': Mediating age and generation in New Queer Cinema. *Feminist Media Studies*, 16(4), 631–647.

Krekula, C., Nikanda, P. and Wilińska, M. (2018). Multiple marginalizations based on age: Gendered ageism and beyond. In L. Ayalon and C. Tesh-Römer (eds), *Contemporary perspectives on ageism* (pp. 33–50). Switzerland: Springer.

Krijnen, T. and Van Bauwel, S. (2015). *Gender and media: Representing, producing, consuming*. London: Routledge.

Lemish, D. and Muhlbauer, V. (2012). 'Can't have it all': Representations of older women in popular culture. *Women & Therapy*, 35(3–4), 165–180.

Livingstone, S. (1998). Relationships between media and audiences: Prospects for future audience reception studies. In T. Liebes and J. Curran (eds), *Media, ritual and identity: Essays in honor of Elihu Katz*. London: Routledge.

Lykke, N. (2010). *Feminist studies: A guide to intersectional theory, methodology and writing*. New York: Routledge.

Montemurro, B. and Chewning, L.V. (2018). Aging 'hot': Images and narratives of sexual desirability on television. *Sexuality & Culture*, 22, 462–478.

Montiel, A.V. (2014). *Media and gender: A scholarly agenda for the global alliance on media and gender*. Paris: UNESCO/IAMCR.

Ross, K. (2011). *The handbook of gender, sex, and media*. Malden, MA: Wiley-Blackwell.

Ross, K. and Padovani, C. (2017). *Gender inequality in the media: A challenge for Europe*. New York: Routledge.

Sandberg, L. (2008). The old, the ugly, and the queer: Thinking old age in relation to queer theory. *Graduate Journal of Social Science*, 5(2), 117–139.

Scarcelli, C.M. (2015). It is disgusting, but … ': Adolescent girls' relationship to internet pornography as gender performance. *Porn Studies*, 2(2–3), 237–249.

Smith, C., Attwood, F. and Barker, M. (2015). Figuring the porn audience. In L. Comella and S. Tarrant (eds), *New views on pornography: Sexuality, politics, and the law* (pp. 277–296). Santa Barbara, CA: Praeger.

Tortajada, I., Dhaenens, F. and Willem, C. (2018). Gendered ageing bodies in popular media culture. *Feminist Media Studies*, 18(1), 1–6.

PART I

Young people, sexuality and gender performance: Texts and audiences

1

FEMINIST YOUTUBERS IN SPAIN

A public space for building resistance

Núria Araüna, Iolanda Tortajada and Cilia Willem

Feminism in Spain

The Spanish feminist movement has recently gained significant relevance both in Spain and outside (Campillo 2019). Through massive demonstrations, the women's strikes on International Women's Day (8 March) from 2018 to 2020 in Spain, and a strong capillarity within diverse local settings and with social movements beyond those focused on gender, feminist collectives have managed to raise awareness and legitimise their claims. As a consequence, the 'feminist' label is now connoted with positive meanings in mainstream culture, after decades of stigmatisation. Journalists have put particular emphasis on the young age of feminist activists during the 8 March marches in Spain highlighting a renewal going on in the Spanish feminist movement without losing previous age groups' claims, thus bridging the generation gap around old demands such as legislation on gender violence, abolishing the pay gap or fighting against the feminisation of precarity. As Galarza Fernández, Castro-Martínez and Sosa Valcárcel (2019) have pointed out, Spanish feminism has benefited from social media and online communication, which has allowed activists to increase their social capital and mobilise young and old. In fact, according to Hunt (2017) the incorporation of young women in the movement and the creation of new networks have allowed for a sense of unity among women, regardless of age, and despite acknowledging their different positions on the axes of inequality. This, in turn, has led to a transnational expansion of the movement, as well as a more sophisticated use of technology contesting discursive strategies online and a more inclusive definition of the term 'women' understood as a political category. We consider this transnationality, intersectionality and technological empowerment to be part of what some authors have called the 'Feminist Fourth Wave' (Cochrane 2013), despite the controversial use of the 'wave' metaphor for referring to the feminist movement and the obvious geographical differences regarding discourses of feminism in different territories (McLean 2020).

The aim of our research is to examine how feminist YouTubers in Spain are forging a digital public space for resistance, by delving into YouTube and analysing videos that share and help spread feminist ideas or actions in Spain. In this chapter, we are focusing on the channels of activists like Andy Asadaf, Towanda Rebels and Irantzu Varela. As a *produsage* platform (Bruns 2008) based on video, YouTube provides many young and digitally savvy people with a chance to participate in the construction of a public debate about gender inequalities, the historical role of feminism, and social transformation strategies (Jouët 2017; Lawrence & Ringrose, 2018). On this platform, new communication formats are being tested that establish relationships both with the feminist tradition and with celebrity culture (Araüna, Tortajada & Willem 2019). At the same time, the online violence, threats and attacks on feminist YouTubers (Döring & Mohseni 2019), and the attempts to silence them are forcing the latter into articulating responses fast and developing sophisticated strategies of resistance and solidarity. We intend to highlight some of these strategies in this chapter.

Capitalising on the achievements of feminism

The recent expansion of feminism into the mainstream as a broad conceptual framework – ranging from a commercial and neoliberal appropriation of feminism to grassroots activism – has come to replace the hegemony of postfeminism as defined by Rosalind Gill, one of the most prominent researchers in postfeminist culture (Gill 2007). We will argue that postfeminism now shares a much more contended understanding of gender roles with this renewed and 'mainstreamed' feminism.

In communication and gender studies, postfeminist representation patterns have been one of the main concerns of Anglo-Saxon and North European academics during the last decade (Gill 2016b; Tortajada & Van Bauwel 2012). Postfeminism is a cultural representation regime, suggesting that feminism has achieved formal 'equality' between men and women while omitting structural and embedded inequalities in cultural systems (McRobbie 2004). Its assumptions somehow arose from the conjunction between neoliberalism and a popularised third-wave feminism. Since the early 2000s it has occupied the substrate of most audiovisual and graphic productions addressing women, establishing narratives that emphasise individual empowerment through competition on the labour market (neoliberal feminism) and encouraging the recovery of some of the traditional values associated with femininity. In this postfeminist spectrum, the concept of beauty and the ability to generate sexual attraction – especially in its cosmetic-commercial realisation – had a central role in the satisfaction of women (McRobbie 2004; Gill 2007), along with their capacity as consumers (Gill 2008). While the meritocratic and liberal notions underlying postfeminism supposedly allowed for a diversification of gender identities and sexualities, in turn, they subsumed this diversity to standards of 'heterosexiness' (Dobson 2011). The postfeminist framework and its liberal optimism have thus participated in rendering the structures of inequality invisible and holding individuals accountable for their own failure and success while promoting mechanisms of self-surveillance and self-demand in performing standard and marketable identities in terms of 'appropriate femininity' (Araüna, Dhaenens & Van Bauwel 2017).

In more recent times, however, and partly as a response to this backlash, the labels and ideas associated with feminism have regained centrality and are now present everywhere, ranging from political discourses to commercial advertisements (Banet-Weiser 2018). Rosalind Gill defines the moment as 'a new luminosity' of feminism (2016a, 2016b). Guerra Palmero (2019), on the other hand, has pointed out that the institutionalisation of feminism goes hand in hand with a hostile, patriarchal and misogynistic reaction from neoliberalism and neoconservatism, against which feminism is now the most significant force of resistance. In summary, we are facing a scenario where feminist and postfeminist media discourses operate simultaneously, while misogyny and antifeminism are also strengthened (Banet-Weiser & Miltner 2016; Keller, Mendes & Ringrose 2016), and where both left and right-wing political parties – at least in Spain – try to capitalise on the achievements of feminism.

Feminism on YouTube

YouTuber videos, along with content on recent platforms such as TikTok or Twitch, are the privileged objects of young people's audiovisual *produsage* practices, understood as actions carried out by people who adopt a double condition of *producers* and *users* (Bruns, 2008). Much of this *produsage* has to do with the presentation of the online Self in its various aspects, including the creation of the Self as a reflective (Genz 2015) and political subject (Tortajada, Cabellero-Gálvez, Willem 2019). At the outset, YouTubers who self-define as such mostly produce videos on their own (or in small teams), focusing on their own image and what they have to say, acting as the enunciator and branding the style of a set of videos uploaded regularly on their channel. In stylistic terms, the camera usually emulates the position of the selfie with a constant medium shot of the YouTuber, who most of the time is sitting in a private space at home. Bedrooms, offices and living rooms are the most common backdrops for this type of videos. The domestic atmosphere, together with the first-person tone of the video, creates an environment of apparent proximity and trust between the performer and the public.

Teenagers have been reported to perceive YouTubers as personalities who are accessible, close and similar to themselves, and with whom they can identify (Pérez-Torres, Pastor-Ruiz & Abarrou-Ben-Boubaker 2018). Adding to this illusion of a direct connection with the YouTuber is the relative possibility of followers to actually interact with them through likes, shares, and comments, or – in the case of other YouTubers – with videos of their own. In some cases, for example in the YouTube row involving the trans community in Spain (Tortajada, Caballero-Gálvez & Willem 2019), dialectic discussions between YouTubers indicate the positioning of their publics regarding the issues raised, tapping into broader debates regarding social and gender inequalities.

YouTubers can have one or several channels, and they sometimes specialise in a specific topic, but each YouTuber establishes a 'marketable' and intentionally styled personality. When successful, YouTubers become micro-celebrities: a kind of public personality who – unlike television or cinema celebrities – needs to constantly and successively upload new content herself (Jerslev 2016). Regardless of the complexity of the content, YouTube videos generally have a 'didactic' or 'common good' aspect, in the sense that they intend to raise issues perceived as useful for a particular social group. In fact, the success of social media platforms like YouTube greatly depends on the social response to its contents, and this often leads to mutual support groups or even learning communities (Araüna, Tortajada & Willem 2019).

According to authors such as Szostak, YouTube 'operates as a support network for women dedicated to the general goal of acceptance and respect' (2013: 56), and so we can assume its feminist potential within the discursive online space. In fact, the number of YouTube channels specifically dedicated to feminist issues has increased dramatically in the last five years. On other social media platforms movements such as #MeToo or #TimesUp have already spoken out against the rape culture (Mendes, Ringrose & Keller 2018), heavily influencing the public opinion on this topic. Likewise, feminist YouTubers focus on making the audience understand the nature and demands of the feminist movement while contesting what they consider to be persistent manifestations of patriarchy and attacks on feminism (Araüna, Tortajada & Willem 2019). Videos produced by feminist YouTubers combine theory with activism and, above all, humour. This kind of feminist practices (Jouët 2017; Lawrence & Ringrose 2018) not only contribute to generating reflective spaces; they also articulate and encourage ironic contestations to antifemisms. The displays of resistance to constant attacks on feminism cover a wide repertoire of digital feminist pedagogies that connect with offline activism (Retallack, Ringrose & Lawrence 2016), for example when YouTubers like Irantzu Varela mobilise a broader audience through a mainstream media outlet (i.e. *Público*). At the same time, these videos contribute to the creation of micro-celebrities or public figures of reference, whose popularity online opens up possibilities in other areas of action. All three YouTubers that we will analyse in this chapter have eventually become an online reference for feminism in Spain.

We will centre attention on Spanish YouTubers Andy Asadaf, Towanda Rebels and Irantzu Varela, all three identifying as feminist. They connect with a young audience, embedded in contemporary feminism: all three are micro-celebrities on YouTube and have been invited for talks and conferences on feminism; Towanda Rebels has published the book *#HolaGuerrera*, and Irantzu Varela is the mastermind behind the feminist collective *Faktoria Lila*, regularly writes for the periodical *Pikara Magazine*, and has directed a documentary about sexist violence. This chapter will focus on the discursive and formal strategies employed by feminist YouTuber activists, and examine their ability to bend the neoliberal logics of YouTube as a personal-brand medium into a tool for awareness-raising and social commitment.

'I used to be an anti-feminist': Social media as a space of awareness and self-reflection

Social media have been claimed as a space for socialisation and exchange, from which young people build their identities and political affinity groups around certain topics or social issues (Szostak 2013; Keller, Mendes & Ringrose 2016). If we look at the particular case of feminism as one of these issues, it is clear that contents produced by young people on social media since 2013 have been key to recovering the popularity of the feminist movement, after about two decades in which the hegemony of postfeminism eroded the knowledge of the history and struggles of the feminist movement (McRobbie 2004).

After years of backlash and negative connotations, it is 'cool' again for a teenager to be a feminist (Retallack, Ringrose & Lawrence 2016). As an example of this, the YouTuber Andy Asadaf addresses youth directly, with her trajectory of more than two years of pedagogical videos about feminism. Taking a reflective perspective about the origins of her online activity, in her video 'I used to be an anti-feminist (+critique and reflection on this channel)', Asadaf recognises that as a teenager she was quite wary and mistrustful of feminism. In this video, Asadaf explains the lack of reliable information about feminism in her formal education, as well as the scarcity of references to women who fought for their rights – or were simply relevant in the political, scientific or cultural field, for that matter – in school curricula. This concern is shared by other YouTubers (e.g. Towanda Rebels), who have publicly recognised this lack of available tools to understand feminism in what they define as a 'patriarchal culture'. The abovementioned video by Asadaf departs from the idea that online interaction allows young people to discuss and learn from each other – as it was through these debates that she 'learnt' the reasons why feminism was important. However, her video also reveals the double-sided nature of online communication: she had considered herself an anti-feminist when she was fourteen precisely because of what she had read and seen online back then. Asadaf goes on to tell her viewers how she fell in the trap of sexist 'fallacies' and, in her down-to-earth style, explains what a fallacy is and how it is built through the partial suppression of data and a very specific and tricky framing of these data. By believing these deliberate misinterpretations, spread by organised groups, she says, she became an anti-feminist. Only later, when some online feminist activists' planted the seed of doubt in her mind, she could reach a feminist awareness by way of rational reasoning.

By recalling and re-telling her experience, Asadaf points to the relevance of social media and YouTube as informal learning tools, which can and should contribute to countering anti-feminist hate speech and messages that maintain inequalities (Tortajada, Caballero-Gálvez & Willem, 2019). In addition, Asadaf emphasises the importance of deliberation, in a Habermasian sense, which occurs in these spaces (Habermas 1987): despite the attacks and insults she receives as a feminist YouTuber, she reads these as a symptom of the need to produce more feminist discourse. As she says when remembering the launch of her channel: 'Precisely because of the attacks I received, I realized that one had to talk about feminism, that my channel had to focus on this.'

It is also interesting how Asadaf states that most anti-feminists do not label themselves as such, but instead use euphemisms such as 'I am not PC' (or 'a freethinker'). These considerations match the current media and political language used by new misogynists, and by admitting that she used to be one of those people and framing their assumptions as a mistake, Asadaf positions herself into the current public debate. The explicitly pedagogical and discursive nature of Asadaf's videos, and her aiming at social transformation, are also materialised in her particular *mise-en-scene*: while the predominant film location of the average YouTuber is a room in the house (as discussed above), we see Asadaf against a flat backdrop of violet fabric that does not reveal any details of her private life and draws the attention exclusively to what she has to say. In the montage of her videos, Asadaf also edits in slides, infographics and bullet points to illustrate her content. In fact, in most of her videos, she points out to her viewers that it is essential to continuously learn and inform and educate yourself, and be responsible.

In conclusion, the video 'I used to be an anti-feminist (+critique and reflection on this channel)' is an example of a process of reflectiveness and self-criticism occurring on social media, as well as an instance of 'authenticity' displayed by YouTubers as part of their reputation and credibility (Szostak 2013; Araüna, Tortajada & Willem 2019). In the same 'authenticity' vein, with videos like 'Branches and currents of feminism (+ what is my feminism?)', Asadaf describes the history of different feminist orientations and defines herself as a 'radical transfeminist'. Recognising herself as someone 'who did not understand feminism before', she opens the door for other people to identify with her without judgement and start a process of change through information and awareness. This feminist consciousness will imply, as Asadaf warns, constant attacks of anti-feminist movements enjoying good health (Jouët 2017). Like other YouTubers we will analyse below, in videos like 'DECONSTRUCTING feminist topics' Asadaf makes explicit the attacks and social constructions around feminism that she has experienced, and unmasks them through gender perspective analysis. Asadaf can be considered part of an online feminist activism that faces 'pervasive misogyny' (Lawrence & Ringrose 2018) through discursive tools and a good sense of humour. Her videos can be seen as a form of resistance, as she does not give in to heterosexy attributes of female YouTubers, and undermines anti-feminist attacks and unpacks stereotypes about feminists – such as the concept of feminazi – using subtle humour and not imposing her point of view in a dogmatic way.

'How do you see it?': Laughs to combat antifeminism

The above shows that social media enable new spaces for feminist practices where anti-feminist discourses are questioned and rejected (Jouët 2017; Lawrence & Ringrose 2018) in many ways, one of which is the use of humour. An example of this is Towanda Rebels' video 'How do you see it? We see it really bad' (2017) in which two YouTubers denounce and criticise the role of the media in disqualifying feminist demands. Teresa Lozano and Zúa Méndez, the two young women behind Towanda Rebels, define their YouTube project as an attempt to deactivate patriarchy with laughs, irony and sharp criticism. Their productions are another example of the potential of YouTube for feminism and resistance (Szostak 2013; Pruchniewska 2018; Araüna, Tortajada & Willem 2019) as they invite viewers to reflect on the multiple daily inequalities faced by women and to identify and subvert misogynist media discourses.

In 'How do you see it? We see it really bad', Lozano and Méndez stage an evening of watching TV, wondering: what are we doing tonight? Should we suffer watching a talk show? They reproduce a piece of a TV show that exemplifies a controversial media practice: inviting people who have absolutely no training or knowledge to talk about gender issues and who simply reinforce misogynist stereotypes and spread rumours against feminists and their achievements on live TV. During the twelve minutes that the piece lasts, they make fun of the supposedly qualified guests who have been invited to the show to talk about sexual harassment, and with a fine sense of humour they make their point that public TV in Spain 'has entered the game of broadcasting debates with little content and a lot of *macho* discourse'. In addition, they offer data to deconstruct the retrograde messages of the show host and the rest of the invited guests (for example, with regard to the myth of 'false accusations' of sexual harassment). At one point in the video, the host asks: '... and you, how do you see it?' To which Lozano and Méndez respond promptly: 'I see it really bad.' Throughout the video, Towanda Rebels make a sharp analysis of the talk show with endless funny comments, laughing and taking out their anger. In addition, they simulate innocence to make a point about the host and the guests, the first ones to kill any males who assault their daughters. After this passage and paraphrasing what has just been said, one of the YouTubers thinks out loud: 'This has been amazing, this show has changed my life. What have I been doing so far? I don't know how to relate to men, I should treat them like this (stiff as a stick), be mean and hate them.' The video ends with a critique of this type of talk show, suggesting they are tabloid and are constantly looking for business along the same line: 'Do you know what line? The *macho* line.'

In their commitment to combat anti-feminist media discourses, Lozano and Méndez fight against a politically void concept of feminism (McRobbie 2004) and the dangers of the 'visibility economy' (Jouët 2017), using their digital skills, self-reflection and humour. Their fresh and plain language is embedded in solid feminist theory and activism and is based on a reflective and supportive identity projected towards the community and the creation of a culture of online support (Keller, Mendes & Ringrose 2016). Towanda Rebels seek viewers' complicity by staging the discomfort we all feel when watching certain kinds of media content. They transport us to our own living room and put the words in our mouths that we would be saying while watching the show. By labelling the reactionary content as 'amazing', they make us laugh and force us to take a therapeutic distance, leading us from anger to reflection. The constant hints and sarcastic jokes about the misogynist talk show not only show us that this is a trickster debate like so many others and that we must keep our eyes open at all times but also capture our interest until the end of the video: a final, pedagogical and political allegation in which Lozano and Méndez criticise the patriarchal commodification of mainstream media. In this video, they make very clear how popular misogyny is running in parallel to the new visibility of feminism (Banet-Weiser & Miltner 2016; Keller, Mendes & Ringrose 2016), and they use a strategy of saturation to re-contextualise sexist discourse and dismantle it from a particular and feminist point of view.

These new generation feminist activists are experts in producing innovative and disruptive content. Moving between political feminism, postfeminist culture and the knowledge economy (Pruchniewska 2018), they somehow manage to confront both the individualistic feminism of neoliberal consumption culture (Rottenberg 2014) and a whole range of postfeminist representations flooding social media (Araüna, Tortajada & Willem 2019). Far from the sophisticated and 'subversive frivolity' of influencers' practices (Abidin 2016), feminist YouTubers in Spain use a casual though articulate discourse, full of political hints. A vital ingredient in their narratives is humour and irony, which were already used by other feminists in the past and now take on a new dimension thanks to the possibilities of social media (memes, cross-media references, digital creativity). Thanks to this combination of hard data and irony, they are contributing to the increase in audience and promoting feminist interconnection (Jouët 2017; Lawrence & Ringrose 2018). Their creative practices re-configure both digital media and the articulation of feminism itself (Zafra 2011; Keller 2012; Rentschler & Thrift 2015; Jouët 2017; Pruchniewska 2018) and, despite attempts of neoliberalism to individualise women's experiences, they render visible a collective feminist struggle using a language of their own (Baer 2016). Towanda Rebels' video as discussed above unmasks the role of the (public) media in a patriarchal agenda and makes the constant attacks on laws preventing gender-based violence, sexual harassment and the invisibility of women in Spain visible through reflection, denunciation and irony. These three intertwined strategies constitute a new way for young feminists to tell their stories on YouTube, ensuring that their cultural and political work on social media will ultimately lead to social transformation.

'Violent feminists': Places on the frontier

Another example of feminists fighting antifeminism on digital platforms is the journalist and activist Irantzu Varela. In her Wikipedia entry, she defines her profession as *feminazi*. Irantzu Varela receives online and offline violence and hate speech daily. Her show *El Tornillo* (The Screw) is a feminist micro space on *La Tuerka*, a programme broadcast online by Público TV. El Tornillo reflects on issues related to feminism while being critical of the feminist movement itself, applies a gender perspective to social analysis, and contests attacks on feminism. Varela's 'El Tornillo and the violent feminists' is a sarcastic monologue on 'violent feminists' in which she deconstructs one of the recurrent attacks on feminism – its supposed violent actions – with facts and figures. At the beginning of the video she appears masked, wielding a drilling tool to announce that 'the program is going to be very brief, as violent feminists do not exist'. Then she explains that in the history of feminism nobody was ever killed, injured, kidnapped or tortured in the name of feminism and that this kind of false discourse is spread by those who feel threatened by a struggle that aims to end all kinds of oppression and privilege. To prove her point she performs two different characters to caricature types of people who are reluctant to support feminism. The first character is a bearded guy embodying a sexist and homophobic masculinity, who defends his ideas vehemently, without applying argument, imposes his judgment and does not expect to be answered. The second is a female character wearing an animal print headband, representing a femininity that considers feminism as 'unnecessary', with no awareness of the feminist struggle, defending a neoliberal discourse (essentialist, naive and anti-feminist). These characters confront Varela's position, although she does not answer them but leaves it up to the audience to judge for themselves.

Irantzu Varela defines 'El Tornillo' as a 'place on the frontier', from where she presents the constant attacks on feminism as absurd and ridiculous, in line with other online feminist practices (Lawrence & Ringrose 2018). Although their visibility is low compared to mainstream popular feminism, these micro spaces promote feminist interconnection and solidarity by defending feminism in a creative and novel way (Jouët 2017; Lawrence & Ringrose 2018). Online feminist sarcasm very successfully serves to expose misogyny and sexism as desperate and old-fashioned attempts to undermine feminism (Rentschler & Thrift 2015). This happens when Towanda Rebels call the talk show guests' *umpalumpa* while beating their chests as if they were Tarzan, or when Irantzu Varela distorts her voice when embodying the bearded man, who tries to be smart but cannot help but look dumb. All of these feminists construct a discourse against oppression and present themselves outside the stereotypes of 'angry' feminists or 'man-haters'. Humour is by large the best strategy for resistance. Far from depoliticising the message, fun-making and irony reinforce the agency of both the performers and their audiences by widening the horizon of what is possible (Álvarez, Platero & Rosón 2014) and giving way to a new form of digital feminist literacy (Lawrence & Ringrose 2018).

Discussion and conclusion

After years of reorganisation, marches and protests – which have led feminism to become a movement with major capacity for mobilisation in Spain and outside – the challenge now is to establish cultural narratives and practices that can counter the rise of sexist violence and neoconservative bigotry globally. Despite frequent criticism of digital activism in terms of 'clicktivism' or 'slacktivism' (for an overview see George & Leidner 2019), we argue that the YouTubers analysed in this chapter prove that digital activism has a real impact on mobilisation both on and offline, their practices an essential element of fourth-wave feminism (Cochrane 2013) and profoundly political. These YouTubers have a fundamental role in the further expansion of feminism into the mainstream and interconnect women of all ages, ideologies and classes. But this is not an easy task: despite the skilfulness and power of the YouTubers we have looked at in this chapter and many other online activists, people who openly identify as feminists are constantly harassed online (Mantilla 2013). There is no doubt that activist YouTubers operate in a hostile environment, where reactionary machismo and misogyny are now hegemonic: content creators who do not respond to gender stereotypes and standards, or who decide to talk about feminism, receive sexist and violent comments instantly

(Döring & Mohseni 2019). One only has to look at Irantzu Varela's YouTube channel or Twitter timeline to realise how many haters and trolls she has to deal with on a daily basis. At one point, in October 2019, Varela's personal details – including her phone number – were made public on Twitter by one of her haters with the aim of threatening her.[1] These attacks are intensifying as populist movements and extreme right-wing parties increase.

The abovementioned YouTubers and their videos establish some features of contemporary feminist digital activists: humour, participation and effectiveness. Although this is a convenience sample of three, it is clear from the outset how content creators adopt some of the features of memetic communication, particularly by using irony and parodic cross-references to patriarchal tropes. Authors such as Cochrane (2013) had already suggested, despite controversies, that sense of humour is one of the features of the so-called fourth-wave feminism. In the case of our YouTubers, humour acts out as a protection against verbal aggression and the social pressures that they receive as a consequence of their online activity. Faced daily with so-called 'gendertrolling', YouTubers like Irantzu Varela release resistant responses based on sarcasm and parody, making sexist attitudes look ridiculous. The three YouTubers we have examined can afford to use humour precisely because they manage a broad set of reliable data and theoretical knowledge about feminism, which allows them to ridicule the insults and attacks disguised as notions of 'common sense' by misogynist opinion-makers.

Indeed, the punch and sarcasm in YouTube videos are features that help messages go viral, but in the case of feminist YouTubers, this may also contain pitfalls. On the one hand, they are at risk of not being understood or not being taken seriously by audiences that are less familiar with the codes of memes and other kinds of humour on social media, which may ultimately lead to a backlash against feminism in specific segments of society or to accusations of banalising the struggle. On the other hand, by entering the field of irony, feminist sarcasm is often paid back with even more sarcasm and ridicule from neoconservative populist movements, which have been managing sexist humour for a very long time. Regardless, feminist activists (should) keep on settling the fight online as they have proven to be skillful navigators on social media, capable of capturing contemporary ways of steering the narrative despite the risks.

From the start, feminism – understood as social activism – has considered occupying the streets as a necessary means for making the struggle visible in public spaces, a site that had always been denied to women. In Spain, this concern for the public space has endured, culminating in the landslide success of women's strikes on 8 March 2018, 2019 and 2020 across the whole country. Currently, feminists everywhere are aware that the public debate and the battle for hegemony are settled not only on the streets but also on social media. Consequently, one of the strategies is exposing feminist debates online, trying to provoke empathy and reflection in a smart albeit informal way. Cool young people declaring themselves feminists on YouTube and producing feminist videos is a personal and political statement that serves both to popularise feminism and to reinforce processes of personal transformation, which until now was difficult to achieve using conventional media outlets. Although feminist YouTubers operate at the margins, their number and plurality of representation attracts and connects other activists – both on and offline – and encourages a broader circulation of feminist demands and struggles.[2]

Future research should look into feminist online activists' fan forums and followers' comments to gain understanding of how their audiences interconnect with feminist discourses.

Acknowledgements

This research is part of the project FEM2017–83302-C3–1-P (2018–2021): 'Produsage juvenil en las redes sociales: construcción de la identidad sexual y gestión de las desigualdades de género' (RESPECT) funded by the MICINN.

Note

1 https://twitter.com/IrantzuVarela/status/1184476029777338369
2 Since the time of writing of this chapter some of the issues raised here have shifted in the public debate. While Feminist *produsers* are still fundamental to spreading claims for equality, we have witnessed a diversification of the debate among different feminist points of view, and a certain degree of polarization. The lockdowns following the COVID-19 pandemics have intensified online discussion in the femininist movement globally. The activists analyzed in this chapter fall into different categories regarding debates on, for example, sex work or queer and transgender expressions. We are tackling these challenges in ongoing and new research.

References

Abidin, C. (2016). 'Aren't these just young, rich women doing vain things online?': Influencer selfies as subversive frivolity. *Social Media + Society*. DOI:doi:10.1177/2056305116641342.

Álvarez, A., Platero, L. and Rosón, M. (2014). El 'estilo de la carne' en Maikrux y Falete: Feminidad, humor y agencia. *Feminismo/s*, 24, 143–162.

Araüna, N., Tortajada, I. and Willem, C. (2019). Discursos feministas yu videos de youtubers: Limites y horizontes de la politizacion yo-centrica. *Quaderns del CAC*, 45, 25–35.

Araüna, N., Dhaenens, F. and Van Bauwel, S. (2017). Historical, temporal and contemporary trends on gender and media. *Catalan Journal of Communication and Cultural Studies*, 9(2), 177–184.

Baer, H. (2016). Redoing feminism: digital activism, body politics, and neoliberalism. *Feminist Media Studies*, 16(1), 17–34.

Banet-Weiser, S. (2018). *Empowered: Popular Feminism and Popular Misogyny*. Durham, NC: Duke University Press.

Banet-Weiser, S. and Miltner, K.M. (2016). #MasculinitySoFragile: Culture, structure, and networked misogyny. *Feminist Media Studies*, 16(1), 171–174.

Bruns, A. (2008). *Blogs, Wikipedia, Second Life, and Beyond: From Production to Produsage*. New York: Peter Lang.

Campillo, I. (2019). 'If we stop, the world stops': The 2018 feminist strike in Spain. *Social Movement Studies*, 18(2), 252–258.

Cochrane, K. (2013). *All the Rebel Women: The Rise of the Fourth Wave of Feminism*. Guardian Shorts Original (ebook).

Dobson, A. (2011). Hetero-sexy representation by young women on MySpace: The politics of performing an 'objectified' self. *Outskirts*, 25.

Döring, N. and Mohseni , M.R. (2019). Male dominance and sexism on YouTube: Results of three content analyses. *Feminist Media Studies*, 19(4), 512–524.

Galarza Fernández, E., Castro-Martínez, A. and Sosa Valcárcel, A. (2019). Medios sociales y feminismo en la construcción de capital social: La red estatal de comunicadoras en España. *Anàlisi: Quaderns de Comunicació i Cultura*, 61, 1–16.

Genz, S. (2015). My job is me: Postfeminist celebrity culture and the gendering of authenticity. *Feminist Media Studies*, 15(4), 545–561.

George, J.J. and Leidner, D.E. (2019). From clicktivism to hacktivism: Understanding digital activism. *Information and Organization*. 29(3), 100249.

Gill, R. (2007). *Gender and the Media*. Cambridge: Polity.

Gill, R. (2008). Empowerment/sexism: Figuring female sexual agency in contemporary advertising. *Feminism and Psychology*, 18(1), 35–60.

Gill, R. (2016a). Postfeminism and the new cultural life of feminism. *Diffractions: Graduate Journal for the Study of Culture*, 6, 1–8.

Gill, R. (2016b). Post-postfeminism? New Feminist Visibilities in Postfeminist Times. *Feminist Media Studies*, 16(4), 610–630.

Guerra Palmero, M.J. (2019). (Des)institucionalización, políticas y movimiento feminista transnacional: una compleja cuestión a la luz de las luchas del presente. *Bajo palabra. Revista de filosofía*, 20, 245–262.

Habermas, J. (1987). *Teoría de la acción comunicativa*. Madrid: Taurus.

Horeck, T. (2014). #AskThicke: 'Blurred lines', rape culture and the feminism hashtag takeover. *Feminist Media Studies*, 14(6), 1105–1107.

Hunt, T.A. (2017).A network of one's own: Young women and the creation of youth-only transnational feminist spaces. *Young*, 25(2), 107–123.

Jerslev, A. (2016). Media Times in the time of the microcelebrity: Celebrification and the YouTuber Zoella. *International Journal of Communication*, 10, 5233–5251.

Jouët, J. (2017). Digital feminism questioning the renewal of activism. *Journal of Research in Gender Studies*, 8(1), 133–157.

Keller, J. (2012). Virtual feminisms: Girls' blogging communities, feminist activism, and participatory politics. *Information, Communication & Society*, 15(3), 429–447.

Keller, J., Mendes, K. and Ringrose, J. (2016). Speaking 'unspeakable things'; Documenting digital feminist responses to rape culture. *Journal of Gender Studies*. DOI:doi:10.1080/09589236.2016.1211511.

Lawrence, E. and Ringrose, J. (2018). @NoToFeminism, #FeministsAreUgly, and misandry memes: How social media feminist humor is calling out antifeminism. In Keller, J. and Ryan, M. (eds), *Emergent Feminisms: Complicating a Postfeminist Media Culture* (pp. 211–232). New York: Routledge.

Lotz, A. (2001). Postfeminist television criticism: Rehabilitating critical terms and identifying postfeminist attributes. *Feminist Media Studies*, 1(1), 105–121.

Mantilla, K. (2013). Gendertrolling: Misogyny adapts to new media. *Feminist Studies*, 39(2), 563–570.

McLean, J. (2020). Feminist digital spaces. In *Changing Digital Geographies*. Cham: Palgrave Macmillan (ebook).

McRobbie, A. (2004). Postfeminism and popular culture, *Feminist Media Studies*, 4(3), 255–264.

Mendes, K., Ringrose, J. and Keller , J. (2019). *Digital Feminist Activism: Girls and Women Fight Back Against Rape Culture*. Oxford: Oxford University Press.

Pérez-Torres, V., Pastor-Ruiz, Y. and Abarrou-Ben-Boubaker, S. (2018). YouTuber videos and the construction of adolescent identity / Los youtubers y la construcción de la identidad adolescente. *Comunicar*, 26(55), 61–70.

Poveda, D. and Morgade. M. (2018). Changing digital media environments and youth audiovisual productions: A comparison of two collaborative research experiences with South Madrid adolescents. *Young*, 26(46), 34–55.

Pruchniewska, U.M. (2018). Branding the self as an 'authentic feminist': Negotiating feminist values in postfeminist digital cultural production. *Feminist Media Studies*, 18(5), 810–824.

Rentschler, C. and Thrift, S. (2015). Doing feminism in the network: Networked laughter and the 'Binders Full of Women' meme. *Feminist Theory*, 16(3), 329–359.

Retallack, H., Ringrose, J.L. and Lawrence, E. (2016). 'Fuck your body image': Teen girls' Twitter and Instagram feminism in and around school. In Coffey, J., Budgeon, S. and Cahill, H. (eds), *Learning Bodies: The Body in Youth and Childhood Studies* (pp. 85–103). New York: Springer.

Rottenberg, C. (2014). The rise of neoliberal feminism. *Cultural Studies*, 28(3), 418–437.

Szostak, N. (2013). Girls on YouTube: Gender politics and the potential for a public sphere. *McMaster Journal of Communication*, 8(10), 46–58.

Tortajada, I. and Van Bauwel, S. (2012). Gender and communication: Contemporary research questions. *Catalan Journal of Communication & Cultural Studies*, 4(2), 143–153.

Tortajada, I., Caballero-Gálvez, A.A. and Willem, C. (2019). Contrapúblicos en YouTube: El caso del colectivo trans. *El profesional de la información*, 28(6), e280622.

Zafra, R. (2011). Un cuarto propio conectado: Feminismo y creación desde la esfera público-privada online. *Asparkía. Investigació feminista*, 22, 115–129.

2

UN/FIT FOR YOUNG VIEWERS

LGBT+ representation in Flemish and Irish children's television

Florian Vanlee and Páraic Kerrigan

Introduction

Analyses of LGBT+ representations on television feature in queer studies since the 1990s (e.g. Fejes & Petrich 1993, Battles & Hilton-Morrow 2002, Chambers 2009, Dhaenens 2012, Marshall 2016) – unsurprisingly, given the field's constructionist perspective. Committed to deconstructing gender and sexuality's (re)creation and regulation through cultural representations (Warner 2000), popular television is a crucial site for queer scholarship. TV remains a formidable force in contemporary culture, validating certain sexual and gender identity configurations while marginalising others. Scholars have discussed how television representations of LGBT + people reiterate the hetero- and cisnormative status quo (e.g. Avila-Saavedra 2009, Kies 2016) or, conversely, subvert heteronormality by queering established representational strategies (e.g. Munt 2006, Dhaenens & Van Bauwel 2012). This is not to say that queer television analyses adopt exclusively textual perspectives. Some address issues of sexuality and gender in relation to organisational aspects of television (e.g. Aslinger 2009, Ng 2013, Kerrigan 2016), while others explore television producers' discourses on creating LGBT+ characters (e.g. Martin 2015, Thorfinssdottir & Jensen 2017).

Despite this demonstrable variety, productions intended for children and adolescents remain dramatically understudied (Kelso 2015), and little is known about LGBT+ portrayals in content consumed by young audiences. TV representations are nevertheless formative resources for young people's attitudes on gender and sexuality, and are therefore a crucial site of analysis. Because queer television studies have predominantly scrutinised US programming (see Vanlee 2019), the dearth of works on LGBT+ portrayals in television content for young audiences is likely related to the invisibility of sexual and gender diversity in US children's television. As Dennis (2009: 751), notes, the 'intentional portrayal [of LGBT+ people] would result in howls of outrage and probable cancellation [of a programme intended for children and/or adolescents]', and the absence of (openly) non-heterosexual or non-cisgendered characters presumably accounts for the scarcity of queer television scholarship on this particular segment of US TV programming. That such LGBT+ representations are structurally absent from US programming by no way means that this situation can be universalised. With Isak, Even and Eskild, Norwegian teen web series *Skam* [Shame] (NRK 2015–2017) – produced and distributed by public service broadcaster [PSB] NRK – features three openly non-heterosexual characters, for instance. Similarly, German PSB children's soap opera *Schloss Einstein* [Castle Einstein] (KiKa 1998–) ran a storyline in 2008 on Marie-Luise entering into a short-lived relationship with her roommate Karla. That these portrayals occurred openly in PSB's programming for young audiences suggests that potential '*howls of outrage*' (Dennis 2009: 751) are less of a consideration, but also allude to TV production cultures that recognise the necessity of featuring LGBT+ roles in content for children and adolescents. Naturally, these are anecdotal examples that support claims about shared progressive discourses on LGBT+ representation in Western European PSB programming for young audiences. For instance, Thorfinnsdottir and Jensen (2017) show that children's programming of some PSBs – in this case, Denmark's DR – '*serves to reinforce heteronormativity*' (413) and rarely undermines it.

Despite qualitative differences demonstrated by aforementioned examples, they suggest LGBT+ televisibility[1] – or the overt presence of LGBT+ people in TV content – in Western European PSB children's and youth offerings. This coincides with historical parallels in mainstream portrayals of LGBT+ people on Western European small screens (see Vanlee 2019), but calls for further analyses of PSBs' engagement with sexual and gender diversity in their young audience schedules. Focused on LGBT+ televisibility in Flanders and Ireland, this chapter offers a comparative analysis tracing the earliest instances of explicit attention for (certain) LGBT+ people to the contemporary role of sexual and gender diversity in children's and youth offerings. First assessing the position of children's and youth programming at VRT[23] and RTÉ[4] – the Flemish and Irish PSBs respectively – it asserts the prominence of this segment in both schedules. Regulating the style and substance of content intended for young audiences was a core consideration herein, both for in-house production and the selection of foreign imports. Turning to the earliest portrayals of same-sex desire, it shows how domestic non-fiction programming offered initial pathways for rare but explicit instances of LGBT+ televisibility in the 1970s. Where these first examples in Flanders and Ireland parallel each other in their contingency on prosocial discourses on PSB responsibilities, subsequent developments in LGBT+ mainstreaming differ significantly. Starting in the late 1990s, VRT fiction productions for young audiences increasingly feature LGBT+ characters and counter their limited visibility in popular imported series broadcast by domestic commercial channels. RTÉ, by contrast, embraced imports with openly LGBT+ characters – primarily British and Australian – to address the subject without risking potential controversy. These contemporary differences notwithstanding, the chapter concludes by asserting the comparability of both cases and the formative role of PSB remits in ensuring LGBT+ televisibility children's content.

Youth programming in Flanders and Ireland

Each a small domestic TV market and industry, Flanders and Ireland have several comparable characteristics. Like most Western European contexts, both currently feature public service, commercial and independent company actors, although VRT and RTÉ historically enjoyed monopolies (see Corcoran 1996, Dhoest 2007). Temporary difficulties to retain dominance upon commercial rivals' entry to the market notwithstanding, both PSBs were and are at the core of their regional media ecosystem. The charters and policy documents structuring their operations keep VRT and RTÉ not only to serving children and young audiences but also to clauses about the substance of content and notions of diversity in representation. This has motivated them to produce and/or commission domestic TV content for their youngest audience segments. Nevertheless, both regions, like many small-scale European media landscapes (see Moran 2007), are subject to global market forces regarding children's TV. High prices in domestic production and the need to fill schedules ensure circulation of international youth content on commercial and public channels in Ireland and Flanders. Accordingly, studying historical and contemporary LGBT+ televisibility on the Flemish and Irish small screens cannot consider domestic productions exclusively, as LGBT+ televisibility may be enacted through imports. Whereas the diversity mandates of VRT and RTÉ underline the relevance of analysing 'homegrown' programming, the Irish case in particular emphasises the importance of purchasing strategies to LGBT+ televisibility.

Initially though, like in other European countries, domestic TV content for young audiences originated in PSB offerings (see Corcoran 1996, Dhoest 2007). Flemish VRT first prioritised youth programming in 1960; creating the Youth and Documentary department in the Directorate for Cultural Programs, which became an autonomous department in 1975 (see Dhoest 2007: 313). In Ireland, the RTÉ Authority's commitment to (domestic) children's programming was evidenced by appointing a Head of Children's programmes, Maeve Conway, in 1962. In the first year of broadcasting there were 253 hours of children's programming, a figure that increased in subsequent decades (Gilligan 1993). Producing and programming content for young audiences was deemed important enough to merit autonomous departments at VRT and RTÉ. This is unsurprising because PSB TV for children is a historical site of concern over appropriateness and demands for 'elevating content'. As Buckingham (1995) notes, 'children's television is not produced by children, but for them', and accordingly, 'children's television is often more of a reflection of adult interests, fantasies or desires' (p. 47). Irish youth programming has always been contentious, both as a site of production and as a vehicle of representation (see Corcoran 1996). That youth content came under the Directorate for Cultural Programs at VRT – rather than under Current Affairs' or 'Film and Entertainment – points to the desire to carefully gatekeep programmes offered to young audiences in Flanders brought by concerns about potential 'nefarious influences' on children (see Dhoest 2007: 313–14).

Paternalism was not confined to the production of in-house, domestic series and shows. Although this composed much of RTÉ's children and young people offerings, imported children's programming has historically filled at least half of the television schedule since the first year of broadcast (see Gilligan 1993, Linehan 2016). Gatekeeping 'appropriate' content therefore took place in acquisition too. For instance, VRT's department of Acquisition of Foreign Fiction – mandated to purchase children's series – intentionally steered clear from portrayals of violence before 22h00 (Dhoest 2007: 314). That the department explicitly contrasted this to Dutch channels available to Flemish audiences (ibid.: 314) points to considerations articulating youth TV programming strategies to tensions between domestically produced and imported content, and the different norms they reflect. Indeed, Flanders and Ireland are examples of dual-reception television markets, with domestic and foreign broadcasters on offer. In Ireland, BBC and ITV were fully available, particularly along the east coast. This became more pervasive in the 1980s, when cable television became established, effectuating a multi-channel reception system simultaneously offering Irish and British terrestrial television (see Kerrigan 2020). Dutch broadcasters – including commercial stations, which did not exist in Flanders before 1989 – formed VRT's competitors. This adds to the relevance of studying portrayals of sexual and gender diversity in Flemish and Irish children's television. The multi-channel media system ensures variety – regarding public/commercial and domestic/imported texts – in the content consumed by children and young viewers. This heterogeneity ensures youthful audiences' exposure to varying ideological frameworks potentially at odds with domestic norms, inviting specific approaches that negotiate contingent circumstances. As the analyses below show, VRT and RTÉ developed distinct strategies to deal with LGBT+ televisibility in their respective markets.

Flanders and Ireland uphold comparable organisational distinctions in youth TV content. The categorisation into pre-school, children's and young people programming throughout RTÉ's existence (Holt and Sheehan 1997) surfaces in the schedule of KETNET – VRT's dedicated children's channel since 1997 – with daytime content for toddlers, afternoon children's programmes and series for adolescents in the early evening (see Vanlee et al. 2018a). Children's television is an expressively globalised programming type (Havens 2007) though, and neither Flanders nor Ireland are exceptional cases. VRT and RTÉ offer a mixture of 'homegrown' content and a selection of foreign imports. In comparison to RTÉ, VRT tends to broadcast more domestic productions intended for children, though. This reflects stagnating funds for public service broadcasting throughout RTÉ's history, but also the institutional position of children's programming in the organisation, which was often not financially prioritised (Gilligan 1993). Additionally, it is related to a linguistic matter, with VRT producing or commissioning more programmes to address viewer demands for content in the regional language (i.e. Dutch) and fulfill its educational mandate vis-à-vis young audiences. This has been exasperated, moreover, by commercial Flemish broadcasters' relative lack of interest in content for young audiences.

An important difference between Flemish and Irish TV content for young audiences is the operationalisation of (government) directives and expectations in output. Since its inception, Irish children's programming follows strict formal categories: story programmes, variety and magazine programmes, information programming and arts and crafts (Gilligan 1993). Divided into genres, Irish programming policy envisions an equilibrium between different kinds of children's TV content, resulting in productions pertaining to identifiable categories. Flemish programming policy for children's TV has historically emphasised central PSB values, not genres. Mandating attention for 'information, education and entertainment' (Dhoest 2007: 313–314) prioritises certain elements for productions, but does not formulate generic expectations. Combining 'information', 'education' and 'entertainment' in one production, therefore, became common practice, resulting in a growing catalogue of domestic fiction series for young viewers since the 1960s (see Dhoest 2007: 314–316) – with educational or informational qualities substantiated by their setting or focus. Compared to Ireland, this permissiveness for youth programming at VRT resulted in increased fiction production at the expense of variety, magazine and information programming. The significant differences between LGBT+ televisibility in Irish and Flemish youth programming are situated on this fault line. Inasmuch as VRT has effectuated a visible presence of LGBT+ characters in children's fiction programming since the 1990s, a survey of the RTÉ Archives reveals a minimal presence in terms of domestically produced content pertaining to queerness and children. Expressively contrasting the Flemish situation, however, those ephemeral, brief traces of LGBT+ visibility in content intended for young audiences are to be found in informational segments since the 1970s. Following the trajectory of much LGBT+ content in contemporaneous Irish broadcasting, particularly within news and current affairs (Kerrigan 2017, 2018), children's information programming fostered prosocial discourses around LGBT+ identities.

'Keeping it real': LGBT+ televisibility in 20th-century youth programming

One of the earliest Irish examples hereof was a special episode on relationships in *Youngline* (1975–1983) – a youth magazine programme composed of various interest pieces that often featured discussions among young audience members. Although the episode itself did not address LGBT+ issues, two of the audience members happened to be gay and used the airtime to discuss similarities between heterosexual and homosexual relationships, noting the added pressure of the oppressive Irish society of the time on those endeavouring to maintain a gay relationship. Their points were positively embraced, but constituted a fleeting instance of visibility. At its founding, *OUT* – Ireland's first commercial LGBT+ magazine – obtained a slot on children's magazine programme *TV Gaga* (1985–1987), a children's magazine programme, for a feature and an interview with founder Edmund Lynch. This presentation of a commercial LGBT+ publication on such a show initiated active acknowledgments of LGBT+ people at RTÉ. A significant moment for LGBT+ visibility was Ciana

Campbell's *Talk It Over* (1987), an intimate discussion programme examining topical issues for young people. One episode's subject centralised a letter sent by a teenager feeling 'homosexual tendencies he could not come to terms with' (RTÉ Archives, 1988). Responding to the letter, Don Donnelly, gay rights activist and director of Tel-A-Friend, a confidential counselling support phone service, offered advice and support, noting that there are services out there and a welcoming gay community when he chose to come out. These moments account for just three instances in RTÉ's early broadcasting history, revealing an undeniable lack of queerness at the broadcaster. Despite its ephemerality, however, children's programming displayed momentary potential to counter exclusionary tendencies in broadcasting.

Composed primarily of fiction series that loosely reflect VRT's core values, Flemish youth programming schedules before the 1990s are decidedly different. Where RTÉ emphasised non-fiction formats, domestic series and serials have long been a staple of VRT youth content – acting as a popular vehicle to address its PSB missions. Historical serials like *Dirk Van Haveskerke* (BRT 1978) – thematising Flemish struggles for emancipation from France in the 14th century – or *Tijl Uilenspiegel* [Till Eulenspeigel] (BRT 1961) – based on the eponymous picaresque character from Low Countries folklore – introduced children to meaningful components of Flemish identity through entertainment, paralleling historical fiction for adults (see Dhoest 2001). Serials with contemporaneous settings – like *Het Veen-mysterie* [The Bog Mystery] (BRT 1982), featuring revived Paleolithic creatures – touched upon scientific subjects while also offering moral examples for young viewers. When surveyed about childhood memories of domestic television, older Flemish audiences invariably refer to fiction series of the 1960s and 1970s (see Dhoest 2015), underscoring the marginal role of non-fiction in youth programming. This strong emphasis on fiction came at the expense of the comparatively greater opportunity to address same-sex desire offered by non-fiction programmes testified to by Irish examples. Instances of implied homosexuality aside, like opera-singing hairdresser Alberto Vermicelli in sitcom *Samson & Gert* (VRT/KETNET 1990–),[5] non-heterosexuality was addressed only once in Flemish youth programming before the surge of LGBT+ televisibility in the late 1990s. In 1970, popular singer Will Ferdy appeared as a guest in *Tienerklanken* [Teenage Sounds] (BRT 1961–1973), a variety show featuring Flemish music intended for adolescent and young adult viewers. During *Inspraak* [Participation], a segment addressing relevant themes to young people, Ferdy revealed his homosexuality (see Herreman 2017). *Tienerklanken* is not strictly youth programming – because it was featured in an 'adult' timeslot – but it is notable to observe that this early instance of LGBT+ televisibility surfaced as something 'relevant to young people'. Clearly, Ferdy's ability to address his homosexuality in a programme watched by young people suggests a degree of permissiveness in VRT attitudes towards homosexuality in the 1970s. He was neither interrupted nor judged by show host Louis Neefs, moreover. Rather, the moment was couched in the prosocial frameworks the PSB had deployed with same-sex desire since the 1966 broadcast of *Diagnose van het Anders-Zijn* [Diagnosis of Being Different] (BRT) (see Borghs 2016) – which addressed the marginalisation Flemish gay men faced. This momentary instance of gay televisibility in Flemish adolescent and young adult programming nevertheless remained an oddity.

The prosocial discourses of children's information programming that affirmed LGBT+ identities in Ireland – but to a lesser extent in Flanders too – did not translate to children's television fiction. These series continued to feature more problematic representations, particularly on gay men. The only inclusion of LGBT+ issues on Irish youth fiction happened in *Finbar's Class* (1994–1996), a drama series on a group of teenagers from a working-class area of north inner-city Dublin. Novice teacher Finbar, taking a vested interest in the youngster's educational endeavours, attempts to encourage them through music and set them on the right, 'respectable' path. None of the main characters identified as LGBT+, but the show's second season introduced a problematic storyline on a predatory sex ring of gay men attempting to groom boys. The sex ring storyline features pop mogul Geoff attempting to recruit teenage boys for his new band, accosting central character Snowy randomly on the street, informing him 'he's exactly what he's looking for'. Initially tempted by the promise of stardom (offered a chance to feature in 'Irelands next boyband sensation'), he declines, with Geoff's project soon uncovered as a gay sex ring. Problematically, this instance of LGBT+ visibility is couched in homophobic stereotypes of predatory older gay men. Deploying these tropes, however brief, infers that gay identities are problematic, articulating associations with criminality and abuse. While fleeting, such portrayals align with early representational strategies noted by Gross (2001), Dyer (1990) and Russo (1981), associating homosexuality with criminality and paedophilia. Such problematic tropes potentially reflect production cultures in RTÉ at the time, with writers not knowing how to write gay characters and falling upon stereotypes (Kerrigan 2020). Flemish youth programming, by contrast, knew few instances wherein LGBT+ people were vilified or ridiculed, but at the cost of invisibility – and youth and adult programming in Flanders differ herein (see Vanlee 2019). In the 1990s, however, domestic portrayals of sexual and (later) gender diversity suddenly became a mainstay in Flemish youth programming. Here, again, Flanders and Ireland show different trajectories of LGBT+ representations in children's TV content.

Important imports: LGBT+ portrayals in 21st-century youth programming

Although imports featured in VRT youth schedules beforehand, the liberalisation of the Flemish market in 1989 (see Raats & Pauwels 2013) the levels of foreign productions on public and private domestic channels – in terms of adult and youth scheduling. Domestic youth television content is almost exclusively produced and distributed by VRT children and youth channel KETNET. Of the 32 domestic youth productions between 2000 and 2016, 27 were produced for and broadcasted by KETNET (see Vanlee et al. 2018a). Commercial broadcasters' limited interest here is likely informed by Flemish legal frameworks on youth programming. These stipulate that segments intended for young viewers cannot be interrupted by advertisements, and enforce a ten-minute embargo for commercial messages before and after broadcasting such productions. Consequently, commercial broadcasters are less incentivised to make investments in domestic productions for young audiences, which cannot generate much advertising revenue. Commercial channel VTM[6] – now a subsidiary of media conglomerate DPG Media – has operated a dedicated youth programming channel since 2000, and has produced and broadcast five children's programmes to this date (see Vanlee et al. 2018a). De Vijver Media, the second commercial Flemish broadcaster – operating channels VIER, VIJF and ZES – has long glossed over domestically produced youth programming, but currently distributes a remake of the Norwegian web series *Skam* called *WtFOCK* (VIER 2018–) online. This is the broadcaster's first domestic production for (pre) adolescents, and other youth programming consists of foreign imports. Finally, international television conglomerates – like Viacom subsidiary Nickelodeon Vlaanderen – offer youth programming but do not produce or programme 'homegrown' content.

More often than not, imports scheduled by Flemish commercial broadcasters originate in the US, ridiculing LGBT+ people or altogether erasing them (see Dennis 2009, Kelso 2015). Reflecting increased visibility and acceptance of same-sex desire in late 1990s/early 2000s Flemish society (see Borghs 2016), KETNET productions suddenly started counteracting the lack of LGBT+ televisibility in imported productions. Since introducing openly gay man Steve in youth sitcom *W817* (KETNET 1999–2003) (see Vanlee et al. 2018b) – 25 openly LGBT+ characters have been included in domestic children's fiction programming. Of this total, 19 featured in content produced for and broadcast by PSB channel KETNET, with commercial productions including LGBT+ characters since 2014 (see Table 2.1). Contrasting commercial portrayals, moreover, LGBT+ characters on KETNET distinguish themselves as prominent, main characters with full-fledged storylines.

W817's first season treated lead character Steve's homosexuality as a mere given – with most characters aware of and comfortable with his sexuality at the series' onset. He and his boyfriend Tony would sometimes kiss or make allusions to their sex life, without this setting them apart from the rest of the sitcom's core group. Rather, the 'difference' of non-heterosexuality was banalised in relation to that of other, straight characters, producing a sense of 'queer normality' (see Vanlee et al. 2018b). Since this first character, explicit attention for same-sex desire has been a consistent theme in KETNET productions. A survey of the LGBT+ characters they have featured over the past twenty years (see Table 2.1) illustrates several representational patterns. Flagship productions like *Spring* (2002–2008), *En Daarmee Basta* (2005–2008) and *D5R* (2014–) include non-heterosexual lead roles, whose romantic encounters are subsequently cast on consecutive side or guest characters. Kathy's bisexuality in *En Daarmee Basta*, for instance, was acknowledged but not 'performed' in the series first season, and concretised in the next season by a fling with neighbour Joost and subsequent stable relation with Lies – a girl from her ice hockey team. Later, her second girlfriend Laura replaced Kathy as a main

TABLE 2.1 LGBT+ characters in Flemish domestic youth fiction programming since 1999 (N=25)

Series	Channel	Genre	Character	Type	Gender	Sexuality	Age	Period
W817	KETNET	Sitcom	Steve	Main	Cis Man	Homosexual	Young adult	1999–2003
			Tony	Side	Cis Man	Homosexual	Young adult	1999–2001, 2003
			Robbie	Side	Cis Man	Homosexual	Young adult	2002–2003
Spring	KETNET	Soap opera	Jo De Klein	Main	Cis Man	Homosexual	Young adult	2005–2008
			Ben	Side	Cis Man	Homosexual	Young adult	2006
			Koen	Guest	Cis Man	Homosexual	Adult	2008
En Daamee Basta	KETNET	Sitcom	Kathy	Main	Cis Woman	Bisexual	Adolescent	2005–2007
			Lies	Side	Cis Woman	Bisexual or Lesbian	Adolescent	2006
			Laura	Side-Main	Cis Woman	Bisexual	Adolescent	2007–2008
Ghost Rockers	KETNET	Soap opera/Musical	Alex	Main	Cis Man	Homosexual	Adolescent	2014–2017
			Jules	Main	Cis Man	Homosexual	Adolescent	2016–2017
Teen Scenes	JIM TV	Scripted reality	Maarten	Side	Cis Man	Homosexual	Adolescent	2014
D5R	KETNET	Scripted reality/ Soap opera	Vincent	Main	Cis Man	Homosexual	Adolescent- Young Adult	2014–
			Bernt	Guest	Cis Man	Homosexual	Young adult	2018
			Jonas	Main	Cis Man	Homosexual	Young adult	2018–
4eVeR	KETNET	Scripted reality/ Soap opera	Marieke	Side	Cis Woman	Lesbian	Adult	2017–2019
			Patje	Side	Cis Woman	Lesbian	Adult	2017–2019

Series	Channel	Genre	Character	Type	Gender	Sexuality	Age	Period
#Likeme	KETNET	Soap opera/Musical	Lewis	Main	Trans Man	?	Adolescent	2019
			Olivier Dubois	Side	Cis Man	Homosexual	Adult	2019-
			Philippe Meusen	Side	Cis Man	Homosexual	Adult	2019-
Vloglab Beach	VTM Kids	Scripted reality/Soap opera	Leandro	Guest	Cis Man	Homosexual	Young adult	2018
			Unknown	Guest	Cis Man	Homosexual	Young adult	2018
WtFOCK	VIER	Scripted reality/Soap opera	Robbe	Main	Cis Man	Homosexual	Young adult	2018-
			Sander	Main	Cis Man	Homosexual	Young adult	2018-
			Milan	Side	Cis Man	Homosexual	Young adult	2018-

character and fell in love with main male role Ruben. Crucially, less frequently featured characters' sexuality – most notably that of their partners – never served comic effect, as happens in sitcoms (see Walters 2003). Instead, their presence simply confirmed the same-sex desire of main roles – which had been established beforehand. The limited seriality of the sitcom genre gave way to representational strategies deemphasising non-heterosexuality's centrality as a narrative device. In *D5R*, Vincent's homosexuality was first addressed by focusing on his unrequited love for his straight best friend Wout. Later, guest character Bernt was introduced to provide Vincent with a romantic storyline, after which he became involved with Jonas – initially cast for a side role but eventually becoming a main character. These examples clearly allude to profound qualitative differences in how same-sex desire has been dealt with in PSB and commercial youth content.

Indeed, *WtFOCK* is the first commercial production to openly deal with same-sex desire – situating the onset of LGBT+ televisibility in Flemish commercial youth programming in 2018. Notably, the sexuality of earlier LGBT+ characters in KETNET series was just a given. Each felt comfortable with their desire, and young viewers learned about it through organic references made by themselves or by other characters throughout the series. This way, non-heterosexuality was not constructed as something to be 'confessed' (see Herman 2005), but as an everyday fact in one's existence. Contemporary domestic commercial and PSB series show different approaches to same-sex desire in youth programming. This relates to genre: early examples such as Steve and Kathy featured in sitcoms – a genre less accommodating to prolonged character development (see Battles & Hilton-Morrow 2002). Later examples like Lewis (*4eVeR*) or Alex (*Ghost Rockers*) surfaced in productions resembling soap operas, and give considerable attention to coming to terms with sexual or gendered difference. Contrasting earlier logics, contemporary tendencies to *develop* rather than *feature* LGBT+ characters allow series to go into the particular hardships (some) LGBT+ adolescents and young adults face. Arguably, this represents a new phase in KETNET's commitment to offer productions resonating with its young viewership. This aligns with aforementioned core VRT values, and negotiates the absence of LGBT+ portrayals in imports with domestic fiction content. This is not to say that Flemish youth programming is without its defaults on this subject. The limited diversity in 'sexual and gender diversity' characteristic of Flemish TV fiction in general (see Vanlee 2019) seems exaggerated in children's content. Lesbian or bisexual characters – female and male – remain underrepresented, for instance, as are trans characters (see Table 2.1). The relative prominence of LGBT+ characters in general cannot be allowed to obscure the inequities within LGBT+ televisibility, which continue to reflect gendered power mechanisms that erase lesbian, bisexual and trans experiences from the smallest screen.

Ireland on the other hand provides an almost inverted image of Flemish tendencies since 1999. Indeed, the Irish situation digresses from European broadcasters altogether. Whereas Flemish children's television has witnessed a tendency to develop LGBT+ characters, rather than only feature them, Irish TV has confined

TABLE 2.2 LGBT+ characters in youth fiction programming broadcast in Ireland since 1992 (domestic and imported programming aimed at youths) (domestic, N=1; imported youth programming, N= 23)

Series	Channel	Genre	Character	Type	Gender	Sexuality	Age	Period
Finbar's Class	RTÉ 2	Television drama	Snowy	Guest	Cis Man	Homosexual	Adult	1996
Grange Hill	BBC 1	Television drama	Mr Brisley	Main	Cis Man	Homosexual	Adult	1992–1999
Home and Away	RTÉ 2/ Channel 7 Australia	Soap opera	Ty Anderson	Main	Cis Man	Homosexual	Adolescent	2018
			Charlie Buckton	Main	Cis Woman	Bisexual	Adult	2008–2013
			Joey Collins	Guest	Cis Woman	Lesbian	Adult	2009
			Christopher Fletcher	Guest	Cis Man	Homosexual	Adolescent	2003
			Dean Silverman	Guest	Cis Man	Homosexual/Bisexual	Adolescent	2006
			Gareth Westwood	Guest	Cis Man	Homosexual/Bisexual	Adolescent	2006
Neighbours	RTÉ 2/ Chanel 10 Australia	Soap opera	Gino Esposito	Main	Cis Man	Homosexual	Adult	2000–2007
			Lana Crawford	Guest	Cis Woman	Lesbian	Adolescent/Adult	2004–2005; 2020 -
			Sky Mangel	Main	Cis Woman	Bisexual	Adolescent/Adult	2003–2007; 2020 -

Series	Channel	Genre	Character	Type	Gender	Sexuality	Age	Period
			Stephanie Scully	Main	Cis Woman	Bisexual	Adult	1999–2018
			Chris Pappas	Main	Cis Man	Homosexual	Adolescent	2010–2015
			Aidan Foster	Main	Cis Man	Homosexual	Adult	2011–2013
			Hudson Walsh	Guest	Cis Man	Homosexual	Adult	2013–2014
			Nate Kinski	Guest	Cis Man	Homosexual	Adult	2014–2016
			Aaron Brennan	Main	Cis Man	Homosexual	Adult	2015 –
			Tom Quill	Guest	Cis Man	Homosexual	Adult	2016–2017
			David Tanaka	Main	Cis Man	Homosexual	Adult	2016–
			Chloe Brennan	Guest	Cis Woman	Bisexual	Adult	2018
			Melissa Lohan	Guest	Cis Woman	Lesbian	Adult	2019
			Rafael Humphries	Guest	Cis Man	Homosexual	Adult	2018
			Rory Zemiro	Guest	Cis Man	Homosexual	Adult	2017–2018
			Mick Allsop	Guest	Cis Man	Homosexual	Adult	2018

LGBT+ characters to information programming for young people, and in one instance, inexorably articulated LGBT+ identities to harmful stereotypes in fiction. Earlier examples notwithstanding, LGBT+ visibility on Irish children's television programming throughout the 2000s and 2010s has been scarce, with a notable anomaly in coverage of the marriage equality referendum, when children's news programme *News2Day* (2003–) included stories on the campaign and eventual 'yes' result. But while domestic programming historically comprised much of RTÉ's children and young people schedule, imported children's programming has comprised more than half of the television schedule since the first year of broadcast (see Gilligan 1993, Linehan 2016).

Accordingly, where LGBT+ representations may have fallen short in domestic fiction programming, mediated images of LGBT+ identities were transmitted to young people in Ireland through imported English-language programming on RTÉ or access to British channels on Irish cable services. Popular children's drama series *Grange Hill* (1978–2008), widely available in Ireland through BBC1, introduced a gay teacher, Mr Brisley, in 1992, who became a central character until his departure in 1999. Although initially subjected to homophobic taunts by students, Mr Brisley's sexuality became widely accepted within the text and explored numerous relationships and difficulties associated with his sexuality, including challenges to obtaining a promotion within the school administration. In the early 2000s, RTÉ2 focused a lot of its resources on children and young people's content and began a teen-orientated programming block from 17:30 to 19:00, featuring international sitcoms and soap operas with a teen appeal. Australian soap operas *Neighbours* (1985 –) and *Home and Away* (1988–) supported this designated teen slot and occasionally offered transgressive LGBT+ fare. Together, both shows included 22 LGBT+ characters since their entry into this teen block. In *Neighbours*, 2004 saw cast regular Sky kiss classmate Alana in the show's first gay kiss. This was followed by a series of LGBT+ storylines from 2008 onwards, with married gay couple Aaron Brennan and David Tanaka becoming main cast members and Sky and Lana's 2020 return and marriage. The show portrayed several teens and their coming-out experiences, including Chris Pappas and David Tanaka. *Home and Away* similarly saw its first overtly gay storyline in 2009, when police officer Charlie Buckton began a brief lesbian relationship with Joey Collins. This was an anomaly, given that much representation on Irish programming has centralised gay male experiences (see Kerrigan 2020), which is also reflected in imported youth programming. This internationalisation of television, particularly in relation to children's television, wrought LGBT+ visibility into the Irish media landscape – reflecting existing patterns of visibility and invisibility. Like domestic productions in Flanders, imports offer a partial image of the LGBT+ community, emphasising white, middle-class gay male couples and underrepresenting lesbian women, bisexual roles and trans characters (see Becker 2006). Nevertheless, imports were certainly at odds with domestic programming, given that some of that content tended to be more transgressive around sexual identity and often conflicted directly with Ireland's cultural conservatism.

Conclusion

With few indications about 'howls of outrage' (Dennis 2009: 751), young television audiences in Flanders and Ireland have increasingly witnessed LGBT+ televisibility on domestic channels since the 1970s. Initially with fleeting instances of
visible queerness – like Will Ferdy's coming out in Flanders or Edmund Lynch's
presence on *TV Gaga* – VRT and RTÉ have since followed contingent trajectories
of growing LGBT+ televisibility on the smallest screen. VRT emphasises domestic
fiction series to meet responsibilities regarding socio-cultural diversity in youth
programming (see Dhoest 2007) – particularly since the increased attention for gay
and lesbian rights in the 1990s (see Borghs 2016). With commercial domestic
broadcasters' children's and youth schedules made up primarily of US imports,
VRT's practice of including LGBT+ characters in its flagship productions has
effectively safeguarded LGBT+ televisibility on the Flemish smallest screen.
Wedged between a conservative socio-cultural climate on the one hand (see Kerrigan 2018) and a demand to be attentive for various forms of diversity on the
other, RTÉ has conversely taken to carefully selecting imports to ensure LGBT+
televisibility. Less involved in fiction production altogether, RTÉ2's youth schedule has and continues to offer an opportunity to materialise prosocial discourses
on sexual and gender diversity in content consumed by children and young audiences. Rather than pursuing creative control over the *production* of imagery and
narratives deemed suitable for young audiences, RTÉ's commitment to LGBT+
televisibility emphasises selection procedures in acquisition. This is not to say that
representations of sexual and gender diversity on the smallest screen in Flanders and
Ireland are without defaults, or that VRT and RTÉ practices are univocally laud-
able. Neither the 'active' system in Flanders nor the 'passive' system in Ireland
necessarily leads to equitable regimes of representation – with a noted over-
representation of gay male characters in both schedules, for instance. It is nevertheless important to emphasise that these PSBs have translated directives in their
respective management agreements (see Vanlee et al. 2018b, Kerrigan 2018) into
observable increases in the frequency with which children and youth audiences
witness LGBT+ televisibility in Flanders and Ireland. More than anything else, this
hints at production cultures centralising the prosocial potential of television representation, and invites domestic queer scholarship to reflect on the contributions it
might make in this regard.

Notes

1 The term 'televisibility' refers to instances of explicit rather than implicit attention for
   sexual and gender diversity. As such, when the term is used, it does not allude to portrayals that invite queer readings or suggest same-sex desire/non-binary gender identification, but to representations overtly coded as such.
2 *Vlaamse Radio- en Televisieomroeporganisatie* [Flemish Radio & Television Broadcasting
   Organization].
3 At the time, VRT was not yet regionalised and was called NIR. For the sake of clarity,
   this chapter will consistently address the Flemish PSB by its current name.

4 *Raidió Teilifís Éireann* [Radio-Television of Ireland].
5 Alberto Vermicelli was outed as gay in 2017 by the actor portraying the role. His same-sex desire was never explicated in the series, however, hence his absence in the overview of LGBT+ character in Flemish children's and youth programming (i.e. Table 2.1).
6 *Vlaamse Televisiemaatschappij* [Flemish Television Company].

References

Aslinger, B. (2009). Creating a network for queer audiences at Logo TV. *Popular Communication*, 7(2), 107–121.

Avila-Saavedra, G. (2009). Nothing queer about queer television: Televized construction of gay masculinities. *Media, Culture & Society*, 31(1), 5–21.

Battles, K., and Hilton-Morrow, W. (2002). Gay characters in conventional spaces: Will and Grace and the situation comedy genre. *Critical Studies in Media Communication*, 19(1), 87–105.

Becker, R. (2006). *Gay TV and straight America*. Newark, NJ: Rutgers University Press.

Borghs, P. (2016). The gay and lesbian movement in Belgium from the 1950s to the present. *QED: A Journal in GLBTQ Worldmaking*, 3(3), 29–70.

Buckingham, D. (1995). On the impossibility of children's television. In C. Bazalgette and D. Buckingham (eds), *In Front of the Children* (pp. 47–61). London: British Film Institute.

Chambers, S. A. (2009). *The Queer Politics of Television*. London: I.B. Tauris.

Corcoran, F. (1996). Children and television advertising. *Irish Communications Review*, 6(1), 83–88.

Dennis, J. P. (2009). The boy who would be queen: Hints and closets on children's television. *Journal of Homosexuality*, 56(6), 738–756.

Dhaenens, F. (2012). Gay male domesticity on the small screen: Queer representations of gay homemaking in *Six Feet Under* and *Brothers & Sisters*. *Popular Communication*, 10(3), 217–230.

Dhaenens, F. and Van Bauwel, S. (2012). The good, the bad or the queer: Articulations of queer resistance in *The Wire*. *Sexualities*, 15(5–6), 702–717.

Dhoest, A. (2001). Peasants in clogs: Imagining Flemish identity in television fiction. *Studies in Popular Culture*, 23(3), 11–24.

Dhoest, A. (2015). Audience retrospection as a source of historiography: Oral history interviews on early television experiences. *European Journal of Communication*, 30(1), 64–78.

Dhoest, A. (2007). Kinder- en jeugdprogramma's. In A. Dhoest (ed.), *Publieke televisie in Vlaanderen: een geschiedenis* (pp. 313–318). Ghent: Academia Press.

Dyer, R. (1990). *Now You See It: Studies in Lesbian and Gay Film*. New York: Routledge.

Fejes, F. and Petrich, K. (1993). Invisibility, homophobia and heterosexism: Lesbians, gays and the media. *Critical Studies in Mass Communication*, 10(4), 395–422.

Gilligan, P. (1993). Box of delights, bridge of feathers: Children's television drama on Telefís Éireann/RTÉ. PhD thesis, Dublin City University.

Gross, L. (2001). *Up from Invisibility: Lesbians, Gay Men and the Media in America*. New York: Columbia University Press.

Havens, T. (2007). Universal childhood: The global trade in children's television and changing ideals of childhood. *Global Media Journal*, 6(10).

Herman, D. (2005). 'I'm gay': Declarations, desire, and coming out on prime-time television. *Sexualities*, 8(1), 7–29.

Herreman, R. (2017) 'We too are specimens of homo sapiens': Holebi culture between agitprop and pop. In L. Mutsaers and G. Keunen (eds), *Made in the Low Countries* (pp. 137–146). London: Routledge.

Holt, E. and Sheehan, H. (1997). *Television in Europe*. Exeter: Intellect Books.

Kelso, T. (2015). Still trapped in the US media's closet: Representations of gender-variant, pre-adolescent children. *Journal of Homosexuality*, 62(8), 1058–1097.

Kerrigan, P. (2016). Respectably gay: Homodomesticity in Ireland's first public broadcast of a homosexual couple. In A. Dhoest, L. Szulc and B. Eeckhout (eds), *LGBTQs, Media and Culture in Europe* (pp. 27–41). London: Routledge.

Kerrigan, P. (2017). Projecting a queer republic: Mainstreaming queer identities on Irish documentary film. *Studies in Documentary Film*, 13(1), 1–17.

Kerrigan, P. (2020). *LGBTQ Visibility, Media and Sexuality in Ireland*. London and New York: Routledge.

Kies, B. (2016). First comes love, then comes marriage: (Homo) normalizing romance on American television. *Journal of Popular Romance Studies*, 5(2), 1–16.

Linehan, H. (2016). Will we miss RTÉ's kids TV? *The Irish Times*, 3 December. Available at www.irishtimes.com/culture/tv-radio-web/will-we-miss-rt%C3%A9-s-kids-tv-1. 2890702 (accessed 1 January 2020).

Marshall, D. (2016). Reading queer television: Some notes on method. *Review of Education, Pedagogy, and Cultural Studies*, 38(1), 85–101.

Martin, A.L. (2015). Scripting black gayness: Television authorship in black-cast sitcoms. *Television & New Media*, 16(7), 648–663.

Moran, K. (2007). The global expansion of children's television: A case study of the adaption of Sesame Street in Spain. *Learning, Media and Technology*, 31(3), 147–179.

Munt, S.R. (2006). A queer undertaking: Anxiety and reparation in the HBO television drama series Six Feet Under. *Feminist Media Studies*, 6(3), 263–279.

Ng, E. (2013). A "post-gay" era? Media gaystreaming, homonormativity, and the politics of LGBT integration. *Communication, Culture & Critique*, 6(2), 258–283.

Raats, T. and Pauwels, C. (2013). 'Best frienemies forever?' Public and private broadcasting partnerships in Flanders. In K. Donders, C. Pauwels and J. Loisen (eds), *Private Television in Western Europe* (pp. 199–213). London: Palgrave Macmillan.

Russo, V. (1981). *The Celluloid Closet: Homosexuality in the Movies*. New York: Harper Collins.

Thorfinnsdottir, D. and Jensen, H.S. (2017). Laugh away, he is gay! Heteronormativity and children's television in Denmark. *Journal of Children and Media*, 11(4), 399–416.

Vanlee, F. (2019). Finding domestic LGBT+ television in Western Europe: Methodological challenges for queer critics. *Continuum*, 33(4), 423–434.

Vanlee, F., Dhaenens, F. and Van Bauwel, S., (2018a). Sexual diversity on the small screen: Mapping LGBT+ characters in Flemish television fiction (2001–2016). Ghent: Working Papers in Film and Television. Available at www.ugent.be/ps/communicatiewetenschapp en/ cims/en/publications/working-papers/sexual-diversity-on-the-small-screen.htm.

Vanlee, F., Dhaenens, F. and Van Bauwel, S. (2018b). Understanding queer normality: LGBT+ representations in millennial Flemish television fiction. *Television & New Media*, 19(7), 610–625.

Walters, S. D. (2003). *All the Rage: The Story of Gay Visibility in America*. Chicago: University of Chicago Press.

Warner, M. (2000). *The Trouble with Normal: Sex, Politics and the Ethics of Queer Life*. Harvard, MA: Harvard University Press.

3

BREAKING THE SILENCE

Young people, sex information and the internet in Italy and Portugal

Daniel Cardoso and Cosimo Marco Scarcelli

Introduction

Social, cultural and technological changes affect intimate aspects of people's lives (Döring 2009, Mowlabocus 2010), especially when it comes to teens and young people (Buckingham & Bragg 2004, Peter & Valkenburg 2006, Scarcelli 2018). Consequently, the internet seems to serve for young people as an environment that adds to the classic agents of socialisation, like schools or families, in terms of how they understand their bodies and sexualities, and it can also represent a source of anxiety for adults in general.

In fact, the internet is often framed (Haddon & Stald 2009) as being quin-tessentially sexual in public and media discourses and a medium providing what are seen as three specific possibilities: accessibility, anonymity and affordability (Peter & Valkenburg 2006). Nevertheless, these three characteristics, often presented as unique regarding online experiences, have been called into ques-tion. In what concerns accessibility, a popular US study from 1971 (so, before the internet existed) showed that 85% of boys and 70% of girls consumed porn (Wilson 1971); as for anonymity, browser cookies, user profiling and data mining continue to be a central concern for those who are concerned about leaving traces behind (Paasonen 2011); as for gratuity, the recirculation of material (Thompson 2017) has long served to detach consumption from spending money.

Another common misconception is the idea that a good deal of data online pertains to porn and/or that most of the use of online resources pertains to por-nography consumption. This too seems to be counterfactual, as research shows that the searches and volume of data dedicated to pornography and other related sexual content is relatively small (Fae 2015, Ogas & Gaddam 2012) in comparison with the total volume of data and online searches.

Even so, there is much media panic surrounding internet and sexuality, and this becomes even more pronounced when children and young people are involved. They are often construed as pure and innocent, their sexuality is seen as something that adults are responsible for regulating in order to ensure a proper reproduction of the heterosexual patriarchal system of gender and sexuality (Cardoso 2018, Egan & Hawkes 2009, 2013, Scarcelli 2015). An example of this is how fears over the 'media effects' that pornography has over youngsters are used to pass legislation, such as proposals to use credit card checks for accessing pornography websites in the UK.

Michel Foucault (1994), in talking about the sexuality *dispositif*, also mentions how the child is made to be a liminal sexual being, whose careful management legitimates actions by the whole of society; he speaks of how 'sexualization of infancy' is fundamental to the social dissemination of the idea of 'sexuality' as an identity (p. 155). In fact, Foucault notes that sexuality has become a cornerstone of identity in contemporary society – that we ask sexuality to tell us 'our truth' about who we 'truly' are (1994, p. 73).

This means that both representations and the subjective work around sexuality involve well-established power relationships that are central to the development of a sense of self and identity in what concerns ones' sexual conduct. The pressure to know oneself is widespread, and that implies both that the individual has to know themselves as a subject (with a given sexuality) and has to have that knowledge recognised by and negotiated with others – governmentality becomes both a way for the subject to deal with themselves and each other (Foucault 2000a, 2000b, 2005).

Within the context of the co-optation of public discourse by media and moral panic (Fahs et al. 2013), internet becomes mainly represented as a hazard for normative sexual development that is expected of young people. This, in turn, erases or obscures how, for many young people, new media can serve as a lifeline out of heteronormativity or cisnormativity and a way to negotiate non-normative sexualities, access sexual health information, access activist spaces and share spaces for personal experiences (Cardoso 2017b, Scarcelli 2015).

A further consequence of this is that young people's 'difficult citizenship' (Robinson 2012) is especially difficult when it comes to gender and sexuality, where they do not see their own worldviews or experiences validated or recognised (Egan & Hawkes 2009), and when the potential for critical education and personal growth is disavowed by parents, educators and the media (Tsaliki 2015). What is at stake, as Breanne Fahs (2014) puts it, is the recognition of young people's sexual citizenship, framed by the societal and structural hurdles around it and by the way young people themselves both reproduce and contest normative systems of meaning and representation. This is particularly so in the case of gender and sexual minorities – because their existence is both less visible and less legally acknowledged. Thus, intimate citizenship (Plummer 1994) can only be fully realised when unfettered and socially validated access to pluralistic modes of literacy can be achieved.

Accessing information is vital, both from a citizenship point of view and from an identity-construction point of view; it is a fundamental right of youth and of people in general, and it is essential to understand the complex dynamics involved in accessing information.

In this chapter we will focus on teens' use of internet resources to look for and find information related to sex and sexuality. To do that we will analyse the results of two different projects carried out in two different, but culturally similar, European countries: Italy and Portugal, by means of discourse analysis of semi-structured interviews.

After a brief comparison of the contexts, we will analyse the roles of family, school and peer groups as sources of sexual information for young people, and then we will focus on the internet and the practices of using different sources by young people. As the two main foci of analysis, we address how online search for information about sex and sexuality relate to other social groups and spaces that are part of young people's lives and how young people talk about the roles the internet plays for them, including the negotiation of gender dynamics.

Contexts in comparison

Both Italy and Portugal belong to a Southern European context that is recognised as such not only from an academic point of view but also from a political and mainstream discourse perspective (e.g. the PIIGS acronym).

The young people that were interviewed in the two projects were directly and indirectly affected by the 2008 economic crisis, coming into their teenage years when it was still playing out, which impacted their education, technological inclusion, literacy and even the material conditions they experienced when growing up.

More broadly, though, both countries can also be considered to be under what some authors call 'late modernity' – that is to say, a mix of traditional and modern sociological traits that coexist in tension (Ponte 2012). According to Leccardi (2006, p. 17, 18), and based on the works of Cavalli and Galland (1996), some of the main traits of this Mediterranean specificity have to do with more time spent in school, followed by a period of professional precarity (which forces youth and young adults to remain living with their parents for longer periods of time) and, frequently, the departure from the parents' house happening within the context of an intimate relationship.

Both countries also share similarities in how their contemporary histories have shaped their societies, in that both were clearly and deeply aligned with the most conservative faction of the Catholic Church, both were clearly concerned with moral puritanism and both were heavily invested in not allowing their citizenry access to education.

Discourse about sexual education in Portuguese schools is still mostly biomedical and about risk avoidance and pregnancy and STI prevention (Marinho et al. 2011), without a critical and empowering gendered perspective (Nogueira et al. 2007). Paula Vieira (2010, p. 128) takes this critique a step further when she flatly states that 'The pedagogy of heterosexuality – not of sexuality – dominates the pedagogic milieu.' Likewise, in Italy there are different and parcelled initiatives that create and reproduce a disjointed legal frame (Marmocchi et al. 2018) and experience. So, in the Italian legal system, sexual education is not mandatory and each headteacher has the power to decide whether or not to include it into the school curriculum.

The other customary source of education on sexuality – family – is also ultimately affected by similarities in modern political events in both countries. Parents are increasingly less formally educated than their children, and especially so when it comes to sexual health. This creates a specific rhetoric within Portuguese and Italian families making 'sex talk' an age-related topic – that it is 'too early' to talk about the topic of sexuality and then 'too late' or unnecessary because parents assume young people are already somehow fully informed. For parents, it seems that there is never a 'right time' to talk about sexuality (Barbagli et al. 2010, Pais 2012). In this context, families leave all sorts of sex talk and discussions about sexuality to other agents, also bearing the task of educating the parents' offspring about sexuality (see also Porrovecchio 2012).

Methods

Even though the two research projects were carried out independently, the results are comparable and connected due to the similar nature of the underlying research questions and the methods used.

Both research projects preferred a qualitative approach to study the phenomena and experiences of teens from their point of view (Flick 1998, Lobe et al. 2008). The researchers prioritised reflexivity and the production of critical knowledge that eschewed classical positivism in order to understand young people's positions as useful to improving the issues that surround and affect them. These methods are the best way to explore the 'sense' that adolescents have of their decisions and experiences.

The empirical section is based on semi-structured, face-to-face interviews and involved young people between 16 and 20 years old – 11 in Portugal and 50 in Italy. In Portugal, recruitment was made via a previous online survey, and there were five young men and six young women, all of them attending undergraduate school, and from middle-class backgrounds. Sexual orientation was not asked, but nevertheless seven of them reported being LGB or having LGB experiences. In Italy, schools were contacted to help with recruiting young participants. There were 25 boys and 25 girls involved in total.

The interviews were transcribed verbatim, sent to the respective adolescents for comments and then analysed using Nvivo10 (for the Portuguese project) and Atlas. Ti (for the Italian project).

Results

This section provides a detail account of the main results found when comparing both projects. The results we analyse have to do primarily with the position that new media take within different social groups, and how youngsters themselves see the role (positive and negative) the internet plays for them. As we will show, the internet operates as a *compensatory system,* a *silent friend* and a *technology of the self,* in an intricate interaction between cultural tendencies, everyday social interactions and their own processes of identity-formation.

Internet and social groups: family, school and peers

Diverse social actors around young people, such as their family, school, and peer groups, inform and impact on what they use the internet for and how they perceive its usefulness regarding their social interactions.

The interviews show a lack of free and relaxed dialogue. Sexuality is often approached with an air of embarrassment and normativity that is so often associated with it. This type of conversation would possibly fulfil the need the young men who were interviewed feel, to find fertile ground in their families in which to plant the seeds of thinking about bodies and sexuality; this is especially relevant in Italy, where our results show that tensions around masculinity seem to be particularly high.

Often, shame is a part of this process, and family is a potential space where shame is felt, or even cultivated, in an attempt (by parents) to avoid the topic altogether, making the domestic context a difficult one where to talk about sexuality.

> When I was younger, I'd look up information about stuff that I was ashamed of asking my parents about, or even of talking openly to my doctor about, out of fear that she would talk to my parents about it.
>
> *(Maria,[1] 20, woman, Portugal)*

According to the interviewees, the schools offer purely health-related information and are not in line with the experiences of young people because they give instructions with respect to the prevention of sexually transmitted diseases and little else and stay on a very superficial level. During the interviews, young people often complained about how the courses offered by their schools are not interesting, which is connected on the one hand to the content of the lessons themselves and on the other hand to how they were managed. Frequently, adolescents' participation is not expected or encouraged, and the schools do not give a lot of space for the adolescents' experiences and stories. Sometimes this type of interaction is present, but it is inhibited by the presence of the teacher in the classroom, a figure that still plays an institutional role, making it more difficult to talk about their intimacy.

> We do sex education at school … Yes, we do but it is useless. They show you reproductions systems, explain you something about venereal illnesses. They remind you to use a condom when you have sex. And that's all. It is difficult to ask for more information or speak about curiosity … the teacher is there. I am ashamed to talk about certain things with my teacher there.
>
> *(Filippo, 17, man, Italy)*

There is also an element of discomfort, since young people feel that their privacy is at risk when accessing information about sexuality, even on school computers – they are afraid of 'getting caught' and suffering negative consequences for it:

Ah, no, [I didn't use the school computers to look up information on sexuality] because there's always the browsing history, that fear of someone coming up from behind and look at what you're looking for.

(Pamela, 20, woman, Portugal)

In Italy in particular, teens' favourite people to discuss intimacy with are peers. In this case, adolescents speak mainly about the subjects that family discussions have no space for and that are connected to practices and sexual experiences or, in general, about subjects that belong to the sphere of desire. In Portugal, however, talking to friends is seen as something that happens mostly when they're extremely worried about something, and is something that is uncommon for them to do – unless it involves addressing older friends. This, in both Italy and Portugal, does not mean they never talk about sexuality with their peers – it means that specifically looking for information (and so creating a power imbalance by admitting to ignorance) is something that is not framed as part of their peer routines.

Talking about sex takes on distinctly different modes according to the group to which the adolescent belongs. In comparison with young men, Italian girls find it easier to speak with other girls about sex and their own experiences. Indeed, their relationships with friends are based on sharing emotions and experiences (Grazzani & Ornaghi 2007), which is an important component in building a relationship of trust, in which hearing others' experiences becomes a way of learning how to cope with specific situations. In Portugal, however, it was mostly young women who explicitly denied talking to friends about sexuality ('If you have doubts about sexuality at 15, you're not going to ask your best friend [...]. In school, since it's during adolescence, it's the worst! You can't ask anything to anyone. [laughs] Because they'll just gang up on you to make fun', Redgi, 19, young woman, Portugal), which is in line with a silencing and desexualisation of women and teenage girls present in families' and institutions' representations of them (Tsaliki 2015).

For the majority of the interviewed young men, the intimate realm is dealt with by keeping more private experiences hidden from the peer group. Among friends, including the closest, matters related to sexuality are frequently talked about in a humorous manner, through anecdotes referring to people outside the group or through jokes with sexual innuendos (Pascoe 2005, Porrovecchio 2012). This is due to the fact that they often have a fear of being laughed at by others and so have to show, in front of the group, self-confidence and skilled expertise in the world of sexuality.

If I show to someone else ... I mean to my friend ... that I don't know any basilar points. [Interviewer: basilar points?] Yes, you know, the important staff about sex. How to do it, or what is a clitoris for example [laugh]. Anyway, if you show yourself ignorant, they will start to mock you. Honestly ... sometimes you have to show them that you know the secrets of sex, even if it is not true.

(Francesco, 17, man, Italy)

The internet: potentials, affordances and challenges

Curiosity

Given the limited information available to them about the topic, young people not only take it upon themselves to look for sexuality-related content online but also turn this search into a self- and other-imposed mandate, surrounding it within a moral obligation to be curious. This means that, according to them, getting informed about sexuality is a personal, subjective responsibility. This curiosity is at the same time a trait of the person looking for the information and an obligation, often also framed heteronormatively: 'People [since they reproduce sexually] must take initiative; they must educate themselves' (Miguel, 20, man, Portugal).

This also means that people who are not well informed are responsible for not being well informed, in young people's perspective; both as demonstrate in this quote, and in several others where they criticised themselves for not having had the initiative to look for more information online.

Curiosity is seen by young people as a twofold phenomenon – on the one hand as the aforementioned moral imposition of having to learn about sex, and on the other hand as a biological reaction that equates hormonal changes in adolescence with physiological responses that develop into curiosity: 'I think it has to do with maturity; once it's attained, [needing information] just isn't an issue' (Miguel, 20, man, Portugal).

As we will show below, this curiosity then interacts with two other elements. First, it is mentioned as being fuelled by the lack of resources from parents, schools and peers, as explained above; second, it is hampered by difficulties that young people sometimes experience when it comes to identifying useful and truthful information.

At the same time, this also means that when they think that growth is finished, many adolescents consider that there is no longer any reason to keep looking for answers or information – that knowledge plateaus (where being a grown-up is intrinsically being knowledgeable): 'No, I've got all the information I need, so I don't need to look for it anymore (Tiago, 19, man, Portugal).

Therefore, adolescents are curious about different kinds of information besides the biomedical paradigm usually offered at school, and yet they struggle with knowing if they can trust the information they find online and deploy several different strategies to cope with this, which we will explore below, and that have to do with finding different sources and types of information.

Categories of sex-related information

Information regarding sex on the internet is usually related to four informational categories (see also Scarcelli 2014): health, knowledge of the body, practices and curiosity.

Information related to health is related mainly to medical knowledge concerning the prevention of sexual diseases or unwanted pregnancy. Women who were presenting as heterosexual seemed to be the most interested in this kind of information, and men seemed interested quite exclusively in contraceptive methods (also according to Donati et al. 2000, Graziano et al. 2012); among gay-identified men, the focus was more on STI prevention. The men, overall, are more focused on information related to their own bodies. They look for this kind of information in line with a certain 'normalization' (Shapiro 2008) of the intimate sphere. An example is one of the interviewees in Portugal He had had had his testicles surgically removed for health reasons and therefore had prosthetics implanted and was taking testosterone. Therefore, he had to renormalise the experience of having a surgically altered body, and part of that process had to do with gathering information online.

Females that look for this kind of information use the internet mostly to better understand their own pleasure mechanisms (the 'G spot', female orgasms, etc.):

> Once I used the internet to understand how orgasm works. Everyone spoke about orgasms, but I did not feel that sensation, so I looked for information to understand if something did not work.
>
> *(Cristina, 18, woman, Italy)*

The type of information connected to practices was read from two different perspectives, especially in the Italian interviews: one perspective concentrating on discovering the pleasure of 'the other' and the other dedicated to understanding the 'techniques' of sexual intercourse. This division tends to follow gender differences (with men more focused on techniques) and the amount of sexual experience of each individual (often associated with age).

Finally, there is the use of the internet to find information 'related to curiosity': information that is connected to terms related to pornographic and medical language but that does not fall within the previous categories. Here, a main focus is on 'the rather strange stuff' (Giulia, 17, woman, Italy). Through the internet, teens try to find answers regarding the world of sexuality and its different practices, looking for images, videos or explanations that can help them to discover or understand what is usually indicated as perversion or paraphilia: 'My friends spoke about fisting and they laughed. I did not know what fisting was and so I looked on the internet' (Alberto, 17, man, Italy).

In fact, showing each other this type of content can also serve as another layer of sexuality regulation (Cardoso 2017a).

Literacy and difficulties parsing online information

Looking for information requires being prepared to look for information (knowing how and where to look for it, and how to identify false information), and young people generally consider themselves ready to cope with false information. According to the latest EU Kids Online report (Smahel et al. 2020), which summarises results from 19 European countries, an average of 59% of youngsters (aged 12–16) say they know how to identify true information online, and 72% say they know which keywords to use when they're looking for information.

Some, however, do not feel so prepared and have personal experiences of finding incorrect information. There is no easy way to identify incorrect information, and several respondents noted that it is characteristic of the internet and so is to be expected. Others shared their strategies for managing incorrect information: comparing different websites, looking at official government websites and looking at the first few Google results that show up on the first page.

In comparison, some interviewees did not use the internet to look for this kind of information and considered the web to be an unreliable source because it contains uncertain information that is too generic. They also consider it a space in which sex and sexuality is presented only in the form of pornography.

The interviewees' words evoke two specific approaches taken by those who say they do not use the internet to find information, both connected to the validity of the source and the contents. In the first case, the interviewees frequently have an idea of sex and sexuality as things that can be handled only by health specialists or another kind of specialist, parents: 'On a first moment, of course I'll use the internet, but often the information is not reliable enough, and so I look for a doctor' (Ivo, 18, man, Portugal).

In the second, case interviewees describe it as something that cannot be useful to fulfil the needs of specific people either in terms of health information or information about specific practices because the internet spreads only generic information that cannot be adapted to the person's situations.

> Because every person is different, for example, all the birth control pills are different, they don't all have the same effect [and so] it's very complicated to know what's real and what isn't, online.
>
> *(Íris, 18, woman, Portugal)*

This shows a lack of experience with respect to web offerings relating to sex and sexuality, including experts' forums, webpages dedicated to sex and sexuality from a medical point of view and forums where individuals can talk about their problems or experiences, etc. It is a rather reductive and negativist view of the internet and is full of prejudices towards the medium, potentially replicating mainstream discourse about new media and sexuality. Furthermore, it serves to question the narrative about youngsters as digital natives, or as acritical consumers of online information.

It is also here where a particular difference between LGB and non-LGB youngsters can be seen – given society's compulsory heterosexuality (Rich 2007), information for queer adolescents is much sparser and community-building much more important. In fact, some of them treated pornography *as a source of information* – not about performance or bodies but about the validity itself of their emotions and desires, the only place where they felt represented, even if sometimes poorly (Cardoso 2017b, Cardoso & Ponte 2017).

Looking for experiences more than 'hard' information

Another interesting topic is the platforms that teens use to find information and the formats they prefer when trying to increase their knowledge about sexuality.

According to a considerable number of interviewees, the internet represents a sort of 'user guide' that they can read immediately: a set of instructions that comes from different platforms and sites that, thanks to multimedia content, affords them a step-by-step explanation of how to manage topics related to sex and pleasure.

But despite the presence of several websites and platforms dedicated to health and sexual information – medical or institutional websites, for example – the interviewees are far from having an intense use of these resources and prefer to pay attention to alternative sources of information that have a common base: the ability to read about (and share) the experiences of people who have had to cope with similar problems, doubts and insecurities.

For teens, looking for experiences instead of what an interviewee called 'cold information' (Patrizia, 17, woman, Italy) is a useful way to find answers to their questions, by inserting themselves into what we could define as an enlarged peer group: a group consisting of people (sometimes not knowing each other) that supposedly belong together because they are the same age:

> You can easily find information when someone like you speaks about what happens to them. I prefer this kind of information. Someone that says, 'I did this', and it worked. Or, 'I had this problem and I solved it'.
>
> *(Pietro, 18, man, Italy)*

All four different informational categories mentioned above (health, knowledge of the body, practices and curiosity) are intersected by different information epistemologies. In fact, for all four different categories, young people mention looking for 'accurate' (or medical/scientific) information but also looking for personal, subjective experiences around those same topics.

As an example, the Portuguese young man who had had his testes removed had received all the information he wanted about the issue from his doctor; however, information about the *lived* experience of other people who had undergone the same kind of treatment was far more available online. Therefore, it is sometimes authenticity and realness of shared experiences that users value in turning to health-related sources.

As another interviewee put it: 'Besides more official information, aimed at informing people, there's something else I think is quite useful as well, which is forums, where anonymous people share their experiences' (Ivo, 18, man, Portugal).

For non-heterosexual adolescents in particular, looking for information is often connected to looking for community and spaces of sociality, and the internet is seen as the 'only place ... with information [on LGBT topics]' (Beatriz, 20, woman, Portugal).

Therefore, some teens prefer peer narratives to complement other types of information, and the internet represents a place rich in narratives, echoing Ken Plummer's (1995) point about the importance of telling stories within intimate citizenship. It is interesting thus to note that while the use of narratives of other people is widespread, its production seems to be much less frequent (Cardoso & Ponte 2017).

Gender, performance and knowledge of the self

There are some differences between men and women in the way they talk about how they use the internet to find information and the kinds of information they look for.

We noticed a dividing line separating those who said they had had intercourse from those who claimed never to have had it. After the 'first times', the differences in the reported behaviour of the young women and men become more prominent: usually young women reported to have stopped using the internet as a source of technical instructions in order to use a different approach based on the comparison between friends' sexual experiences and their own direct experiences. Women show less anxiety connected to performance compared to men, and the most commonly researched information is related to body care, focused mainly on resolving and preventing, on the one hand, undesired pregnancy and, on the other hand, sexually transmitted diseases, especially in the case of women presenting as heterosexual or bisexual. This reflects mainstream dynamics about how girls and women will often bear the brunt of contraceptive and sexual health responsibility, and how masculinity is construed on notions of power, prowess and performance (hooks 2004). This helps understand men's concerns with issues like penis length and the 'normal' duration of intercourse. It is also important to remember that mainstream narratives around the relationship between young women and the media posit it as intrinsically problematic and harmful (Bale 2010, 2011).

As for men, the internet represents an important source of information that becomes useful in preparing for the first experience of intercourse, for which they could not arrive 'unprepared':

> Before my first time I read information about sex on the internet.
> [Interviewer: Can you please explain better to me what you mean by 'sex information'?]
> Of course, I mean ... what to do. Positions, how it works the first time, how long is the intercourse, etc. We can say I studied [laugh].
>
> (Michele, 17, man, Italy)

Men then act as the gatekeepers of sexual information and performance and as those who have the power to introduce girls to sexuality – in stark contrast with what women think, since they don't feel dependent on men to access sexuality; however, work on sexual scripts and gatekeeping shows that there are conflicting narratives about who is seen as having control and initiative over sexual experiences (Sakaluk et al. 2014).

However, young men who claim to have some sexual experience seem to shift their focus to women's bodies and libidos:

> I used the internet to … improve the technique [laugh]. To better understand how to do things.
>
> [Interviewer: Things?]
>
> You know … how to touch, how to make my girl crazy. Everyone knows there are some tricks. Then, of course, it is different for everyone … but I want my girl to say, 'You are the best' [laugh].
>
> *(Luca, 17, man, Italy)*

Information becomes useful for enacting the idea of the 'great lover', and the internet, thanks to anonymity and personal-narrative resources where people can explain step by step what to do, becomes teens' favourite source.

As we have seen, then, the internet plays a multitude of roles for youngsters, and such roles interact heavily with other available resources (or the lack thereof) such as family or school support, their self-perceived media literacy, and their own gender or sexual orientation. Youngsters do not necessarily see themselves as inherently competent in navigating online experiences, but include it in a multi-layered approach to information seeking and, in fact, seek out different kinds of information.

Conclusions

We hope to have shown that young people's use of the internet for seeking information regarding sexuality and sexual health is complex and deeply intertwined with their contexts and cultural milieus. Markers like gender and sexual orientation are fundamental in understanding adolescents' positionality. Furthermore, the comparison between Portugal and Italy also demonstrates that cultural and historical markers, which impact the way sexuality is perceived and experienced, interact with technology and its role in young people's lives.

Our research makes evident three important aspects of the internet related to information about sex and sexuality. The internet operates as a *compensatory system*, a *silent friend* and a *technology of the self*.

The internet is an important source of information related to sex and sexuality for teens, but not the only one, and not unambiguously positive or negative (Tsaliki, Chronaki & Ólafsson 2014). Adolescents do a continuous *bricolage*, trying to cope with their insecurities from failure and the anxiety deriving from the 'first times' they have to face. They can ride out these insecurities through a meta-experience accessible by different channels, each with a specific contribution. The internet represents one of these many channels (Morrison et al. 2004). They can also challenge the kinds of information adults think are appropriate for them and how they are used, thus demonstrating an autonomous experience of sexuality.

The internet then operates as a *compensatory system* for gaps in other spheres of life (school, family, friends). The internet becomes a risk-avoidance strategy and is easier to access. However, some young people did mention that being fully anonymous was complicated, given the specific knowledge required about digital traces, but still easier than having to go through someone else.

The internet also offers something that more formal sources of information cannot offer as effectively that being, different kinds of information. For example, several adolescents (especially those who identify as LGBTQ) noted that the internet was where they could find testimonies of people going through specific situations (such as coming out or having a specific STI) through fora and social networks; some also mentioned that pornography in itself could be seen as a way to find information in a different way. In this context, young people are not looking for accuracy or scientific validity; they are looking for the subjectivity of personal experience, for representation of non-hegemonic sexualities and bodies and for different epistemologies.

To do that, teens frequently insert themselves into a space that allows them to speak not only with experts but also with what we define as an extended peer group. It is formed by other adolescents probably around the same age and could help them have access to experiences more so than to hard information. The difference between this kind of space and the peer group is that the ability to have a medium that can respond to the teens' questions without mocking the individual asking the question or affecting the young person's everyday peer group makes the internet a sort of *silent friend* (paraphrasing Goffman 1959). The anonymity assumes a specific peculiarity: it is not just a way to find information without parental control but is also a way to access a sphere similar to the one composed of friends but in which adolescents have no risk of being embarrassed, perceived as having made a mistake or seen as incapable of managing their own bodies. And it is clearly connected to the importance of the performance mentioned above.

We see that online information is framed as having both opportunities and limitations. From the interviews, we can see that, for respondents in general, information *must* be sought and young people *must* be competent and capable of dealing with it (emotionally and physically); it *allows* some level of anonymity and safety, *allows* teens to fight the fear of the unknown or of problems associated with sexuality (such as STIs and pregnancy) and becomes a *key conduit* in establishing a 'truth' about how to perform sexuality.

This is to say, the internet operates as a technology of the self in the Foucauldian sense – as a way for young people to tap into narratives that purport to give access to a truth about sex and sexuality. As we have seen though, part of why the internet is so relevant pertains to how different social spheres concurrently circulate different epistemologies on what can constitute a truth about sexuality. Therefore, even though there is an association between adulthood and sexual maturity, young people negotiate their sexual identities by seeking information but also evaluating its trustworthiness or effectiveness.

In the cultural and social backgrounds that we described, the internet becomes a way for young people to modulate the silencing around sex and sexuality, re-appropriating discourses that contradict how adult society constructs youth sexuality. This happens, as we saw, by reconnecting the internet's characteristics with young people's culture and playing with ancient gender models, redefining and challenging them.

Therefore, sexual citizenship and identity-development are connected – since speaking positions around citizenship are often predicated on specific identities – but accessing information is a fundamental aspect of both, as both are in fact intersubjective processes. As we have shown, there is a dialectical process between information-seeking and forms of sociability – and so to consider accessibility is to consider the social conditions under which access occurs: the social, economic, cultural and epistemic frameworks around information and its intelligibility as such.

Note

1 Respondents were asked to choose pseudonyms for themselves.

References

Attwood, F. (2010). *Porn.com. Making Sense of Online Pornography*. New York: Peter Lang.

Bale, C. (2010). Sexualised culture and young people's sexual health: A cause for concern? *Sociology Compass*, 4(10), 824–840. https://doi.org/10.1111/j.1751-9020.2010.00316.x.

Bale, C. (2011). Raunch or romance? Framing and interpreting the relationship between sexualized culture and young people's sexual health. *Sex Education*, 11(3), 303–313. https://doi.org/10.1080/14681811.2011.590088.

Barbagli, M., Dalla Zuanna, G. and Garelli, F., (2010). *La sessualità degli italiani*. Bologna: Il Mulino.

Buckingham, D. and Bragg, S. (2004). *Young People, Sex and the Media: The Facts of Life?* Basingstoke and New York: Palgrave Macmillan.

Cardoso, D. (2017a). Gazing upon the (disgusted) gaze: The abnormal regulation of 'normal' sexuality. *Porn Studies* [online], 4(4), 468–472. Available from: doi:10.1080/23268743.2017.1398678.

Cardoso, D. (2017b). 'I sort of knew what I was, so I wanted to see what awaited me': Portuguese LGB youngsters and their situated experiences with new media. In A. Dhoest, Ł. Szulc and B. Eeckhout (eds), *LGBTQs, Media and Culture in Europe* (pp. 208–223). London and New York: Routledge.

Cardoso, D. (2018). Notas sobre a Criança transviada: Considerações queerfeministas sobre infâncias. *Revista Periódicus* [online], 1(9), 214–233. Available from: doi:10.9771/peri.v1i9.25755.

Cardoso, D. and Ponte, C. (2017). Género, sexualidade e ativismo online: Um olhar interseccional para o papel da participação cívica na internet por jovens portugueses. *Ex aequo* [online], (35), 49–64. Available from: doi:10.22355/exaequo.2017.35.04.

Cavalli, A. and Galland, O. (eds) (1996). *Senza fretta di crescere*. Napoli: Liguori.

Donati, S., Andreozzi, S., Medda, E. and Gandolfo, M.E. (2000). *Salute riproduttiva tra gli adolescenti: conoscenze, attitudini e comportamenti*. Rome: Istituto Superiore di Sanità.

Döring, N.M. (2009). The internet's impact on sexuality: A critical review of 15 years of research. *Computers in Human Behavior* [online], 25(5), 1089–1101. Available from: doi:10.1016/j.chb.2009.04.003.

Egan, R.D. and Hawkes, G. (2009). The problem with protection: Or, why we need to move towards recognition and the sexual agency of children. *Continuum* [online], 23(3), 389–400. Available from: doi:10.1080/10304310902842975.

Egan, R.D. and Hawkes, G. (2013). Disavowal and foundational fantasies: A psychosocial exploration of the class, race and the social construction of the sexual child in the Anglophone West. *Sexualities* [online], 16(5–6), 635–650. Available from: doi:10.1177/1363460713488285.

Fae, J., (2015). *Taming the Beast.* Letchworth Garden City: Berforts Information Press.

Fahs, B. (2014). 'Freedom to' and 'freedom from': A new vision for sex-positive politics. *Sexualities* [online], 17(3), 267–290. Available from: doi:10.1177/1363460713516334.

Fahs, B., Dudy, M. and Stage, S. (eds) (2013). *The Moral Panics of Sexuality.* Basingstoke and New York: Palgrave Macmillan.

Flick, U. (1998). *An Introduction to Qualitative Research.* London: Sage Publications.

Foucault, M. (1994). *História Da Sexualidade 1: A Vontade de Saber.* Lisbon: Relógio d'Água.

Foucault, M. (2000a). *Sex, Power and the Politics of Identity.* In P. Rabinow (ed.), *The Essential Works of Michel Foucault, 1954–1984: Ethics* (pp. 163–173). London: Penguin.

Foucault, M. (2000b). *Technologies of the Self.* In P. Rabinow (ed.), *The Essential Works of Michel Foucault, 1954–1984: Ethics* (pp. 223–251). London: Penguin.

Foucault, M. (2005). *The Hermeneutics of the Subject: Lectures at the College de France 1981–1982.* Edited by F. Gros and F. Ewald. New York: Picador.

Goffman, E. (1959). *The Presentation of Self in Everyday Life.* New York: Doubleday Anchor.

Graziano, F., Pertosa, M.A. and Consoli, A. (2012). Educare alla sessualità e all'affettività in preadolescenza: Le fonti di informazioni e le domande dei ragazzi e delle ragazze. *Psicologia della Salute*, 2, 1–16.

Grazzani Gavazzi, I. and Ornaghi, V. (2007). *La narrazione delle emozioni in adolescenza.* Milan: McGraw-Hill.

Haddon, L. and Stald, G. (2009). A comparative analysis of European press coverage of children and the internet. *Journal of Children and Media* [online], 3(4), 379–393. Available from: doi:10.1080/17482790903233432.

hooks, b. (2004). *The Will to Change: Men, Masculinity, and Love* (reprint edn). Washington Square Press.

Leccardi, C. (2006). Facing uncertainty: Temporality and biographies in the new century. In C. Leccardi and E. Ruspini (eds), *A New Youth? Young People, Generations and Family Life* (pp. 15–40). Aldershot and Burlington: Ashgate.

Lobe, B. et al. (2008). *Best Practice Research Guide: How to Research Children and Online Technologies in Comparative Prospective.* London: EU Kids Online.

Marinho, S., Anastácio, Z. and Carvalho, G.S. (2011). Desenvolvimento e implementação de projectos de Educação Sexual: Análise das dimensões biológica, psicológica e social da sexualidade. In Atas do VI Congresso Internacional. Maia: AGIR (Associação para a Investigação e Desenvolvimento Socio-Cultural), May 2011, Chaves, Portugal [online]. (Accessed 4 March 2012). Available from: http://repositorium.sdum.uminho.pt/handle/1822/12639.

Marmocchi, P., Raffuzzi, L. and Strazzari, E. (2018). *Percorsi di educazione affettiva e sessuale per preadolescenti: il progetto 'W l'amore'.* Centro studi Erickson.

Morrison, T.G., Harriman, R., Morrison, M.A., Bearden, A. and Ellis, S.R. (2004). Correlates of exposure to sexuality explicit material among Canadian post-secondary students. *Canadian Journal of Human Sexuality*, 13, 143–156.

Mowlabocus, S. (2010). Porn 2.0: Technology, social practice and the new online porn industry. In F. Attwood (ed.), *Porn.com: Making Sense of Online Pornography* (pp. 69–87). New York: Peter Lang.

Nogueira, C., Saavedra, L. and da Costa, C.E.V. (2007). (In)Visibilidade do género na sexualidade juvenil: Propostas para uma nova concepção sobre a educação sexual e a prevenção de comportamentos sexuais de risco. *Pro-Posições*, 2(19), 59–79.

Ogas, O. and Gaddam, S. (2012). *A Billion Wicked Thoughts: What the Internet Tells Us about Sexual Relationships.* New York: Plume.

Paasonen, S. (2011). *Carnal Resonance: Affect and Online Pornography.* London: MIT Press.

Pais, J.M. (2012). *Sexualidade e afectos juvenis.* Lisbon: Imprensa de Ciências Sociais.

Pascoe, C.J. (2005). 'Dude, you're a fag': Adolescent masculinity and the fag discourse. *Sexualities* [online], 8(3), 329–346. Available from: doi:10.1177/1363460705053337.

Peter, J. and Valkenburg, P.M. (2006). Adolescents' exposure to sexually explicit material on the internet. *Communication Research* [online], 33(2), 178–204. Available from: doi:10.1177/0093650205285369.

Plummer, K. (1994). *Telling Sexual Stories: Power, Change and Social Worlds.* New York: Routledge.

Ponte, C. (2012). *Crianças & Media: Pesquisa Internacional e Contexto Português Do Século XIX à Actualidade.* Lisbon: Imprensa de Ciências Sociais.

Porrovecchio, A. (2012). *Sessualità in divenire: Adolescenti, corpo e immaginario.* Milan: FrancoAngeli.

Rich, A. (2007). Compulsory heterosexuality and lesbian existence. In R. Parker and P. Aggleton (eds), *Culture, Society and Sexuality: A Reader*, 2nd edn (pp. 209–236). London: Routledge.

Robinson, K.H. (2012). 'Difficult citizenship': The precarious relationships between childhood, sexuality and access to knowledge. *Sexualities* [online], 15(3–4), 257–276. Available from: doi:10.1177/1363460712436469.

Sakaluk, J.K., Todd, L.M., Milhausen, R. & Lachowsky, N.J. (2014). Dominant heterosexual sexual scripts in emerging adulthood: Conceptualization and measurement. *Journal of Sex Research*, 51(5), 516–531.

Scarcelli, C.M. (2014). 'One way or another I need to learn this stuff!' Adolescents, sexual information, and the Internet's role between family, school, and peer group. *Interdisciplinary Journal of Family Studies*, 40–59.

Scarcelli, C.M. (2015). 'It is disgusting, but …': Adolescent girls' relationship to internet pornography as gender performance. *Porn Studies*, 2(2–3), 237–249. Available from: doi:10.1080/23268743.2015.1051914.

Scarcelli, C.M. (2018). Young people and sexual media. In P.G. Nixon and I.K. Düsterhöft (eds), *Sex in the Digital Age.* London: Routledge.

Smahel, D., Machackova, H., Mascheroni, G., Dedkova, L., Staksrud, E., Olafsson, K., Livingstone, S., and Hasebrink, U. (2020). EU Kids Online 2020: Survey results from 19 countries. EU Kids Online.

Shapiro, T. (2008). Masturbation, sexuality, and adaptation: Normalization in adolescence. *Journal of the American Psychoanalytic Association*, 56(1), 123–146. https://doi.org/10.1177/0003065108315687.

Thompson, M. (2017). *Rubbish Theory: The Creation and Destruction of Value*, 2nd edn. London: Pluto Press.

Tsaliki, L. (2015). Popular culture and moral panics about 'children at risk': revisiting the sexualisation-of-young-girls debate. *Sex Education* [online], 15(5), 500–514. Available from: doi:10.1080/14681811.2015.1022893.

Tsaliki, L., Chronaki, D. and Ólafsson, K. (2014). Experiences with sexual content: What we know from the research so far. EU Kids Online, LSE.

Vieira, P. (2010). Silêncios simultâneos: Currículo e sexualidades. Master's thesis, Universidade do Minho. Available from: http://repositorium.sdum.uminho.pt/handle/1822/14155 (accessed 21 March 2012).

Wilson, W.C. (1971). Facts versus fears: Why should we worry about pornography? *The ANNALS of the American Academy of Political and Social Science* [online], 397(1), 105–117. Available from: doi:10.1177/000271627139700113.

4

COVID-19 PANDEMIC AND DISCOURSES OF ANXIETY ABOUT CHILDHOOD SEXUALITY IN DIGITAL SPACES

Despina Chronaki

Introduction

This chapter unpacks discourses of anxiety about childhood sexuality, focusing on concerns about how young people hang out and socialise in online spaces during the COVID-19 quarantine. COVID-19 national lockdowns have generated fears and anxieties about individuals' bodily, social and sexual wellbeing. Alongside concerns about how the virus might affect individuals' health (including the risk of death), societies and institutions have also been focusing on how people would continue being active and productive during the quarantine. Campaigns about physical exercise indoors, online fitness training, cooking and DIY tutorials, distance learning for young people and teleworking were offered as ways of filling one's day. In a sense, in such times of imposed social distancing, such strategies aimed at motivating people to be productive and creative. Not surprisingly, discussions and concerns about pornography consumption across European media online have been at the centre of attention – for example, in titles like 'The COVID-19 pandemic gave us free premium accounts on Pornhub' (*Screenshot*, 18 May 2020) or, more critical and concerned, 'Porn use is up, thanks to the pandemic' (*Theconversation.com*, 8 April 2020). Reading newspaper titles warning about sexuality consumed or performed online during the pandemic, we might easily assume that concerns become even greater when young people are involved. Titles such as 'A breeding ground for abuse: Children at risk behind the closed doors of COVID-19' (*thejournal.ie*, 21 April 2020) imply fears about children consuming sexual information while in quarantine, but also their risk of falling victim to sexual abuse because of their increased use of social media. In effect, what is of interest here is how sexuality appears to become a major concern during a time of social turbulence and persists as a site of regulation and self-regulation.

When it comes to sexuality, non-normative or unregulated forms of consumption, performance and identities are understood in terms of promiscuity and raunchiness. Having said that, sexuality performance in a digital context is frequently defined in terms of how it does not comply with socially acceptable ways of engaging in relationships, of falling in love, or of negotiating the sexual self (e.g. see the critical work of Paasonen et al. 2007, Attwood et al. 2013). In this sense, online dating, sexting, online porn consumption or webcam sex fall within this category of promiscuous, inappropriate and more broadly 'problematic' versions of sexual expression. At the same time, childhood has been a contested term at a social, cultural and political level because of its inherently constructed nature across time and space. Researchers have, for almost two decades now, been stressing the need for children's voices to be heard in research about children (e.g. Buckingham 1993, Tsaliki & Chronaki 2020), given that even as this chapter is being written, knowledge about their experiences with media is mostly based on adults' or adult researchers' accounts. In effect, children's relations with media (mainly online media) have been explored pretty much out of the socio-cultural context in which they are actually lived and understood, and it is among the aims of this chapter to contribute to the discussions from this critical perspective.

In what follows, I first provide a review of the main epistemological arguments around children's sexuality as raised by effects and mass communication researchers, and I then unpack such anxieties via a cultural studies perspective. At an empirical level, I chose to approach an illustrative sample of press articles online analytically, raising a number of points about young people's sexuality in relation to media.

Anxieties about sexuality performed and consumed online

Dominant discourses about media are primarily informed by effects-laden research, aiming at proving a linear relationship between media use and cognitive, attitudinal, developmental or behavioural effects on audiences. Almost fifty years of effects studies attempt to establish a notion of causality in online/offline media audiences' consumption of pornography and its short- or long-term effects (e.g. Miller et al. 2018, de Alarcón et al. 2019). Alongside those, the proliferation of social media and dating/meeting apps has also led to a mushrooming of studies on the assumed effects of online dating (e.g. De Vries et al. 2016). In what particularly concerns children's sexuality and the media, there is an equally large body of effects research, trying to prove a causal relationship between young people's experiences with mediated sexual or sexualised content (mainly online), or sexting, and their assumed effects (e.g. Quadara et al. 2017).

From a more critical perspective, the communication risk paradigm addresses issues of online risk: more specifically, sexual content, sexting, and communication with strangers online are seen as risks possibly enabling harm for the young users (Livingstone et al. 2011). This approach is more child-specific, given that the work of the communication risk paradigm is informed by pedagogical and sociological perspectives, compared with the media effects paradigm. Nevertheless, even in the context of this paradigm sexuality is per se defined as a potential risk for young people online.

The running thread in such arguments is usually anxieties about audiences' sexual conduct and the dangers emanating from unregulated, socially inappropriate or promiscuous sexual information. Having said that, I should bring in here the cultural studies perspective, which underscores the need to contextualise discussions and concerns about sexuality in historical and cultural terms. In fact, cultural studies scholars prioritise a cultural-historical contextualisation of sexuality in relation to childhood (Egan & Hawkes 2010, Tsaliki 2016) and more broadly of sexuality per se, especially when performed in the highly unregulated space of the internet (Attwood, 2010). In studies situated within this paradigm, sexuality and childhood but also technology itself are cultural platforms upon or through which people perform identities and project certain selves, within varied sexual, cultural, social or political contexts.

For example, Masanet and Buckingham (2015, p. 486) explore the pedagogical potential and limitations of online fan forums as a source of informal sex education, in ways that motivate young people to discuss this potential out of ordinary discourses about sex. Hasinoff (2015) and Scarcelli (2020) explore the ways in which young people negotiate gendered, agentic and sexual selves in the context of private versus public in sexting practices. In fact, cultural studies work explores the diverse constructions of childhood as they appear in public discourse, in the domestic versus public space, in different cultures. Following scholars like Buckingham and Bragg (2004) and Tsaliki (2016), I argue in this chapter that young people's experiences with any sort of sexual information broadly reflect eighteenth and nineteenth-century anxieties about childhood.

Constructing sexuality in the context of digital culture and the issue of leisure

My main argument in this chapter is to show that sexuality, technology and childhood (both combined and in themselves) are inherently understood in a governing and self-governing context because of their relation to the concept of *leisure*. In raising the issue of leisure, one needs to address the perspective of 'time' and the ways it defines and is defined by everyday experiences (Shove et al. 2009). A pandemic affecting affluent consumer societies is a major disruption impacting upon the complex temporal organisation of the collective, the individual and the everyday. Therefore, time and its 'emotional, moral and political dimensions' (2009, p. 2) change in ways that urge individuals to adapt in sometimes uneasy modes. Although the case of leisure, and youth leisure more particularly, has been understood within a productive-unproductive binary since the 19th century, we need to acknowledge that as a bundle of social practice, youth leisure is also subject to time production and consumption. Therefore, the disruption in time management caused by COVID-19 might well have reiterated concerns about children's free time.

Concerns about children's leisure and 'unstructured leisure' more particularly, are rooted in Victorian times, when children's free time was thought as a cause of juvenile deviance (Blackman 2011). Given that the family has been already constructed as a regulatory space for children, 19th-century elites focused on reorganising the notion of the domesticated family, within which poor children would keep safe from the immorality of the streets (Rose 1999). As Tsaliki (2016) comments, leisure drawing upon popular culture has been targeted as inappropriate and promiscuous, leading in effect in further regulation of young people's activities outside the formal context of education (and of factory work for the working classes). Regulation of this sort was reinforced in the form of policymaking, in defining unstructured leisure as a social problem, but also as a health problem (leading in effect in the pathologisation of childhood), at the level of the individual (Blackman 2011). Such policy and social advances in relation to childhood and the domesticated family, reorganised the space of the home as a highly regulated space – in fact as a space of regulation and self-governing. Following this argument, it comes as no surprise that ample time available to children during COVID-19 lockdowns – even taking some schooling time into account – raised concerns about how this would be spent in creative and productive ways.

Along these lines, children's online media use as a form of leisure is frequently dealt with anxiety, for the line between productive time and unproductive leisure is assumed to be thin. In fact, the ease with which children use online media for different reasons, to hang out, flirt, play or just wander around, sometimes replacing the offline sites in which such practices take place with online ones, are met with suspicion. In this respect, Pascoe (2010) argues that social media is for young people a private sphere where they can deploy a range of communication and consumption activities (including exploring content, meeting friends, partners, strangers), without parents or any authority figures watching over their shoulders. And when it comes to intimacy and sexuality in specific, digital communication plays a key role in how young people express themselves or perform their sexual conduct (2010, p. 123). However, to follow Slater's (2009) argument about the ethical nature of routine: although these might be youth's everyday routines in the same way as taking one's coffee at a café or flirting at a bar, they are even more subject to ethical framing and connotations of self-governmentality because they take place in the highly contested space of the internet. Therefore, youth's everyday life wherein online media use is an integral part becomes even more intensively scrutinised in a condition like that of COVID-19 where parents' and children's extended co-existence at home further exacerbates calls for effective parenting.

Overall, at the public and policy level, childhood sexuality raises anxieties about the child at risk and its pathologised sexual body and reinforces calls for regulation and self-regulation in this respect (Tsaliki & Chronaki 2020). As aptly put by Egan and Hawkes (2010), anxieties about the sexual child go back to the 19th-century purity reform movement, revolving around health, wellbeing and proper guidance towards adulthood. Also, as Jackson (1982) argues on the same matter, the emergence of childhood as a social category coincides with the emergence of sexuality as a social construction, continuing since then in tandem. The discursive equilibrium between the (socially expected) asexual and Freudian inherently sexual child emerged as a convenient platform for discourses about childhood sexuality control and management, and not least self-regulation. Such constructions make sexuality 'a key dimension of the distinction between childhood and adulthood, and 'despite Freud's "discovery" of infantile sexuality, the image of the sexual (or "sexualised") child fundamentally threatens our sense of what children should be' (Buckingham & Chronaki, 2014, p. 303).

Alongside concerns about children's sexuality sit alarming voices arguing for regulation of children's technological capital – for fear of unstructured leisure becoming an excessive habit. Therefore, instead of being understood as 'sites for the exploration of self-identity, lifestyle and consumption' (Bramham 2011, p. 12), young people's hanging out, messing around or geeking out online – to use Ito et al.'s (2010) terms – become invariably defined as casual, non-serious and unstructured leisure, calling for expert intervention and effective parenting.

Methodological note

For this small-scale qualitative study, an illustrative sample of 50 news items on the topic of sexuality during the pandemic were collected from online news media across Europe (mostly the UK). *The Guardian, Metro, Insider, The Telegraph* and *The Times* are just a few newspapers online where I found articles for this analysis. Although it was not my intention to focus on how the topic is covered in the UK, it is possible that most articles appeared in those media because childhood and sexuality is a key topic in public, political and academic agendas in the UK since 1980s (Pilcher 1996).

To identify the articles of the sample, I used the 'most popular' and 'most recent' filters, available on Google News, and entered keywords like 'children and porn', 'children and pornography', 'Pornhub and COVID-19'. Although many of the articles found also addressed adult sexuality, online dating, pornography addiction, marriage, relationships and sex, they have been left out of the final dataset as not related to the topic discussed. Nevertheless, as a future step in this sort of research, it would be interesting to look comparatively at how discourses of anxiety about sexuality overall cross-cut age constructions of the sexual subject during the COVID-19 pandemic.

Given that sample collection took place during the COVID-19 quarantine, most articles were published between mid-March to mid-May 2020. This was a convenient element in the sampling process given that my interest is mainly on how discourses of anxiety about childhood sexuality have been exacerbated further during COVID-19 lockdowns. Initially a sample of 100 articles was collected; after removing reprints, as well as articles where sexuality was a peripheral and not a central topic, 50 items were included in the final dataset.

The sample has been processed analytically via thematic analysis (Clarke et al. 2015). This analytical strategy allows researchers to offer an overview of a core list of themes appearing in the dataset and – in this specific case – highlight how media and public agendas have framed childhood sexuality amid the pandemic. Although thematic analysis is not an analytical strategy allowing an exhaustive discursive approach to data, it is a useful analytical tool to provide a mapping of the key thematic areas available in the dataset. In the process, researchers may engage partly with discourse analysis (for example of the sort Potter and Wetherell (1987) do) to make their arguments more succinct.

The regulatory context of the public discourse about sexuality in digital spaces

Drawing upon the epistemological discussion offered above and processing stories that specifically address children and sexuality during the COVID-19 pandemic, news search revealed three groups of stories between mid-March and mid-May – that is, the most widespread period of COVID-19 lockdown across Europe. Among the top stories in relation to children that stirred a lot of attention and public debate in European online media were:

- Pornhub's offer of free access to its premium service to countries most affected by the pandemic (e.g. the Wuhan region in China, Italy, Spain, France)
- Fears of online sexual child abuse (amidst incidents of online depictions of child sex abuse)
- Porn 'zoom bombing'

A review of the news items found, brought two main themes that reflect well-established concerns about childhood sexuality forward: *fear of the predator* and *toxic sexuality – toxic youth*. Such umbrella themes were pretty much expected to emerge given that childhood serves as a platform of anxieties about the use and ownership of technology and about the negotiation of children's sexual conduct; matters to do with agency, regulation and practices of self-governmentality (Tsaliki & Chronaki 2020).

Fear of the predator

One of the most popular issues appearing in online news during lockdown has been the rise of incidents of child sexual abuse content or the risk of quarantined children experiencing 'grooming' online. According to Livingstone et al. (2011, p. 88), meeting strangers online is one of the least frequently reported risks for children online: out of 25,000 children 9–16 across Europe, 'although nearly one third (30%) made new contacts online that they have not met face-to-face, the percentage who have gone to meet that person offline is far smaller – 9%'. No matter if the person who these children have met might be a common friend, a peer or someone else, the fear of 'stranger danger' is persistent in the discourse around childhood and has been exacerbated even further during lockdowns. News items have been mostly focusing on a blurred idea of deviant, abusive persons who either exploit lockdown in order to sexually abuse children or bombard them with sexually abusive content: 'The internet has become a defacto babysitter to keep kids entertained or to keep them learning. Predators are also at home and have more time on their hands' (Rappler, 18 April 2020).

Hinting at how children seem to have been left to use screens unsupervised while parents were working (indoors or outdoors), a significant part of the public discourse worked on the idea of 'stranger-danger' posing a threat to children's wellbeing at home. Most news items revolved around five subthemes: *parental mediation, regulation of unstructured time, the non-agentic child, state interventions* and *the risk-averse online culture*. In the way of making the domestic space inherently public in these times − not just in terms of media use but in health management overall − a notion of surveillance society has emerged through the ways media advised and motivated parents, and children themselves, to regulate children online:

> This lockdown is a time for parents to be proactive in speaking to their children about online safety, how to change settings to 'private, friends or contacts only', or prevent spam or unwanted sexual content.
>
> *(IT web, 15 April 2020)*

Parental mediation is not a recent discourse regarding childhood. As discussed above, the emergence of childhood into a distinct social category led to defining and organising the domesticated family, thereby sharing the regulation and supervision of childhood between parents and the state (Rose 1999). Parental mediation as a form of knowledge that parents need to have in order to regulate the conduct of their children when it comes to media use can be seen as a product of the 19th-century preoccupation with the child as a target of moral discourse (Tsaliki & Chronaki 2020). Therefore, the proliferation of online technologies enabling individualised, anonymous and private use led to an intensification of advice on parental mediation informing public, media and academic agendas (see the work of Livingstone & Helsper 2008). During the COVID-19 pandemic, more particularly, effective parenting included supervising children's schoolwork online and, even more, regulating leisure practices:

> The closure of schools and nurseries has led to children spending much of their day online, including time spent on educational activity, contact with friends and entertainment, but the NSPCC warned that it could increase the risk of sexual abuse.
>
> *(The Guardian, 2 April 2020)*

As King (1980) notes, the organisation of industrial societies in terms of time and space in the 19th century and their social organisation, meant a strict organisation of citizens' time and daily routine. The space-time that social life possesses − time-space in Schatzki's (2009) terms − is vital to the existence and smooth running of society. This time-space, within which the social life of individuals is organised, is according to Schatzki a social feature and depends on certain, well-established social practices, including working, learning, dining, sleeping. A disruption due to instances like a pandemic 'alerts us to how rhythms need to be situated within both technological and political cultures' (Trentmann 2009, p. 76). In effect, such circumstances lead to collective and imposed changes to the notion of time-space, therefore impacting on our perceptions about the working order of society and about how people are expected to adapt to them as well. In this sense, children's routine includes school time – an evolving condition since the 19th century – as the main source of training, socialisation and discipline (although working-class children joined formal education later on). A disruption of this social practice generates fears of social disruption, given that schooling is considered as the appropriate pursuit for them. In Shove's terms, such a disruption impacts upon the 'sociotemporal' invention of childhood, which is 'in structuring the days and doings not only of young people but of adults too' (2009, p. 27).

As in most discourses about children's risks online, the media usually address children's parents and carers as those responsible for regulating the non-agentic child; advice about strict parental mediation and discourses of the non-agentic child, lacking the skills to keep safe online, emerged in most news items:

> For most parents, protecting their children from online sexual predators means banning certain sites. But you can also protect your kids through these ways.
> *(Rappler, 18 April 2020)*

> [P]arents are more than ever at the forefront of keeping their children safe online and offline, and knowing where to get help and support is vital.
> *(Metro, 3 April 2020)*

Discourses about the non-agentic child underlie most of the information provided in the sample, given that news items mainly target adults. In cases such as the above, children's voices are – obviously – missing. Bringing parents to the forefront of children's safeguarding and supervision reiterates the notion of neoliberal 'responsibilisation', where individuals are expected to handle risk situations themselves through developing ethical decision-making processes based on risk awareness (Cradock 2004): 'Parents and schools urged to supervise children on Zoom amid fears over child sex abuse risk' (*The Telegraph*, 18 April 2020).

Such claims show how 'stranger danger' may easily breach not just domestic online privacy but also penetrate mainstream – if not mundane – online practices. The policy discourses that emerge in due course, serve to safeguard childhood and the nation itself:

> The government is set to send a text message to every parent and carer in the country amid fears that the lockdown is encouraging online abuse
> *(The Times, 20 April 2020)*

> British campaigners against 'revenge porn' say parents have contacted them in desperation, unable to get non-consensual videos of their children removed from the site.
>
> (The Guardian, *25 March 2020)*

Griffin (2014) argues that youth can be seen as a result of neoliberal governmentality (especially in a globalised context), defining both parents and young people in relation to their consumption practices but in ethical terms. Similarly, Tsaliki and Chronaki (2020) comment that at an institutional level as well, narratives of anxiety about youth are shaping parental cultures and public policy towards young people. If we take a step back, one may find Paterson's (1980) discussion of how the penetration of the welfare state in the family – through the domestication of the media, the proliferation of consumer culture, and the rise of the white appliances and media market – aimed at securing and regulating the family and children's daily routines. In fact, as Shove (2009) discusses through the example of prime-time TV, media programming (by producers) and media consumption (by audiences) contribute to the structuring routines, habits and days, that is social life overall. Therefore, calls for state interventions and effective parenting seem to fit the public narrative of 'child protection' and sit firmly within a context of family regulation and monitoring, but also of regulating free – unstructured – time in the domesticity.

Toxic sexuality – toxic youth

As expected, national lockdowns followed by school closures and work suspension, would sooner or later bring forward concerns about pornography consumption. Under the umbrella theme of 'toxic sexuality – toxic youth' three subthemes emerge: the *demonisation of pornography and pornification of culture, industry regulation* and *toxic youth*. In fact, Pornhub's offer for free premium accounts to users in countries most affected by COVID-19 was rarely welcomed, and the service has been heavily criticised for its 'exploitation of the pandemic' – for example: 'Pornhub owners Mindgeek have used the coronavirus lockdowns to promote their site, giving free Premium access to people living in isolation in Italy, Spain and France' (*The Guardian*, 25 March 2020).

The porn industry is usually contextualised as a raunchy culture, within which money made does not reflect ethical or socially acceptable ways of earning (Tsaliki & Chronaki 2016). As seen above, verbs like 'used' and 'promote' signify exploitation or profit-making on behalf of the company, regardless of the fact that Pornhub has pledged that part of its earnings would be donated to hospitals and pandemic-related causes. In fact, one of the first commentaries published during the quarantine discussed the potential effects of pornography use in the context of COVID-19 pandemic drawing upon Pornhub's published figures (Mestre-Bach et al. 2020). Pornhub's increased traffic, subscriptions and overall economic growth during the pandemic has given rise to criticism regarding the adequacy of state regulation and the industry's self-regulation. Discussion about Pornhub was broadly framed within anxieties that wide lockdowns have inevitably led to more porn consumption;

> The porn site recently published insights tracking user engagement in different countries from the time global concern about COVID-19 began and found traffic across the site has grown exponentially – with daily use to the site increasing by 11.6% since February 24 to March 17.
>
> (Insider, *23 March 2020*)

Especially in this article from the Insider, the discourse around the risk of attitudinal effects from pornography took flesh in the argument about 'coronavirus porn', a thematic category of porn drawing upon the pandemic's impact on Asia. As a result, allegations about the xenophobic representation of Asian people have been made:

> Videos like 'Hot Chinese girl likes to s— coronavirus out of him' […] combine xenophobic tropes about Asian people being 'diseased' and 'foreign' with the existing fetishizing of Asian women that occurs in porn.
>
> (Insider, *23 March 2020*)

The fetishisation of pornography is a rather popular anti-porn argument, mainly within the feminist thought, and primarily because of its implications about the sexual objectification of the (feminine) body (Chronaki 2014). In effect, arguments that Pornhub promotes biased representations against Asian people created a platform upon which assumptions about the industry's objectifying nature sit firmly. Along similar lines, calls for industry regulation emerged amidst allegations of posting revenge porn or non-consensual sexual content on the Pornhub platform, which preceded the company's provision of free accounts:

> Along with more clicks, however, have come renewed complaints about the video-sharing platform and questions about whether all the content available online is consensual. […]. Women's rights experts have urged governments for tighter regulation to tackle abuse online and accused Pornhub of failing to act quickly enough to remove content when reported.
>
> (Reuters, *26 March 2020*)

Regulation of the sex industry – especially amidst allegations of sexual abuse content – makes the issue of these public manifestations of sexuality an inherently political issue. Although frequently part of radical feminist agendas, the debate about the regulation of the pornography industry was a central issue of the 1980s sex wars and has been part of discussions around pornography since the late 1970s (Segal & McIntosh 1993). Such discourses about regulation point towards ethical claims that have to do with both those who produce and those who consume pornography, picturing porn audiences in terms of otherness and problematic behaviour (Attwood 2007). In effect, these public discussions about the problematic nature of the porn industry itself and its corruptive forces reflect assumptions about its audiences and, more specifically, not only the fear of being exploited or influenced but also the fear of exposing one's own problematic sexual conduct.

Alongside the news about Pornhub, news about hacking attacks on Zoom meetings led to the new term 'zoombombing'. As reported, individuals hacked educational or recreational online meetings, throwing pornographic content and allegedly engaging in offensive behaviour towards zoom participants: "'As large numbers of people turn to video-teleconferencing (VTC) platforms to stay connected in the wake of the COVID-19 crisis, reports of VTC hijacking (also called 'Zoom-bombing') are emerging nationwide," the agency said' (*Metro*, 3 April 2020).

Popular free applications, but also the need to go to an online environment to continue one's professional, social and cultural practices during COVID-19 lockdown, gave rise to concerns about privacy breach and the need for further regulation (so that privacy is protected). As mentioned above, the domestication of media but also the proliferation of online technologies brought calls for regulation – of media and the users themselves – even more to the fore (Hepp & Krotz 2014). Going back to the concept of neoliberal responsibilisation, zoombombing brought discourses of risk awareness to the forefront, thereby reminding the neoliberal citizen of their obligation to ethical decision-making amid such risk. An inherent part of such safeguarding processes as risk-management decisions obviously concerns childhood. In the case of zoombombing, this related both to the children whose classes have been disrupted and to childhood more broadly: 'Many angry parents took to social media to express their shock at the images they and their children were subjected to' (*Daily Record*, 14 April 2020).

Dominant scholarship on young people's online experiences focuses a lot on the potential effects of hacking, porn or other 'inappropriate' forms of content and find firm ground for policymaking in terms of content and audiences' regulation (e.g. O'Neil et al. 2011). To this end, academic and policy agendas on children's digital rights and safety online emerge as a response to the need for child protection (Livingstone & Third 2017); and as a result, children are expected to become themselves agents of ethical decision-making by being informed about a risk-averse culture wherein they should be cautious.

The zoombombing incidents – especially those related to disruption of higher education online lectures by students – regenerated the toxic youth discourse:

> The cases come after the University of Derby suspended six students over 'degrading and offensive' comments allegedly made about their female peers in an online group chat, and a leaked report found Warwick University lacked internet filter software to block students and staff from accessing inappropriate or illegal material.
>
> *(The Guardian, 22 April 2020)*

The concept of toxic youth seems to envelope young people who do not conform with or cause disruptions tp the normative way educational or leisure practices work during the pandemic. Failing to fit the master narrative of the 'moral' young individual (in this case emerging adults) whereby moral regulation of everyday routine and culture consumption is included reiterates discourses about corrupt youth, youth as trouble. With assumptions about youth being per se wrongdoers if not guided otherwise, the 'rhetoric of control and constraint follows, with morality becoming a tool for maintaining order' (Tsaliki & Chronaki 2020, p. 8). I am here returning to Blackman's (2011) discussion of troubled youth and her argument that dominant explanations of young people's engagement with risky or inappropriate forms of leisure are seen as disturbing, 'a causal factor in the generation of social problems' (p. 97):

> A group of pranksters has been using Discord to organize 'Zoom-bombs' of online classes. The 'raids' not only involve disrupting the video conferences with insults, racial epithets, and porn, but also recording the sessions and posting them on YouTube, TikTok and Twitch.
>
> (PCmag.com, *31 March 2020*)

In this article, the use of the word 'pranking' – a form of joking of schadenfreudian nature (see Portmann 2000) – is framed in terms of 'raiding'. Pranking, usually defined as a 'childish', 'inappropriate' or even 'offensive' practice, connotes youth as trouble in this particular case and regenerates Victorian discourses about maladjusted beings. Again, free or unstructured time (also a result of lockdown) is seen as a cause of deviance. Even more, given that it takes place in the public space of a Zoom meeting in the context of higher education and is therefore subject to regulation and authority (Blackman 2011), such practice is seen as a potential social problem.

Apparently, youth and its connotations when combined with the notion of sexuality denote a problematic condition – even more so when these are discussed in the context of technology use and leisure. Although illustrative, the analysis of a small sample of online news items supports argumentation that youth becomes a platform of social control but also for the reiteration of the neoliberal risk-aware – and thus self-governed – ethical subject.

Conclusions

The COVID-19 pandemic disrupted the rather normative way of the multi-tasking, 24-hour day of life and the ever-expanding set of indoor, outdoor, online, offline set of practices performed. In adapting to this disruption, societies moved most of the everyday practices such as work, education and leisure indoors and into online spaces. Much of the overall concern in the context of the pandemic inevitably focused on children – who reflect the future of every society – and revolved around youth leisure at home and more particularly online leisure. Soon enough, and occasioned by incidents such as zoombombing and Pornhub's offer of free accounts during the pandemic, concerns focused on children's online encounters as a space of potential risk and harm. In effect, childhood sexuality and childhood more broadly have been once again put under the public, policy and expert microscope, with pressure to intensify regulatory and self-regulatory practices.

Media, as agents of such discourses of anxiety, raised a number of issues having to do with stranger danger, problematic forms of porn consumption and production, as well as toxic youth. Although such concerns have spread in media agendas across the globe, a closer look at a small, illustrative sample of news items in European online media reveals again obsessive concerns with how children's daily routines at home are organised. In this respect, parents' efficacy to organise, supervise and regulate this routine is also addressed, and in fact takes the form of guidance around effective parenting. To draw upon Schatzki's (2009) and Shove's (2009) discussions about time-space production and consumption, sexuality becomes, in this case, a platform for concerns about how normative time-spaces have been disrupted and reorganised, rather than a concern itself.

In effect, everyday routines become even more subject to ethical framing, also through technologies like sexuality, youth and media use, emerging as forms of self-government and neoliberal responsibilisation. To return to Slater's argument, given that 'everyday life is constructed within a larger division between public and private domains' (2009, p. 220), youth's self-governing through everyday routines during COVID-19 became a matter of intensive supervision and regulation at a public level even more than before.

References

Attwood, F. (2007). 'Other' or 'one of us'?: The porn user in public and academic discourse. *Participations: Journal of Audience and Reception Studies*, 4(1).

Attwood, F. (ed.) (2010). *Porn.com: Making Sense of Online Pornography*. New York: Peter Lang.

Attwood, F., Bale, C. and Barker, M.J. (eds) 2013. The sexualization report. Available at https://thesexualizationreport.files.wordpress.com/2013/12/thesexualizationreport.pdf (retrieved 9 May 2020).

Blackman, S. (2011). Rituals of intoxication: Young people, drugs, risk and leisure. In P. Bramham and S. Wagg (eds), *The New Politics of Leisure and Pleasure* (pp. 97–118). Basingstoke: Palgrave Macmillan.

Bramham, P. (2011). Choosing leisure: Social theory, class and generations. In P. Bramham and S. Wagg (eds), *The New politics of leisure and pleasure* (pp.11–31). Basingstoke: Palgrave Macmillan.

Buckingham, D. (1993). *Children Talking Television: The Making of Television Literacy*. London: Falmer Press.

Buckingham, D. and Bragg, S. (2004). *Young People, Sex and the Media: The Facts of Life?* Basingstoke: Palgrave Macmillan.

Buckingham, D. and Chronaki, D. (2014). Saving the children? Pornography, childhood and the internet. In S. Wagg and J. Pilcher (eds), *Thatcher's Grandchildren* (pp. 301–317). Basingstoke: Palgrave Macmillan.

Chronaki, D. (2014). Young people's accounts of experiences with sexual content during childhood and teenage life. PhD thesis. Loughborough University, UK.

Clarke, V., Braun, V. and Hayfield, N. (2015). Thematic analysis. In J.A. Smith (ed.), *Qualitative Psychology: A Practical Guide to Research Methods* (pp. 222–248). London: Sage.

Cradock, G. (2004). Risk morality and child protection: Risk calculation as guides to practice. *Science, Technology & Human Values*, 29(3), 314–331.

de Alarcón, R., de la Iglesia, J.I., Casado, N.M. and Montejo, A.L. (2019). Online porn addiction: What we know and what we don't: A systematic review. *Journal of clinical medicine*, 8(1), 91.

De Vries, D. A. (2016). Meeting expectations: The effects of expectations on self-esteem following the construction of a dating profile. *Computers in Human Behavior*, 62, 44–50.

Egan, R. and Hawkes, G. (2010). *Theorizing the Sexual Child in Modernity*. New York: Springer.

Fabiani, A. (2020). 'The COVID-19 pandemic gave us free premium accounts on Pornhub'. *ScreenShot*, 18 May. Available at https://screenshot-magazine.com/technology/sex-tech/covid-19-free-pornhub/ (retrieved 13 June 2020).

Griffin, C. (2014). 'What time is now?': Researching youth and culture beyond the 'Birmingham school'. In D. Buckingham, S. Bragg and M.J. Kehily (eds), *Youth Cultures in the Age of Global Media* (pp. 21–36). Basingstoke: Palgrave Macmillan.

Grubbs, J. (2020). 'Porn use is up, thanks to the pandemic'. *The conversation.com*, 8 April. Available at https://theconversation.com/porn-use-is-up-thanks-to-the-pandemic-134972 (retrieved 13 June 2020).

Hasinoff, A.A. (2015). *Sexting Panic: RethinkingCcriminalization, Privacy, and Consent*. Urbana, IL: University of Illinois Press.

Hepp, A. and Krotz, F. (eds) (2014). *Mediatized Worlds: Culture and Society in a Media Age*. London: Springer.

Jackson, S. (1982). *Childhood and Sexuality*. Oxford: Blackwell.

Ito, M. et al. (2010). *Hanging Out, Messing Around and Geeking Out: Kids Living and Learning with New Media*. Cambridge, MA: MIT Press.

King, A. (1980). A time for space and a space for time. In A. King (ed.), *Buildings and Society*, London: Routledge.

Livingstone, S. and Helsper, E.J. (2008). Parental mediation of children's internet use. *Journal of Broadcasting & Electronic Media*, 52(4), 581–599.

Livingstone, S., Haddon, L., Görzig, A. and Ólafsson, K. (2011). Risks and safety on the internet: The perspective of European children. EU Kids Online. LSE, London.

Livingstone, S. and Third, A. (2017). 'Children and young people's rights in the digital age: An emerging agenda', *New Media and Society*, 19(5), 657–670.

Masanet, M.J. and Buckingham, D. (2015). Advice on life? Online fan forums as a space for peer-to-peer sex and relationships education. *Sex Education*, 15(5), 486–499.

Mestre-Bach, G., Blycker, G.R. and Potenza, M.N. (2020). Pornography use in the setting of COVID-19 pandemic. *Journal of Bhavioural Addictions*, doi:10.1556/2006.2020.00015.

Miller, D.J., Hald, G.M. and Kidd, G. (2018). Self-perceived effects of pornography consumption among heterosexual men. *Psychology of Men & Masculinity*, 19(3), 469–476.

O'Neill, B., Livingstone, S. and McLaughlin, S. (2011). Final recommendations for policy, methodology and research. EU Kids Online. LSE, London.

Paasonen, S., Nikunen, K. and Saarenmaa, L. (2007). *Pornification: Sex and Sexuality in Media Culture*. Oxford: Berg.

Paterson, R. (1980). Planning the family: The art of the television schedule. *Screen Education*, 35, 79–85.

Pascoe, J. (2010). Intimacy. In M. Ito et al., *Hanging Out, Messing Around and Geeking Out: Kids Living and Learning with New Media* (pp. 117–132). Cambridge, MA: MIT Press.

Pilcher, J. (1996). Gillick and after: Children and sex in the 1980s and 1990s. In S. Wagg and J. Pilcher (eds), *Thatcher's Grandchildren* (pp. 78–94). London and Washington, DC: Falmer Press.

Portmann, J. (2000). *When Bad Things Happen to Other People*. London: Routledge.

Potter, J. and Wetherell, M. (1987). *Discourse and Social Psychology: Beyond Attitudes and Behaviour*. London: Sage.

Quadara, A., El-Murr, A. and Latham, J. (2017). The effects of pornography on children and young people. Australian Institute of Family Studies, Melbourne.

Rose, N. (1999). *Governing the Soul: The Shaping of the Private Self*. London: Free Association Books.

Scarcelli, C.M. (2020). Teenage perspectives on sexting and pleasure in Italy: Going beyond the concept of moral panics. In L. Tsaliki and D. Chronaki (eds), *Discourses of Anxiety over Childhood and Youth across Cultures* (pp. 297–322). Cham: Palgrave-Macmillan.

Schatzki, T. (2009). Timespace and the organization of social life. In E. Shove, F. Trentmann and R. Wilk (eds), *Time, Consumption and Everyday Life: Practice, Materiality and Culture* (pp. 35–48). Oxford: Berg.

Segal, L. and McIntosh, M. (eds) (1993). *Sex Exposed: Sexuality and the Pornography Debate*. New Brunswick, NJ: Rutgers University Press.

Shove, E. (2009). Everyday practice and the production and consumption of time. In E. Shove, F. Trentmann and R. Wilk (eds), *Time, Consumption and Everyday Life: Practice, Materiality and Culture* (pp. 17–34). Oxford: Berg.

Shove, E., Trentmann, F. and Wilk, R. (2009). *Introduction*. In E. Shove, F. Trentmann and R. Wilk (eds), *Time, Consumption and Everyday Life: Practice, Materiality and Culture* (pp. 1–11). Oxford: Berg.

Slater, D. (2009). The ethics of routine: Consciousness, tedium and value. In E. Shove, F. Trentmann and R. Wilk (eds), *Time, Consumption and Everyday Life: Practice, Materiality and Culture* (pp. 217–230). Oxford: Berg.

Thejournal.ie (21/04/2010). 'A breeding ground for abuse': Children at risk behind the closed doors of COVID-19. *Thejournal.ie*, 21 April. Available at www.thejournal.ie/domestic-a buse-investigation-coronavirus-crisis-part-two-5079167-Apr2020/ (retrieved 10 May 2020).

Trentmann, F. (2009). Disruption is normal: Blackouts, breakdowns and the elasticity of everyday life. In E. Shove, F. Trentmann and R. Wilk (eds), *Time, Consumption and Everyday Life: Practice, Materiality and Culture* (pp. 67–84). Oxford: Berg.

Tsaliki, L. (2016). *Children and the Politics of Sexuality: The Sexualization of Children Debate Revisited*. Basingstoke: Palgrave Macmillan.

Tsaliki, L. and Chronaki, D. (2016). Producing the porn self: An introspection of the mainstream Greek porn industry. *Porn Studies*, 3(2), 175–186.

Tsaliki, L. and Chronaki, D. (eds), 2020. *Discourses of Anxiety about Childhood and Youth Across Cultures*. Cham: Palgrave MacMillan.

PART II

Adults, sexuality, gender and the media in research perspective

5

HIV-RELATED STIGMA IN THE EUROPEAN CINEMA

Conflictive representations of a cultural trauma

Sergio Villanueva Baselga

Introduction

Since the beginning of the HIV epidemic in 1981, approximately 1,000,000 people have been diagnosed with the virus in the European Region according to the World Health Organization (WHO). While the infection rate has declined, almost 80,000 new cases were reported in adults in Western and Central Europe in 2017, and the prevalence of HIV in Europe will continue to increase in the foreseeable future as people living with HIV (PLWH) can now expect to have a normal lifespan. In 2014, the Joint United Nations Programme on HIV and AIDS (UNAIDS) and its partners launched the ambitious 90–90–90 targets strategy for 2020 as a commitment to improve access to antiretroviral therapy (ART), a lifesaving treatment, a transmission prevention measure and a human right. The first of the three targets is the successful diagnosis of 90% of all HIV-positive people. The second target involves delivering ART to 90% of those diagnosed; and finally, the third target is viral suppression for 90% of those on treatment (Levi et al. 2016). In 2017, 79% of PLWH in the European region knew their status, of which 79% were accessing therapy and 81% were virally suppressed.

The UNAIDS 90–90–90 targets have required innovative, multidisciplinary strategies to diagnose, treat, and promote adherence to antiretroviral drug prescriptions. However, this strategy has been mainly directed towards biochemical solutions and overlooks other important issues that PLWH face in their daily lives. As an example, PLWH have a 29% higher risk of reduced quality of life due to comorbid health conditions like cardiovascular diseases, osteoporosis and depression (Evans-Lacko et al. 2012) which can also affect their adherence to medication regimens (Markovitz et al. 2000, Gao et al. 2010). Many of these comorbidities are related to mental health and how adult PLWH interpret, deal with, and contextualise their life with HIV overall. In other words, how they negotiate with

HIV-related stigmas and cultural traumas but also with being PLWH and the ways this identity progresses and evolves with age. Based on this insight, researchers and activists have highlighted the necessity of adding a fourth '90' to the UNAIDS targets: improved quality of life – that is, reaching a 90% of PLWH with a high standard of quality of life that is free of HIV-related comorbidities (Lazarus et al. 2016).

Many PLWH have internalised the negative societal narratives surrounding HIV and fear that healthcare professionals (HCPs) treating such comorbidities will discriminate against them (Kinsler et al. 2007, Lekas, Siegel and Leider 2011). Hence it is clear that negative narratives of HIV spread by the media constitute one of the structural drivers of stigma that PLWH face in their everyday co-habitation with HIV. As Lupton and Tulloch (1996) explain, when PLWH narrate the impact of HIV in their lives, they use frequent and concurrent images that they got from media. In this sense, there is an urgent need to study how the media, and specifically cinema, has portrayed HIV to develop negative narratives surrounding the virus. In the last decade, most films that depict HIV still deal with the epidemics of the 1990s, portraying troubled characters who become emotionally detached from their friends and lovers to fight against the damaging consequences of HIV infection and ultimately die in a sad ending. In fact, a great number of the European films about HIV fall into the melodrama genre, in which their characters die during the story because of the HIV infection or get infected by their sexual partners or lovers. These representations are frequently associated with biased and stereotyped pictures of gay love and gay sexualities, that serve as a moral labelling that feeds HIV-related stigmas (Attinelo 2013, p. 108; Martín Hernández 2013, p. 123).

In order to shed light on how media, and especially cinema, may impact on PLWH's quality of life and perception of their co-habitation with HIV, this chapter sets out to problematise how European cinema has portrayed adult people living with HIV and gay sexualities in the last decades. By analysing the films *Drôle de Félix* (2000), *Pride* (2014), *Theo et Hugo dans le même bateau* (2016) and *Bohemian Rhapsody* (2018), this chapter seeks to demonstrate that, despite the advancements in the treatment of HIV and the reach of undetectability as a guarantee of untrasmitability – that is, the success of the 90–90–90 goals – the public conversation about HIV as narrated in films is still relying in the trauma of the origins of the epidemic and focuses on a simplistic and overtly stereotyped of men who have sex with men (MSM), neglecting women living with HIV and sustaining a pretty much biased and conflictive picture of PLWH.

The four films approached analytically in this chapter have been selected upon two main criteria: (i) they provide a socio-historical trajectory of how adult PLWH have been portrayed in the last two decades in European films; and (ii) they portray gay characters in their adult life, i.e. living with HIV or sharing their lives with someone HIV+. My analysis focused on how HIV+ characters navigate along their adulthood and struggle with the impact of HIV in their lives. In the same vein, this analysis looks at the asynchronous representation of the pandemic and the way representations of the 1980s and the 1990s HIV epidemic are still evoked in 21st-century texts, reproducing a portrayal still pierced by cultural trauma. It is relevant at this point to declare that this research does not attempt another effects study on the matter of HIV reception as it does not address how audiences respond to the films discussed (like, e.g. Farrell (2006). Instead, it seeks to question and challenge how HIV is portrayed in such texts in order to examine how PLWH might read themselves in a mediated relation with cinema, in the same way as Pocius (2016, p. 32) or Dean (2007).

Identity, stigma and health, or why we should worry about cinema

The study of identity is complex and numerous scholars have devoted considerable intellectual and scientific energy to understand strategies of identity construction and how these in effect contribute to the formation of beliefs, attitudes and behaviours. Identity impacts upon many spheres of our daily life, health being one of them. Many scholars have studied how identity determines individuals' health choices, values and actions, under the assumption that identity and health are inextricably entwined (e.g. Haslam et al. 2009). *Being healthy* often becomes an identity and defines or is defined by other dimensions of identity, such as gender or age. Ideas about what it means to be a healthy person pierce many media outlets. In this sense, it is necessary to bear in mind that media and cinema have the potential to shape how we understand health and, thus, how we think of illness and being sick (Gough 2006).

It is impossible to understand the personal experience and social meaning of HIV without considering the concept of 'stigma' and its relation to adult life. Whenever the sociological or psychological aspects of HIV are considered, 'stigma' is quickly evoked – indeed, the social experience of living and ageing with HIV may be entirely encompassed by the term 'stigma'. This is as true when it comes to academic discourse such as sociological studies, as it is when it comes to the work of community 'stakeholders'. 'People living with HIV endure stigma' is, quite simply, a truism. But as common as the notion of 'HIV stigma' may be, definitions or explanations of what is meant by the term are equally uncommon. A gesture toward Goffman's (1963) classic treatise on the subject may be made before returning to the implicit or tacit sense that we know what HIV stigma is. Indeed, the discourse of HIV stigma is so pervasive that one could argue that it imposes a specific meaning to one's condition upon people living with ageing HIV, one that they may or may not recognise.

Major et al. (2018, p. 42) define stigma as 'entirely contingent on access to social, economic, and political power that allows the identification of differentness, the construction of stereotypes, the separation of labelled persons into distinct categories and the full execution of disapproval, rejection, exclusion, and discrimination'. People perceived to suffer from certain illnesses have, in most cases, been considered not capable or worthy of fulfilling certain duties (Taggart et al. 2015). In effect it is possible that negative stereotyping that comes with the profiling of a given disease could potentially lead to their being rejected even in jobs that they have the qualifications for; and this situation worsens with ageing. The media has undeniably played a critical role in spreading information about the negative impact of the labelled activities, conducts, or illnesses (McGinty, Kennedy-Hendricks & Barry 2019). And among media, film has an immense power to articulate representations, discourses and identities, thus feeding stigmas and shaping health perception.

Taking this idea a bit further, and assuming that cinema and popular culture inform a historical project in which ideologies, confrontations and ontological positions are tumultuous and conflicting, the analysis of health in cinema emerges as a way to understand how collective identities have been constructed under specific historical, political and geographical contexts. In this sense, cinema can be considered not only as an industry that includes companies, producers, directors and actors, but a social institution that evolves alongside the society in which it is produced and viewed (Dyer 2013). Therefore, by examining film representations and framings of traumas such as the HIV pandemic, it is possible to puzzle out the political and social implications of specific readings on concrete conflicts and how they are interwoven in the construction of health identities (Kelly and Millward 2004, p. 5). This is what makes film analysis so crucial for understanding how film viewers can have their health identity moulded, with the result of either fostering or mitigating the stigmas associated with certain diseases or health conditions, albeit recognising other influxes of their cultural contexts (Herrmann et al. 2018, McGinty, Kennedy-Hendricks & Barry 2019).

In the case of HIV, most of the studies addressing the matter have focused on documentary films (Hart 2013, p. 74), where there is a relationship of trust between the filmmaker and the spectator based on the veracity of the events depicted. According to Bill Nichols (1991, pp. 42–43), the relationship of trust between spectator and filmmaker is established mainly through two fundamental features of the genre: the filmmaker has limited control over the story, and the textual logic of a documentary is argumentative rather than narrative. Documentaries such as *Killing Patient Zero* relate to a scenario where an HIV+ patient was demonised as dangerous and capable of negatively influencing other people (Röhm, Hastall & Ritterfeld 2017). The other actors in the film expressed fear and neglect towards the patient who was perceived to be an HIV patient. Videos of this nature tend to attract a huge audience due to the quality of entertaining in the contents; nonetheless, the deeper meaning embedded in the story is the negative depiction of HIV/AIDS victims.

The above articulations prove that, indeed, the mainstream media has the ability to control the spread of stigma among the affected groups in diverse social settings. However, in the case of fiction films, the mediation between filmmaker and spectator is enacted through narrative mechanisms designed to elicit emotions that trigger stigmas (Hatzenbuehler, Nolen-Hoeksema & Dovidio 2009). This highlights the need for further analysis of fiction films in order to understand the relationship between identity, stigma, and health.

Internalised and enacted stigma in *Theo et Hugo dans le même bateau* (2016) and *Drole de Félix* (2000)

Stigma can manifest mainly in two forms: internalised and enacted. Internalised stigma refers to an individual's own adoption, consciously or unconsciously, of the negative societal beliefs and feelings associated with his or her stigmatised status (Lee, Kochman & Sikkema 2002, Simbayi et al. 2010, Turan et al. 2017). Internalised stigma is commonly fuelled by narratives and cultural devices that propagate negative portrayals of stigmatised groups and, thus, foster harming attitudes towards those belonging to those groups. And this is how one can think *Theo et Hugo dans le même bateau* (2016), a French film directed by Olivier Ducastel and Jacques Martineau, deals with HIV-related stigma while watching its impactful opening scene.

This film tells the story of two lovers, Theo and Hugo, in their most graceful adulthood, who meet at a sex club called *L'Impact* in central Paris. The film begins with an explicit group sex scene lasting more than twenty minutes, in which Theo and Hugo meet in a poorly lit place crowded with naked men, and fall in love; from the outset, this is possibly suggesting that the film takes a promiscuous view of gay love (Çakirlar & Needham 2019). The lovers' romance unfolds amidst the bodies of the other men and, overwhelmed by excitement, the two make love without using condoms. Theo is HIV positive, takes medication and has an undetectable viral load; however, when he confesses this to Hugo, the latter is overcome with doubt and fear. His internalised stigma has been triggered and he doesn't know how to react or how to treat Theo. It is 4:27 a.m., and the two decide to leave the club and take a long bike ride through Paris to get to know each other better.

Nevertheless, the film *Theo et Hugo dans le même bateau* does not dwell on Hugo's doubts or on Theo's explanations. Instead, the relaxed conversation between the lovers gradually begins to dissolve the negative narratives on which Hugo has constructed his imaginary of HIV. Riding their bikes, Theo and Hugo transcend the fear and reaffirm their love, born out of an erotic spark. The lovers do not fall into the simplistic dualism of a patronising view of the HIV epidemic of the 1990s, nor do they wallow in pain they haven't experienced to offer an outdated portrayal of HIV. In their two-hour ride through the centre of Paris, Theo and Hugo shatter the internalised stigma. However, wanting to reassure Hugo, Theo decides to accompany him to a hospital to receive post-exposure treatment, and it is here that the directors, Olivier Ducastel and Jacques Martineau, present to us an example of enacted stigma.

When they get to the hospital, Theo and Hugo confront enacted stigma when the doctor who attends them adopts a negative, critical stance towards them. Theo has an undetectable viral load, which means it is non-communicable and cannot be transmitted to Hugo. But the doctor does not explain this, instead choosing to reproach the lovers, and especially Theo, for their careless attitude. Enacted stigma is defined as negative biases in feelings toward and evaluations of stigmatised groups and unfair treatment of those groups by healthcare professionals or the general public (Kinsler et al. 2007, Lekas, Siegel & Leider 2011). In other words, it is the stigma perceived and spread by those unaffected by the stigma themselves but who frequently deal with stigmatised individuals: doctors, nurses, dentists, etc. After a brief lecture designed to make them feel guilty, the doctor prescribes Hugo a post-exposure treatment, which once again fills him with doubt. Enacted stigma operates as a constant reminder of negative, guilt-inducing narratives. While internalised stigma can be reduced by personal experience or direct contact with others who have suffered from the stigma and have overcome it, enacted stigma returns stigmatised individuals to their condition of discrimination. Hugo's renewed fear is once again calmed by Theo as they continue their ride, eat a kebab, and meet a woman on the Paris Metro. By the time their bike ride is over, at 5:59, there is no stigma separating the two lovers.

How Ducastel and Martineau framed stigma in the film *Theo et Hugo dans le même bateau* contrasts with their second film *Drôle de Félix* (2000), directed 16 years before. This film chronicles the life of the eponymous character Félix, a HIV-positive gay man of mixed race who shares an apartment with his boyfriend Daniel in his hometown, the city of Dieppe. After losing his job as a ferry steward, Félix uses some of his free time to clean his mother's home. While cleaning her apartment he discovers a box of letters and photographs that include a Marseille-based address of his long-lost father of Maghrebi origin. This finding triggers a road-movie to the south of France that is divided into five short adventures that take Felix through several provincial settings where he meets several characters who become part of his surrogate family.

As Provencher (2008, p. 2) states, 'the film presents Félix as a character who is comfortable with his sexuality, HIV+ status, as well as his stable, healthy, and open relationship with Daniel'. On one of the stops in his journey, at the home of an elderly woman who lives in the mountains, Félix openly shows how he takes his medication, sharing the moment with his host, who also takes her own medication for her blood pressure. In this scene, Félix explains to his companion what his life with HIV is like, and how the medication allows him to have a long and happy life. The woman responds enthusiastically and without a hint of surprise, quite different from Hugo's first reaction triggered by internalised stigma. In this way, *Drôle de Félix* (2000) offers a de-stigmatised perspective of HIV that abandons the negative, guilt-inducing visions pursued in contemporary narratives of HIV.

The HIV pandemic and cultural trauma: *Bohemian Rhapsody* (2018) and *Pride* (2014)

According to Alexander (2004, p. 34), collective identities are constructed over cultural traumas, which are 'horrendous events that leave indelible marks upon group consciousness, impacting memories forever and changing collective identities in fundamental and irrevocable ways'. Cultural trauma is first and foremost an empirical, scientific concept, suggesting new, meaningful causal relationships between previously unrelated events, structures, perceptions, and actions. But this concept also sheds light on an emerging domain of analysis. It is by constructing cultural traumas that social groups not only cognitively identify the existence and source of human suffering but also take on board some significant responsibility for it (Sztompka 2000, Kansteiner 2004). In this sense, it has been theorised that cultural trauma even becomes interwoven with health identities when a community evolves out of a health situation, such as the HIV community (Hudnall Stamm et al. 2004, Gailienė 2019, Shea et al. 2019).

It is clear that the rapid expansion of the HIV epidemic in the 1980s and 1990s was a crisis of such dimensions that it has become a cultural trauma that has laid the foundations of the HIV community's collective identity. At this point one might question how stigma and cultural trauma might be connected, and the answer can be found in the history of HIV epidemic. Hence, HIV cultural trauma could be revealed through an analysis of the representations of the disease in contemporary cultural productions and the impact they had on their audiences. With this in mind, at this point it is worth analysing and discussing how HIV is represented in one of the most successful European productions of recent years: *Bohemian Rhapsody* (2018).

This British film, directed by Bryan Singer, is a biopic on the life of Freddy Mercury, the lead singer of the rock band *Queen*, a film that made more than 900 million euros at the box office and won the BAFTA and the Oscar for best actor for the performance of Rami Malek. The film's huge success, however, did not prevent it from being criticised for its treatment of the singer's sexuality and its slanted view of the HIV pandemic. As McCleerey (2019, p. 4) suggests, '[t]he movie is intriguing on one level: its engagement with recent discourse on same-sex relationships in relation to heterosexual relationships, heteronormativity in particular'. The new heteronormal is shown in the film in the constant conflict between Freddy Mercury's hedonistic lifestyle with other men and the constant reminder of the possibility of returning to 'normalcy' represented by Mary, Freddy's ex-wife. In this way, the film, even it does not explicitly portray Mercury's sexual identity, locates the beginning of the singer's fall at the same point as the beginning of his relationships with men, while Mary is depicted as his salvation.

In addition to linking the source of the singer's fall to his journey into hedonism, the film's heteronormal vision diverts the impact of Mercury's HIV towards culpability, and it is increased as Mercury gets older. The film thus encourages a reading in which the brilliant artist is dragged to his doom by other men incapable of controlling their sexual desire, leading to the HIV infection that ended his life. The link between gay promiscuity and HIV also present in *Theo et Hugo dans le même bateau* is expressed in *Bohemian Rhapsody* in the placement of blame on the artist's non-heterosexual lifestyle. This view of the early days of the epidemic delves into the cultural trauma that continues to exist today in relation to HIV; it is a view still caught up in the stereotype that associates the virus with promiscuity, sin with deviant relations.

In contrast to the mainstream view presented in *Bohemian Rhapsody* (2018), another British film, *Pride* (2014), written by Stephen Beresford and directed by Matthew Warchus, tells the story of the Lesbians and Gays Support the Miners (LGSM) movement; an alliance of LGTB rights activists who decided to join the miner's struggle that began with the general strike in 1984 against the policies of the Thatcher government. The film's protagonist, young, fresh LGMS founder Mark Ashton, is depicted as a fervent activist who notices that the police have stopped persecuting the gay movement because their attention is focused on the miners' struggle. In a quest for allies, Ashton manages to convince the members of his movement to join the miners, helping them raise funds and even confronting the police in their heavy-handed tactics against the demonstrators. This wins them the friendship and trust of the miners, who subsequently march in London's Gay Pride parade the following year in support of their comrades in the LGMS.

Pride portrays a socially committed, politically active protagonist who, in contrast with Freddy Mercury in *Bohemian Rhapsody*, is not absorbed in a life of hedonism. Mark Ashton is sexually active, and during the film we meet several of his lovers, but the narrative construction of the film does not delve into his sex life or place it above other aspects of his life. As a result, when a former lover's confession reveals to Ashton that he might have contracted HIV, the film does not invoke the simplistic dualist narrative of the origins of the pandemic. In this way, *Pride* effectively evades the cultural trauma associated with HIV and, although Mark Ashton ends up dying of AIDS two years later, we are offered an alternative reading divorced from the promiscuity, culpability and hedonism that so many other films have repeatedly depicted.

As a mode of conclusion: HIV, age and cinema in the time of undetectability

As mentioned at the beginning of the chapter, approximately 1,000,000 people have been diagnosed with HIV in the European Region since the start of the epidemic. In the last decades the infection rate has declined, but almost 80,000 new infections were reported in 2017. While these figures decrease, life expectancy of PLWH increases and they have more and more normal adulthood lives. Nevertheless, in 2016, the Prevention Access Campaign, a health equity initiative with the goal to end the HIV/AIDS pandemic as well as HIV-related stigma, launched the Undetectable = Untransmittable (U = U) initiative. U = U signifies that individuals with HIV who receive ART and have achieved and maintained an undetectable viral load cannot sexually transmit the virus to others. This idea, based on strong scientific evidence, has broad implications for the treatment of HIV infection from a scientific and public health standpoint, and for the self-esteem of individuals by reducing the stigma associated with HIV (Rendina & Parsons 2018, Eisinger, Dieffenbach & Fauci 2019).

The U=U campaign has great potential to drastically reduce the stigma associated with HIV and has emerged as a game changer for HIV prevention (Patel, Curoe & Chan 2020). The fact that individuals with an undetectable viral load cannot pass on the virus reduces their moral burden in relation to culpability for transmission. Since, 2016, huge efforts have been made to expand the scope of the U=U initiative, thereby reducing discrimination against PLWH. However, despite this huge push by numerous activist associations and organisations to eradicate HIV, the media impact of the initiative has been very limited and it is still largely unknown to the general population (Meanley et al. 2019). This situation is reflected in cinema, as very few contemporary films have included this message and there are very few HIV+ characters who talk about their undetectability in order to deconstruct the stigma associated with HIV. There is therefore a huge need to develop fiction narratives that offer readings of HIV in the new moral context of undetectability that could thus reinforce an educational strategy to reduce internalised and enacted stigma and lay to rest the cultural trauma of the epidemic.

As said, stigma has become a normal occurrence within the contemporary social scene. And as life expectancy gets larger, stigma in adult life is getting more important as a health issue to tackle. The media transformation and evolutions have brought about immense challenges leading to an adverse impact on the stigmatised victims. Some studies (e.g. Villanueva Baselga 2020) have shown that health issues have been strongly stereotyped, leading to negative perception and publicity among the affected groups. A major observation made in the impact of the media in stigmatizing different health conditions is the lack of standards for determining the controversies in the information posted on the media. The above challenges have led to the absence of oversight on the information posted by different groups Similarly, media education should be introduced to create awareness of the stigmatisations and the need to prevent them from occurring. Acknowledging that the cases of stigma are inevitable, however, the cultivation of useful and responsible practices may enable the users to affect positively the stigmatised victims sharing similar narratives (Winskell et al. 2015). The above analysis could prove that, indeed, fiction cinema is a structural source of stigma for adults in the current social setting. The impact of stigma on the victims makes them continuously suffer discrimination in the workplace, learning institutions, religious settings and political groups, among others. Elimination of such stereotypes could improve the efficiency of interactions in the public domain.

References

Alexander, J.C. (2004). Toward a theory of cultural trauma. In Alexander, J.C., Eyerman, R., Giesen, B., Smelser, N.J. & Sztompka, P. (eds), *Cultural Trauma and Collective Identity.* Berkeley and London: University of California Press.

Attinelo, P. (2013). Who dies? Transformations in Derek Jarman's last films. In Subero, G. (ed.), *HIV in World Cultures: Three Decades of Representations.* New York: Routledge.

Çakirlar, C. & Needham, G. (2019). The monogamous/promiscuous optics in contemporary gay film: Registering the amorous couple in *Weekend* (2011) and *Paris 05:59: Theo & Hugo* (2016). *New Review of Film and Television Studies*, 18(4), 402–430.

Dean, J.J. (2007). Gays and queers: From the centering to the decentering of homosexuality in American films. *Sexualities*, 10(3): 363–386.

Dyer, R. (2013). *The Matter of Images: Essays on Representations.* London: Routledge.

Eisinger, R.W., Dieffenbach, C.W., Fauci, A.S. HIV (2019). Viral load and transmissibility of HIV infection: Undetectable equals untransmittable. *JAMA*, 321(5), 451–452.

Evans-Lacko, S., Brohan, E., Mojtabai, R. & Thornicroft, G. (2012). Association between public views of mental illness and self-stigma among individuals with mental illness in 14 European countries. *Psychological Medicine*, 42, 1741–1752.

Farrell, K.P. (2006). HIV on TV: Conversations with young gay men. *Sexualities*, 9(2), 193–213.

Gailienė, D. (2019). When culture fails: coping with cultural trauma. *Journal of Analytical Psychology*, 64(4), 530–547.

Gao, X., Nau, D.P., Rosenbluth, A., Scott, V. & Woodward, C. (2010). The relationship of disease severity, health beliefs and medication adherence among HIV patients. *AIDS Care*, 12(4), 289–398.

Goffman, E. (1963). *Stigma: Notes on the Management of Spoiled Identity*. New York: Simon & Schuster.

Gough, B. (2006). Try to be healthy, but don't forgo your masculinity: Deconstructing men's health discourse in the media. *Social Science & Medicine*, 63(9), 2476–2488.

Hart, K.-P. (2013) *Queer Males in Contemporary Cinema: Becoming Visible*. Plymouth: Scarecrew Press.

Haslam, S.A., Jetten, J., Postmes, T. & Haslam, C. (2009). Social identity, health and wellbeing: An emerging agenda for applied psychology. *Applied Psychology: An International Review*, 58, 1–23.

Hatzenbuehler, M.L., Nolen-Hoeksema, S. & Dovidio, J. (2009). How does stigma 'get under the skin'? The mediating role of emotion regulation. *Psychological Science*, 20(10), 1282–1289.

Herrmann, L.K., Welter, E., Leverenz, J., Lerner, A.J., Udelson, N., Kanetsky, C. & Sajatovic, M. (2018). A systematic review of dementia-related stigma research: Can we move the stigma dial? *American Journal of Geriatric Psychiatry*, 26(3), 316–331.

Hudnall Stamm, B., Stamm, H., Hudnall, A. & Higson-Smith, C. (2004). Considering a theory of cultural trauma and loss. *Journal of Loss and Trauma*, 9(1), 89–111.

Kansteiner, W (2004). Genealogy of a category mistake: A critical intellectual history of the cultural trauma metaphor. *Rethinking History: The Journal of Theory and Practice*, 8(2), 193–221.

Kelly, M and Millward, L (2004). Identity and illness. In Kelleher, D. & Leavey, G. (eds), *Identity and Health*. London and New York: Routledge.

Kinsler, J.J., Wong, M.D., Sayles, J.N., Davis, C. & Cunningham, W.E. (2007). The effect of perceived stigma from a health care provider on access to care among a low-income HIV-positive population. *AIDS Patient Care and STDs*, 21(8), 584–592.

Lazarus, J.V. et al. (2016) Beyond viral suppression of HIV: The new quality of life frontier. *BMC Medicine*, 14(1), 1–5.

Lee, R.S., Kochman, A. & Sikkema, K.J. (2002). Internalized stigma among people living with HIV-AIDS. *AIDS Behaviour*, 6, 309–319.

Lekas, H.-M., Siegel, K. & Leider, J. (2011). Felt and enacted stigma among HIV/HCV-coinfected adults: The impact of stigma layering. *Qualitative Health Research*, 21(9), 1205–1219.

Levi, J., Raymond, A., Pozniak, A., Vernazza, P., Kohler, P. & Hill, A. (2016). Can the UNAIDS 90–90–90 target be achieved? A systematic analysis of national HIV treatment cascades. *BMJ Global Health*, 1(2). doi:10.1136/bmjgh-2015-000010

Lupton, D. & Tulloch, J. (1996). 'Bringing home the reality of it': Senior school students' responses to mass media portrayals of HIV/ AIDS. *Australian Journal of Communication*, 23(1), 31–45.

Major, B., Dovidio, J., Link, B. & Calabrese, S. (2018). Stigma and its implications for health: Introduction and overview. In Major, B., Dovidio, J. & Link, B. (eds), *The Oxford Handbook of Stigma, Discrimination, and Health*. New York: Oxford University Press.

Markovitz, J.C., Spielman, L.A., Scarvalone, P.A. & Perry, S.W. (2000). Psychotherapy adherence of therapists treating HIV-positive patients with depressive symptoms. *Journal of Psychotherapy Practice and Research*, 9(2): 75–80.

Martín Hernández, R. (2013). Within the limits of the body: Artistic images of HIV/AIDS in Spain and its relation with the cultural industry. In Subero, G. (ed.), *HIV in World Cultures: Three Decades of Representations*. New York: Routledge.

McCleerey, M. (2019). Bohemian normativity: *Bohemian Rhapsody* and the new heteronormal. *Film Criticism*, 43(3).

McGinty, E.E., Kennedy-Hendricks, A. & Barry, C.L. (2019). Stigma of addiction in the media. In Avery, Jonathan and Avery, Joseph (eds), *The Stigma of Addiction* (pp. 201–214). Cham: Springer.

Meanley, S., Connochie, D., Bonett, S., Flores, D.D. & Bauermeister, J.A. (2019). Awareness and perceived accuracy of Undetectable = Untransmittable: A cross-sectional analysis with implications for treatment as prevention among young men who have sex with men. *Sexually Transmitted Diseases*, 46(11), 733–736.

Nichols, B. (1991). *Representing Reality: Issues and Concepts in Documentary*. Bloomington, IN: Indiana University Press.

Patel, R.R., Curoe, K.A. & Chan, P.A. (2020). Undetectable equals Untransmittable: A game changer for HIV prevention. *Clinical Chemistry*, 66(3), 406–407.

Pocius J. (2016). Of bodies, borders, and barebacking: The geocorpographies of HIV. In Randell-Moon, H. & Tippet, R. (eds), *Security, Race, Biopower*. London: Palgrave Macmillan.

Provencher, D.M. (2008). Tracing sexual citizenship and queerness in *Drôle de Félix* (2000) and *Tarik el hob* (2001). *Contemporary French and Francophone Studies*, 12(1), 51–61.

Rendina, H.J. & Parsons, J.T. (2018). Factors associated with perceived accuracy of the Undetectable = Untransmittable slogan among men who have sex with men: Implications for messaging scale-up and implementation. *Journal of International AIDS Society*, 21(1), e25055.

Röhm, A., Hastall, M.R. & Ritterfeld, U. (2017). How movies shape students' attitudes toward individuals with schizophrenia: An exploration of the relationships between entertainment experience and stigmatization. *Issues in Mental Health Nursing*, 38(3), 193–201.

Shea, H., Mosley-Howard, G.S., Baldwin, D., Ironstrack, G., Rousmaniere, K. & Schroer, J.E. (2019). Cultural revitalization as a restorative process to combat racial and cultural trauma and promote living well. *Cultural Diversity and Ethnic Minority Psychology*, 25(4), 553–565.

Simbayi, L., Kalichman, S., Strebel, A., Cloete, A., Henda, N. & Mqeketo, A. (2010). Internalized stigma, discrimination, and depression among men and women living with HIV/AIDS in Cape Town, South Africa. *Social Science and Medicine*, 64(9), 1823–1831.

Szomptka, P. (2000). Cultural trauma: The other face of social change. *European Journal of Social Theory*, 3(4), 449–466.

Taggart, T., Grewe, M.E., Conserve, D.F., Gliwa, C. & Isler, M.R. (2015). Social media and HIV: A systematic review of uses of social media in HIV communication. *Journal of Medical Internet Research*, 17(11), e248.

Turan, B., Budhwani, T.B., Pariya, H., Fazeli, L., Browning, W.R., Raper, J.L., Mugavero, M.J. & Turan, J.M. (2017). How does stigma affect people living with HIV? The mediating roles of internalized and anticipated HIV stigma in the effects of perceived community stigma on health and psychosocial outcomes. *AIDS Behaviour*, 21, 283–291.

Villanueva Baselga, S. (2020). Interactive documentaries and health: Combating HIV-related stigma and cultural trauma. *Catalan Journal of Communication and Cultural Studies*, 12(2), 273–285.

Winskell, K., Holmes, K., Neri, E., Berkowitz, R., Mbakwem, B. & Obyerodhyambo, O. (2015). Making sense of HIV stigma: Representations in young Africans' HIV-related narratives. *Global Public Health*, 10(8), 917–929.

6

BUILD IT AND THEY WILL COME

Sex toys, heteronormativity and age

Paul G. Nixon and Anja Selmer

Introduction

This chapter explores the marketing of sex toys and relates this to broader sociocultural trends, as it aims to understand how sex toys are socially and culturally constructed and how they get embedded into peoples' sex lives.

The definition of sex toys is broadly accepted as relating to sexual enhancement products with the intent of improving sexual experiences (Rosenberger et al., 2012) The Oxford English Dictionary defines it as '[a]n object or device used for sexual stimulation or to enhance sexual pleasure' (OED, 2020). It is important to note that no object is precluded from being used as a sex toy irrespective of its original purpose and function. However, here we focus on artifices which are either exclusively or primarily designed for use in sexual interaction. In the digital age we have morphed some sex toys together with technology to create a new type of responsive sex toy that falls under the broad umbrella term of teledildonics.

The chapter examines how modernisation processes relating to sex toys were influenced by modifications in the cultural understanding of sexuality, and how sex toys and the marketing thereof have intensified and steered these transformations. Subsequently, it discusses the findings from a series of surveys and interviews carried out by the authors during differing research projects examining how sex toys are viewed by users and how their sentiments respond to and reflect changes in the marketing of sexual technologies.

Although the modernisation of sexuality has wrought a move from a male-dominated and heteronormative model of sexual experience, other parameters of sexual exclusion are reinforced by the increasingly segmented sex market and promises of embracing sexual and bodily diversity. As such, active sexuality as expressed through sex toy use remains the prerogative of those who legitimately qualify as 'sexual beings' on several parameters, most significantly age and disability.

The origins of sex toys

Sex toys have been around for up to 30,000 years. Sex toys have evolved from their primitive ancestors and transformed via developing technologies, materials and the cultural norms within which they were interpreted. Vibrators were depicted as a 19th-century cure for 'hysteria' by Maines (2001) although this interpretation has been rebutted by Lieberman & Schatzberg (2018). Devices were developed by numerous companies and their sexual potentialities were hinted at in advertising with vibrators being sold as medicinal devices in order not to offend prevailing morals (Lieberman, 2016), though many of these devices were adaptable for sexual purposes and most companies offered additional phallic-like attachments for sale (ibid.). Paradoxically, the vibrator, which is nowadays perceived as emblematic of female sexual liberation, was initially accepted as it ostensibly served to control women's sexuality thus maintaining a patriarchal gender hierarchy.

Maines (2001) argued that as vibrator usage became widespread in pornography they lost respectability. A further potential issue was that of perceived male inadequacy with the vibrator being more capable of delivering orgasm than the male, potentially destabilising traditional heterosexual norms. Post-World War Two, as technologies evolved, smaller, lighter and more powerful appliances were created. Society also changed, specifically women's rights and their changing role in the workplace led to economic independence for some, albeit with much inequity. The sexual revolution that followed, particularly influenced by developments in contraceptives, led to an upsurge in the recognition of sex as a key issue in equality politics, and enhanced the role of females as consumers and in terms of a recognition of their sexuality. Sex toys were recognised by sex positivists as tools of sexual discovery and manifested women's right to sexual expression and satisfaction.

Despite the seemingly positive connotations to sex toys, Dworkin (1981) saw them as contributing to the patriarchal domination of women grouping sex toys in with the sex industries, including pornography, and regarded them as replacing the cult of the penis. Moreover, it has been argued that sex toys symbolise the inherent violence against women present in those industries. Many feminists rejected sex toys as they 'represented the "technologization" of sex, the coming together of the natural and the mechanical' (Juffer, 1998, p. 29).

Sexual liberalisation

These cultural transformations were followed by changes which furthered the development of liberal attitudes towards sex. Associated changes such as the LGBTQ movements in the 1970s; the emergence of AIDS in the 1980s and open discussions about sexual health including condom marketing fostered the acceptability for other sexually related products to be advertised (Wilson & West, 1995); the emergence of online technologies created spaces for sexual debate, invigorated the sex toy market and facilitated the burgeoning pornography industry. Social media has now accentuated the personification of the self and created spaces such as

Tinder which facilitate sexual encounters in a way our recent ancestors would have considered unthinkable.

Cultural norms reflect more acceptance of the range of sexualities partially helped by the normalisation of sexual practices such as sex toy use (Television series such as 'Sex in the City' extolling the virtuosity of the Rabbit vibrator) and BDSM (books and films of *Fifty Shades of Grey*, which launched a range of themed sexual products) whereby 'sexual fantasy itself becomes commodified via the transition of fictional objects in the book into real commodities for sale' (Martin, 2013, p. 982). One can even find sex toys themed after rock bands, such as Motörhead, with a range of vibrators featuring logos and associated artwork, emphasising the crossover of cultures between sex and the mainstream and an increased societal acceptance of sex as no longer taboo.

Heteronormative sexualities: refashioning the 'charmed circle'

As the sexual industry has modernised, so it has seemingly embraced more progressive values. It is thus interesting to consider to what extent it has disrupted cultural attitudes pertaining to sexuality, and whether it remains influenced by traditional perceptions surrounding sexual behaviour. Conventionally, sexuality has been defined by heteronormativity, which is in abstract terms understood as 'the suite of cultural, legal, and institutional practices that maintain normative assumptions that there are two and only two genders, that gender reflects biological sex, and that only sexual attraction between these "opposite" genders is natural or acceptable' (Schilt & Westbrook, 2009, p. 441). Importantly, heteronormativity contributes to persistent inequalities, upholding heterosexuality as a distinct and privileged sexual identity (Mulholland, 2011, p. 123). Gayle Rubin's (1984) sex hierarchy diagrams are often used as a reference point by scholars theorising about heteronormativity in relation to sexual practices. Rubin organised sexual practices according to their hierarchical positions. As such they show 'how a relationship between acts and identities works to produce certain sexualities as good, normal and healthy, and others as bad, unhealthy and scary' (Mulholland, 2011, p. 121). Plain, marital and procreative intercourse is located neatly within the 'charmed circle' signifying 'permissible' sex, whereas alternate sexual behaviours are located in the 'outer limits' denoting impermissible sex. Rubin's 'outer limits' includes sexual behaviours such as pornography and sex with manufactured objects. Recent cultural changes have arguably disrupted Rubin's sex hierarchies, yet the new reality appears more complex and intricate. Mulholland has reworked Rubin's sex hierarchy circle to align this with contemporary sexual norms. In the revised version, manufactured objects such as sex toys are recognised as acceptable, along with 'stereotypical homosexuality' and mainstream porn. Despite the seeming liberalisation of sex, Mulholland argues that 'while many of the acts and expressions of heterosexual practice are changing shape, a heteronormative culture remains front and centre' (p. 119). That is to say, '"Good Sex" remains at its heart still attached to a normative heterosexual identity, [...] flirting with public displays of raunch and promiscuity as long as they are "respectable", and remaining true to highly codified and standardised gendered conventions' (p. 131).

Evidently, the idealisation of heterosexuality privileges both certain sexual acts and ways of constructing the self and of being. Heteronormativity has been studied extensively by scholars under a rubric which has become entitled 'doing gender'. Informed by Butler (1990), this body of literature sees gender as a performance, specifically an 'interactional process of crafting gender identities that are then presumed to reflect and naturally derive from biology' (Schilt & Westbrook, 2009, p. 442). According to Butler, 'doing gender' produces a gendered identity through repetition of 'specific bodily gestures, practices, declarations, actions and movements' (Lloyd, 2007, p. 48). As a construction of the self this process is independent of biology and sexual desire. Yet, people are socially judged on the extent to which their biological sex, gender and desire appear to align. In their study of pornification culture, Mulholland (2011) notes how certain female identities and non-normative bodies are absent from pornified displays. This includes women of larger-sized people, disabled women, cross-dressers and older people (p. 129). Correspondingly, only those who are young, white, heterosexual and conventionally attractive are accorded sexual subjecthood (ibid.). Although a wider variety of sexual acts are tolerated, heteronormativity is maintained through a 'coded imagery' limiting sexual subjects to those exhibiting a 'conventional gender aesthetic' (p. 127).

Intersectionality refers to the confounding of multiple oppressors, i.e. the 'multidimensionality of marginalized subjects lived experience' (Nash, 2008, p. 2). The concept highlights how institutions, most prominently those of race, gender, class and ableism, interconnect and conjointly condition individuals' social identity and location. Not only does heteronormativity figure as an institution that treats heterosexuality as the ideal (2011, p. 123), sexual subjecthood is also determined by other oppressive institutions (idem). Because the stylisation demanded by heteronormativity's coded imagery – which is predicated on a highly rigid gender dichotomy – is bound up with a range of factors beyond the performance of sexual acts, certain people are ultimately deprived of sexual subjecthood.

Furthermore, social groups may not have equal access to consume sexual technologies. Piha et al. (2018) discuss the taboo experienced by some consumers related to the acquisition of sex toys. For people living with disability or people of old age the taboo could feel intensified because of the stigma surrounding their sexuality, which might hinder them from acquiring sexual material – especially if they rely on the assistance of carers.

While the sex market has made strides to address more audiences, helped redefine feminine subjecthood and expanded the range of permissible sexual acts, heteronormativity may still loom large in the design, marketing and consumption of sex toys. This will be considered in the following sections.

Changing patterns of distribution and consumption

As sex toys have evolved, the method and physical location of their commodification have also developed. While sex shops are changing from 'shady back street to shiny high streets' (Comella, 2010, p. 296) and becoming more welcoming (Martin, 2013), sex toys are on open sale in major European chemist shops and other outlets. Crewe and Martin (2017) note the increasing normalisation of sexual consumption, particularly in major conurbations, attributing this partly to increased acceptability of women's sexuality. Though there is a strange sexism attached to the display and advertising of male sex toys, such as sex dolls, or those for use by the LGBT+ community. These products are not given the same shelf space or placed front of house and seem to be representing the less socially acceptable face of sex toys (Nixon, 2018), though as attitudes become more accepting, this is becoming less pronounced.

As women were targeted as sexual consumers (Attwood, 2005), a range of new female-owned and female-oriented sex outlets emerged that invoke feminist values. Their branding contrasts with conventional sex shops and the male-dominated sex market by bringing together design innovation, sexual health expertise (Bardzell & Bardzell, 2011), increased accessibility, greater visibility and aestheticisation of the toys and related marketing material (Attwood, 2005). Ann Summers, Coco de Mer and Sh! are reflective of this expansion of the sexual market, striving to incorporate the interests of previously sexually marginalised groups, particularly women. This expansion is reflected in the visuality and content of the outlets' marketing strategies and material that transmit ideas about sexual practices. The marketing of women's sex toys contains strong gendered scripts both in advertising and in media that address sex toy usage. For instance, vibrators are frequently depicted as a means to empower women sexually by helping them achieve orgasm, through which they may approximate stereotypical definitions of empowered femininity promoted by fashion-oriented outlets such as *Cosmopolitan* (Fahs & Swank, 2013, pp. 668–669). Attwood (2005) argues that women-oriented sex retailers draw on established discourses of fashion, consumerism, sexuality and bodily pleasure in their marketing strategies, whereby they indeed reference the contemporary ideal of femininity which privileges active selfhood, self-fashioning and sexual agency.

Transforming sex toy designs

Döring & Pöschl (2018) delineate between three main forms of sex toys. The first group encompasses toys which are broadly designed to stimulate erogenous zones, including vibrators, dildos and masturbatory sleeves. Second there is BDSM equipment such as spanking paddles, nipple clamps and restraints. Third there is the ancillary area of erotic lingerie, costumes and associated regalia.

The diversification of sex toys' designs is reflective of new gender understandings as companies attempt to become more responsive to the needs and demands of diverse genders and physiques, especially women. Sex toy designs, particularly of vibrating toys, have to some extent started to depend less upon graphic reproduction of life-like penis dimensions and contours negating male conceptions of size and power and move towards designs that are shaped to fit the contours of female bodies to satisfy their needs. Thus, the traditional focus on copying human forms so that a vibrator resembles a penis is being if not challenged then remodelled into more amorphous artistic representations that are not immediately phallic in their appearance (such as the 'Form 8' vibrator) to meet new and differing market segments. As female sexuality comes out into the open, toys that are focused on clitoral stimulation also emerge. Smith notes how sex toy developers sought to create a new range of toys that 'exploit qualities, new materials, technologies' (2007, p. 147) – for example, the male-oriented masturbatory sleeves such as 'Fleshlight'. Notably, many of the sex toys on sale, while often perceived as being predominantly for women, can be used by anyone regardless of gender. Additionally, there is a rise in the development of gender-neutral toys (Cookney, 2019) along with a range of toys that are more gender specific.

There is also a move towards high-tech sex toys. Through teledildonics, one can connect devices to each other so that remote touching can send sensations via the internet to a partner, creating a shared sexual experience freed from the limitations of distance. Recently, androids that can replicate human intercourse and other sexual acts have emerged, which posits a future of robotic-partnered sex. Their availability may address Wagner and Broll's (2014) findings, which indicated that respondents, in particular the male respondents, disliked many sex toys as they were seen as disembodied items that lacked a full body that they deemed necessary for pleasure.

Methodology

The chapter presents the findings from two separate research projects that were carried out by the authors to examine the ways in which sex toys are viewed by their users. The two projects were carried out independently of each other and used differing methodologies. The first research study took place during the winter of 2018/19 and nine people were consulted for in-depth interviews. Of the nine, four people gave permission for their data to be used in this work. All four were aged 40 and above and came from both Europe and the United States. The interviewees were or had been active consumers of sex toys as well as pornographic material for a longer period.

The second set of data is drawn from questionnaires and interviews of a group of students who took the module 'Sex, The Body and Cyborgs' at Masaryk University, Czech Republic in December 2019. Seventy-four students, all between the ages of 19 and 27, completed the course and were asked to take part in the survey; 36 (50.7%) did so. Twenty-four identified as female, nine as male and three did not wish to identify their gender. To anonymise responses, each student was allocated a random identifying number. With reference to the participants of both research projects, the names used are pseudonyms. The findings of the studies are presented and analysed below.

The integration of sex toys into sexual practice

The survey data relating to the students shows that 68.6% of students had used some form of sex toy. Reasons given for doing so were in order of the number of responses; solely for my own sexual relief; to help learn about my own body and its responses; to enhance my sexual enjoyment with a partner; to enhance my partner's sexual enjoyment; to help my partner learn about my own body and its responses. As additional responses the following comments were gleaned:

> my partner became porn addicted and my sexual libido has always been quite high and he didn't want to have sex with me, because he rather watched porn, so I got myself a sex toy so I would be able to fully please myself without my partner.
>
> *(Female, 22)*

> I can't have an orgasm otherwise.
>
> *(Female, 24)*

Our respondents had tried a variety of sex toys. The aspiration to use sex toys in the future was quite mixed, with a relatively high proportion seeming to rule out trying. The students who had not used sex toys explained that they had either not yet had the opportunity or found the costs prohibitive. One respondent found it unnatural, commenting:

> Even though sex toys might enhance the sex experience, I think I can very well get by with the use of my body and my partner's body and it's awesome and natural. Don't the sex toys mostly just substitute things we can actually do also with our body?
>
> *(Female, 20)*

Fan (2015) identified user segmentation within the sex toy market as somewhat immature, holding a promise of future opportunities for sex toy developers and marketeers. The students' responses indicate that there may indeed be latent demand that might be stimulated to purchase should, for example, price and availability alter. One said:

> Am looking to try them soon, I mean I'm 20 it's not like I got bored with sex just yet and I don't think it's happening soon, but I'm curious how they might improve my sex life so I will try.
>
> *(Male, 20)*

Diversifying the sex toy market

Traditionally, the consumption of sex toys and imagery was deemed a private and secretive affair. However, as contemporary society sees an expansion and increased visibility of the sex merchandise industry, the nature of the industry, retailing mechanisms and with that cultural connotations are also transforming. The already thriving mail order business, which removed some of the taboos around entering sex shops, has been bolstered by the advent of online shopping. (Daneback et al., 2011, Piha et al., 2018). This may also have increased sales of sex toys. One of the male respondents to the student survey said that he had ordered his silicon female torso masturbatory aid online as he wished to be discreet. Other interviewees echoed this need for discretion and the lack of embarrassment from purchasing the item in a traditional shop. Though this may be changing as, reflecting the changes in wider society with the increasing acceptance of non-traditional lifestyles and sexual expressions, sex shops and online retailers attempt to create more inclusive spaces that appeal to a more diverse, sexually fluid and increasingly experimental customer base.

According to Attwood (2005), the traditional sex industry was developed with regard to stereotypical male sexuality, and was perceived as dark and exploitative and therefore demanded regulation. Coulmont and Hubbard (2010) argue that governmental attempts at restricting access to pornographised products in Britain and France influenced the 'design, management and marketing' of sex toys. Restrictive legislation, including expensive licensing fees and regulations imposed on the store layout, resulted in sex shops that were reproduced as male preserves, repelling female consumers due to the lurid appearance and peripheral locations.

The narrative of 'Sandra', an interviewee from the first study, corroborates with Smith's description of traditional sex shops as 'oases of ugliness' (2007, p. 169). During Sandra's first experience shopping for sex toys in Paris over two decades ago, she recounts inappropriate approaches and receiving intense stares by the male clientele and neighbourhood residents. Being of Asian origin, her appearance had also inspired sexually fetishising remarks:

> The sex shops were creepy. I was in Paris at the time, and you go to these sex shops around Pigalle or something you see these creepy dudes looking around, giving you funny looks and then I had the comfort of giving you funny looks as well, cause there's this young, single woman. ... That was where I got uncomfortable, sometimes. You know because […] some guys come up and go like 'oh I love Asians' or like 'Asians are hot'. I mean it's 'yuck!' you know (chuckles). So I didn't like that part of acquiring it, but nicer sex shops were usually the ones where women were selling the items because it didn't feel so creepy.

Sandra's experience suggests that traditional sex shops were defined by place and space as much as their merchandise. Due to their marginalised status, these shops were pushed to the periphery of cities and into designated neighbourhoods. Their position, literally at the margins of society, rendered them hostile environments to women and possibly also to people of alternative sexualities. Paradoxically, this restrictive legislation was later the main reason for the rise of the generation of upscale, highly visible and accessible sex shops in the gentrified areas of London and across France. Largely women-focused, they managed to avoid impeding legislation by branding themselves in opposition to the traditional sex shops. Thus, the 'oases of ugliness' (Smith, 2007) were complemented by 'female friendly' and 'couple friendly' outlets (Coulmont & Hubbard, 2010). Although the female-headed and feminist-oriented sex shops constitute an important addition to the contemporary sex industry, they retain a tenuous position by reinforcing somewhat narrow conceptions about gender and sexuality.

New feminine sexualities and the upscaling of sex toy consumption

Through their marketing, these novel sex outlets steer cultural attitudes regarding sexuality. Attwood (2005) demonstrates how sex retailing and the meanings attached to sexual products are structured by relations of class and gender. 'New' female sexualities intermingle with consumerism (Fahs & Swank, 2013, p. 671) and class relations whereby the 'sexually liberated female consumer imagined and addressed by much of contemporary media culture' (Attwood, 2006, p. 85) is often white and middle class, as epitomised by the television show *Sex and the City* (Mulholland, 2011, p. 130). Smith demonstrates how class hierarchies are invoked and reproduced in relation to the rise of designer sex shops, which present a 'poshing up' of sex where design and innovativeness matter more than functionality and cost. In this context a 'sexual elite' emerges, distinguishable by the fashionableness, independence, intellect and ethics of the boutique's proprietors, who foreground the luxury and designer dimensions rather than their sexual nature when describing their brand. Sex toy consumption is considered 'a feminine thing to do; stylish, sophisticated and adventurous' (Smith, 2007, p. 177). They note how consumers who are willing and able to pay the higher costs associated with the products show a commitment to sex and self-exploration. Notably, by positioning themselves as luxury companies, the designer sex brands catering to this modern feminine sexuality discredit cheaper, yet possibly more accessible, sex merchandise, including that sold by mainstream female-centred outlets.

The ability to purchase sex toys is already a luxury. For moderate to highly active sex toy users this can result in high expenditures. Thus, the creation of an upscale market intensifies an already existing class divide. Sandra's perception of the female-catered sex boutiques confirms their ambiguous nature; while the boutiques give female clients a better experience, their merchandise is 'five times as expensive'. Ultimately these alternatives are rendered as inaccessible to people with lower incomes. The upscaling of sex toys is not exclusive to female-dominated shops. For instance, the *Fifty Shades of Grey* phenomenon spurred BDSM equipment designed with references to the trilogy with significantly higher prices as a premium is placed on the branding (Martin, 2013).

Towards embracing sexual and bodily diversity?

Within feminist analyses the sex industry is evaluated based on its outcomes, especially with regard to implications for patriarchy/heteronormativity (Smith, 2007). In their study of sexual spaces in Soho, London, Sanders-McDonagh and Peyrefitte (2018) argue that the rise of sex businesses in the neighbourhood presents a spatial queering where 'sexual fluidity is part of the urban fabric' and 'a wide range of sexual citizens (including women, LGBTQ and the kink community) can access sex shops without being threatened with the restrictive norms that govern 'appropriate' patterns of sexual practices' (Sanders-McDonagh & Peyrefitte, 2018, p. 364). An article by 'Kinkly' draws a parallel between female-fronted and inclusivity: 'more women are stepping up to bring the female perspective to the helm of new sex-toy companies [...] and finding new ways to make sure everyone has a good time' (Dancyger, 2017). Most stores listed in the article possess a dual role as both distributors of sex toys and educators, legitimising the sales of sexual products by drawing on discourses of empowerment, attempting to convince the audience that they facilitate sexually healthy behaviour and self-discovery. What has replaced porn stars promoting traditional merchandise are curated drawings of non-gendered couples, people of colour, natural and tattooed bodies, non-heterosexual intimate scenes, all aesthetically put together. The changing sex toy industry is slowly transforming the way consumers think about sex toys and sexual practices. However, while representing a step away from a narrow, patriarchal-inspired view on sexuality, as noted, this expanding market does not necessarily entail uniform commitment to diversity and inclusivity.

On the face of it, these companies represent progressive values; yet their acceptability can render people blind to more subtle forms of heteronormative ideology as expressed in beauty norms. Arguably, heteronormativity is also predicated on a form of aestheticisation of gender relations that inspire beauty ideals. Beauty ideals are still largely informed by the sex dichotomy and heterosexuality that create unique expectations for men and women. This is perhaps most evident in relation to physique; while men are rewarded for building muscular bodies that signify masculinity, conflating strength with authority and power (Drummond, 2011), the ideal female body is in contrast slender but not profoundly muscular (Markula, 1995). Adherence to beauty standards – voluntary or not – can be seen as expressing compliance with gender norms and thus with heterosexuality, by which the individual is interpreted as 'acceptable' and may gain social recognition (Anderson, Grunert, Katz, & Lovascio, 2010).

While there has been a push in recent years towards more inclusive beauty standards, there remain conflicting versions of interest in porn stars and the need for an expanded understanding of what is beautiful. As a teenager, 'Felix', who is in his early forties, used to gather pornographic material including sex shop catalogues. He explains: 'I enjoyed [...] that I could see photos of naked men. I didn't even care about seeing them in the act of sex, I just wanted to see good-looking men nude.' Even though he clearly expresses discomfort with his own body, as it deviates from standards of male beauty, he still appreciates male beauty ideals and presents precise criteria when asked to detail his aesthetic preferences:

> Caucasian, 5'8"–6'1", under 200 lbs, dark hair, dark eyes, dark complexion. Non-receding, no thin hair. Symmetrical face, well groomed. A nice set angular jaw line on an inverted pyramid-shaped face. No facial hair. Good teeth. Only a moderate Adam's apple.

In contrast to this rationale, Sandra spurns sex toys designed to resemble human features, such as realistically phallic dildos and plastic dolls, referring to the intensification of bodily insecurities:

> some of the artificial looking ones, things like clamps [...]. I think they're really meant more to enhance the experience that people are having either alone or with someone else, but I think that supposedly realistic looking ones, like either penises or flashlights, for example, or sex dolls, they're all copies of what [...] media tells us is attractive. Or media tells us is a perfect body, [...] in that sense I'm not a fan of them.

Her narrative is supported by 58-year-old 'Martin', who appreciates the appearance of 'everyday people' rather than the kind of male beauty idealised by media, commenting: 'I feel that this perception of male beauty is actually damaging to the esteem of many men, especially teen boys, [...] so I don't relate well to it.' However, in spite of the critical attitude towards homogenous beauty standards, Martin had still worked through personal body image issues and expresses continued dissatisfaction with his body.

Notwithstanding, users' preference for the representation of 'average' bodies in sexual imagery and sex toys can also spring from a basic desire to enhance sexual experience, without being underpinned by a conscious relationship to the conundrum of beauty ideals. Herbenick et al. (2015) note that many sex toy users seem to prefer toys that are average in their dimensions, in contrast to the desire in pornography for larger penis size to be the norm.

We have seen that people position themselves differently in relation to conventional beauty standards, and some sex toy companies do embrace more inclusive forms of beauty and aesthetic appeal. Yet these are equally prone to ageism and ableism, two particular forms of discrimination that pervade Western (sexual) culture, which most current sex toy advertising seems to reproduce. People of mature or old age are largely absent from visual material, and instead young people in their teens and early adulthood populate marketing imagery. It can be derived from this that youthfulness functions as a signifier of sexuality that is largely interpreted as the prerogative of the young. This is at odds with our survey results, noted above, which showed that younger people viewed toys as something to experiment with in later life.

Furthermore, the sexuality of people living with impairments is similarly neglected, with hardly any displays of disabilities or signifiers thereof and no substantial offer of products that cater to this group, reflecting how people with disabilities are often denied sexual subjecthood. While there is a limited offer of sex toys that cater to people living with disabilities, people with visible illness or impairment remain excluded from sexually explicit imagery used in marketing and sales strategies. Although female-headed and feminist-oriented sex outlets incorporate values of inclusivity and diversity, there is a tendency to neglect the sexuality of people with impairments, consequently they perpetuate the conflation of sexuality with conventional parameters of attractiveness.

Conclusion

This chapter reviewed the development of sex toys and traced concurrent changes in cultural understandings pertaining to gender and sexuality. It then discussed results from two separate studies that collected qualitative and quantitative data on people's experiences with, and perceptions of, sex toys. The limitations of the small-scale nature of our research means that further, larger-scale research is needed to produce more representative findings. We acknowledge that we have simply given a snapshot of views from two differing age groups. Given the limited resources available for this research, we have been unable to address other aspects of intersectionality such as race.

It is argued that although the modernisation of sexuality has wrought a necessary move from a male-dominated and heteronormative model of sexual experience, other parameters of sexual exclusion are reinforced by the increasingly segmented sex market and a failure to embrace sexual and bodily diversity. As such, active sexuality as expressed through sex toy use is often only viewed as the prerogative of those who are seen to qualify as 'sexual beings', excluding those who are judged not to qualify in several parameters, most significantly age and disability. As much as the retailing strategies and marketing techniques of new sex companies represent a step in the right direction, the changes which they spearhead are not uniformly progressive as they remain influenced by established social conventions constructed around heteronormative and sexually repressive ideologies which influence the categorisation of people and their ability to engage in sexual activities of their choice.

References

Anderson, T.L., Grunert, C., Katz, A. & Lovascio, S. (2010). Aesthetic capital: A research review on beauty perks and penalties. *Sociology Compass*, 4(8), 564–575.

Attwood, F. (2005). Fashion & passion: Marketing sex to women. *Sexualities*, 8(4), 392–406.

Attwood, F. (2006). Sexed up: Theorizing the sexualization of culture. *Sexualities*, 9, 77–94.

Bardzell, J. & Bardzell, S. (2011). 'Pleasure is your birthright': Digitally enabled designer sex toys as a case of third-wave HCI. Proceedings of the SIGCHI Conference on Human Factors in Computing Systems, Vancouver. DOI: doi:10.1145/1978942.1978979

Butler, J. (1990). *Gender Trouble: Feminism and the Subversion of Identity*. New York: Routledge.

Carpenter, V., Homewood, S., Overgaard, M. & Wuschitz, S. (2018). From sex toys to pleasure objects. Proceedings of EVA Copenhagen 2018, 15–17 May, Politics of the Machines – Art and After. doi:10.14236/ewic/EVAC18.45

Comella L. (2010). Remaking the sex industry: The adult expo as a microcosm. In R. Weitzer (ed.), Sex For Sale: Prostitution, Pornography and the Sex Industry. New York: Routledge, pp. 285–306.

Cookney R. (2019). "In the growing sex toy market, gender-neutral toys are finding a place on the shelf". Forbes, 27 August. Online at www.forbes.com/sites/frankicookney/2019/08/27/gender-neutral-toys-in-the-growing-sex-toy-market/#49e36c4e226f.

Coulmont, B. & Hubbard, P. (2010). Consuming sex: Socio-legal shifts in the space and place of sex shops. Journal of Law and Society, 37(1), 189–209.

Crewe, L. & Martin, A. (2017). Sex and the city: Branding, gender and the commodification of sex consumption in contemporary retailing. Urban Studies, 54(3), 582–599.

Daneback, K., Mansson, S.A. & Ross, M.W. (2011). Online sex shops: Purchasing sexual merchandise on the internet. International Journal of Sexual Health, 23(2), 102–110.

Dancyger, L. (2017). These 5 female-fronted sex toy companies are shaking things up. Kinkly, 7 September. Online at www.kinkly.com/these-5-female-fronted-sex-toy-companies-are-shaking-things-up/2/14972.

Döring, N. & Poeschl, S. (2019). Experiences with diverse sex toys among German heterosexual adults: Findings from a national online survey. Journal of Sex Research, 57(7), 1–13.

Döring, N. & Pöschl, S. (2018). Sex toys, sex dolls, sex robots: Our under-researched bedfellows. Sexologies, 27(3), e51-e55.

Drummond, M. (2011). Reflections on the archetypal male heterosexual body. Austrialian Feminist Studies, 26(67), 103–117.

Dworkin, A. (1981). Pornography: Men Possessing women. London: The Women's Press.

Dworkin A. & MacKinnon C.A. (1988). Pornography and civil rights: A new day for women's equality. Online at www.nostatusquo.com/ACLU/dworkin/other/ordinance/newday/TOC.htm.

Fahs, B. & Swank, E. (2013). Adventures with the 'Plastic Man': Sex toys, compulsory heterosexuality, and the politics of women's sexual pleasure. Sexuality & Culture, 17(4), 666–685.

Fan, L. (2015). International segmentation of the sex toy market. International Journal of Arts and Commerce, 4(5), 30–39.

Heljakka, K. (2016). Fifty shades of toys: Notions of play and things for play in the Fifty Shades of Grey canon, Intensities: The Journal of Cult Media, 8, 59–73.

Herbenick, D., Reece, M., Schick, V., Jozkowski, K.N., Middelstadt, S., Sanders, S., Dodge, B., Ghassemi, A. & Fortenberry, D.J. (2011). Beliefs about women's vibrator use: Results from a nationally representative probability survey in the United States. Journal of Sex & Marital Therapy, 37(5), 329–345.

Herbenick, D., Barnhart, K.J., Beavers, K. & Benge, S. (2015). Vibrators and other sex toys are commonly recommended to patients, but does size matter? Dimensions of commonly sold products. Journal of Sexual Medicine, 12(3), 641–645.

Jannini, E.A., Limoncin, E., Ciocca, G., Buehler, S. & Krychman, M. (2012). Ethical aspects of sexual medicine. Internet, vibrators, and other sex aids: Toys or therapeutic instruments? Journal of Sexual Medicine, 9(12), 2994–3001.

Juffer, J. (1998). At Home with Pornography: Women, Sex, and Everyday Life. New York: New York University Press.

Lieberman, H. (2016). Selling sex toys: Marketing and the meaning of vibrators in early twentieth-century America. Enterprise & Society, 17(2), 393–433.

Lieberman, H. (2017). Buzz: The Stimulating History of the Sex Toy. New York: Pegasus Books.

Lieberman, H. & Schatzberg, E. (2018). A failure of academic quality control: The technology of orgasm. *Journal of Positive Sexuality*, 4(2), 24–47.

Lloyd, M. (2007). *Judith Butler: From Norms to Politics*. Cambridge: Policy Press.

Maines, R.P. (2001). *The Technology of Orgasm: 'Hysteria,' the Vibrator, and Women's Sexual Satisfaction*. Baltimore, MD: Johns Hopkins University Press.

Markula, P. (1995). Firm but shapely, fit but sexy, strong but thin: The postmodern aerobicizing female bodies. *Sociology of Sport Journal*, 12(4), 424–453.

McCaughey, M. & French, C. (2001). Women's sex toy parties: Technology, orgasm and commodification. *Sexuality and Culture: An Interdisciplinary Quarterly*, 5(3), 77–96.

Martin, A. (2013). Fifty shades of sex shop: Sexual fantasy for sale. *Sexualities*, 16(8), 980–984.

Mulholland, M. (2011). When porno meets hetero: Sexpo, heteronormativity and the pornification of the mainstream. *Australian Feminist Studies*, 26(67), 119–135.

Nash, J.C. (2008). Re-thinking Intersectionality. *Feminist Review*, 89(1), 1–15.

Nixon, P.G. (2018) Hell Yes!!!!!: Playing away, teledildonics and the future of sex. In P.G. Nixon & I.K Düsterhoft (eds), *Sex in the Digital Age*. London: Routledge.

Oxford English Dictionary (OED) (2020) 'Sex toy'. Online at www.oxforddictionaries.com/definition/english/sex%20toy.

Piha, S., Hurmerinta, L., Sandberg, B. & Järvinen, E. (2018). From filthy to healthy and beyond: Finding the boundaries of taboo destruction in sex toy buying. *Journal of Marketing Management*, 34(13–14), 1078–1104.

Rosenberger, J.G., Schick, V., Herbenick, D., Novak, D.S. & Reece, M. (2012). Sex toy use by gay and bisexual men in the United States. Archives of sexual behavior, 41(2), 449–458.

Rubin, G. (1984). Thinking sex: Notes for a radical theory of the politics of sexuality. In C. Vance (ed.), *Pleasure and Danger: Exploring Female Sexuality* (pp.143–179). Boston: Routledge & Kegan Paul.

Sanders-McDonagh, E. & Peyrefitte, M. (2018). Immoral geographies and Soho's sex shops: Exploring spaces of sexual diversity in London. *Journal of Feminist Geography*, 25(3), 351–367.

Seale, A. (2013). Diverting dildos: A Toronto co-op has started Canada's first sex toy recycling program. *Alternatives Journal*, 39(5), 40–42.

Schilt, K. & Westbrook, L. (2009). Doing gender, doing heteronormativity: 'Gender normals,' transgender people, and the social maintenance of heterosexuality. *Gender & Society*, 23(4), pp. 440–464.

Smith, C. (2007). Designed for pleasure: Style, indulgence and accessorized sex. *European Journal of Cultural Studies*, 10(2), 167–184.

Wagner, M. & Broll, W. (2014) I wish you were here – not! The future of spatially separated sexual intercourse. Online at http://doc.gold.ac.uk/aisb50/AISB50-S16/AISB50-S16-Wagner-paper.pdf .

Weitzer, Ronald (ed.) *Sex for Sale: Prostitution, Pornography, and the Sex Industry*, 2nd edn. New York: Routledge.

Wilson, A. & West, C. (1995) Commentary. Permissive marketing: The effects of the AIDS crisis on marketing practices and messages. *Journal of Product & Brand Management*, 4(5), 34–48.

7

FUELLING HATE

Hate speech towards women in online news websites in Albania

Emiljano Kaziaj

Introduction

Hate speech is a relatively new term in international legislation. Explicitly, it is only mentioned in a few cases. One of these is the Recommendation (97) 20, of the Committee of Ministers to the member states of Council of Europe, adopted on 30 October 1997. In this document hate speech is defined as:

> covering all forms of expression which spread, incite, promote or justify racial hatred, xenophobia, anti-Semitism or other forms of hatred based on intolerance, including: intolerance expressed by aggressive nationalism and ethnocentrism, discrimination and hostility against minorities, migrants and people of immigrant origin.

Hate speech, as defined here, mostly refers to issues of race and ethnicity. This is also true for other legal instruments such as the International Covenant on Civil and Political Rights (ICCPR), which is seen by many as the most important and comprehensive document when addressing hate speech (Gagliardone et al. 2015) due to article 19's focus on freedom of speech. This article states that

> Everyone shall have the right to freedom of expression; this right shall include freedom to seek, receive and impart information and ideas of all kinds, regardless of frontiers, either orally, in writing or in print, in the form of art, or through any other media of his choice.

In article 20/2 of the same document it is stated that 'Any advocacy of national, racial or religious hatred that constitutes incitement to discrimination, hostility or violence shall be prohibited by law.'

Additionally, when considering online media, the Council of Europe's (CoE) General Policy Recommendation on Combating the Dissemination of Racist, Xenophobic and Anti-Semitic Material via the Internet, issued in 2000, does not target hate speech specifically. Only race, nationality and religion are identified as subjects in both these important documents. Other social categories are not directly covered and protected from hate speech, as should be the case. One of these categories is women (see Bartow, 2009). Even international mechanisms that have a special focus on women's rights – such as the Convention on the Elimination of All Forms of Discrimination against Women (CEDAW) – make no explicit mention of hate speech, even though, as Gagliardone et al. (2015) point out, 'hate speech continues largely to be used in everyday discourse as a generic term ... .' (p. 7).

Several research projects on women and media have called for a greater consideration of sexist language in media and the need to categorise it as hate speech (see Simona et al. 2019, Bartow 2009, Lillian 2007). This is of immense importance for Albania; a country where violence against women is a pervasive phenomenon, as stated in a recent national survey (Haarr 2019). Additionally – as this book chapter reveals – hate speech against women in Albanian online media might be playing an important role in further reinforcing vulnerabilities of women.

Research on hate speech

It being a relatively new term, studies focusing on hate speech have come to the fore in media studies only in the last two decades. Researchers first focused on similar phenomena, such as racist speech or dangerous speech in the media. Matsuda (1989) drafted some criteria in an attempt to address the objections of critics under the First Amendment by focusing on how racist speech can be actionable. Moran (1994) also elaborated a definition of hate speech, building on Matsuda's work and looking to both public debates on hate speech and regulation (see Sellars 2016). Her definition of hate speech is presented as 'speech that is intended to promote hatred against traditionally disadvantaged groups'.

Only a limited number of studies have attempted to unveil the rationales of people who engage in inciting hatred online. A study carried out by Erjavec and Kovačič (2012) analysed hateful messages in the comments' section of several Slovenian news websites. Likewise, studies on internet trolling (Buckels et al. 2014, Shin 2008) have offered insights on how opportunities provided by online media are abused by people, or even institutions, to spread propaganda and misinformation.

Few studies on hate speech and online media have focused exclusively on women. Lillian (2007), in her article on sexist discourse, states that 'amid all the published works on hate speech, the question of sexist discourse as hate speech is rarely even addressed' (p. 719). More recently, Pinto and Singh (2019) focus on Twitter and provide an approach on how to identify misogynistic and sexist language, which they classify as hate speech.

As this brief literature review shows, research that focuses on hate speech and online news websites is scarce. The reason might be that it is not easy for researchers to operationalise such indicators into workable definitions for monitoring media and identifying hate speech language.

Benesch (2013) explored a definition for hate speech, in the process coining the term 'dangerous speech'. She elaborated on five variables in her attempt to provide concrete indicators for identifying hate (or 'dangerous') speech. The variables ask whether there is: (1) a 'powerful speaker with a high degree of influence'; (2) a receptive audience with 'grievances and fear that the speaker can cultivate'; (3) a speech act 'that is clearly understood as a call to violence'; (4) a social or historical context that is 'propitious for violence, for any of a variety of reasons'; and (5) an 'influential means of dissemination'.

Benesch's elaboration on hate speech is very important for researchers studying media in general and online media in particular as it emphasises several important elements in media content, including the speaker, the speech, the audience and the medium of dissemination. By identifying all these elements and focusing on them separately, it becomes easier to analyse content in both qualitative and quantitative terms. Furthermore, as online media is indeed becoming an influential medium, especially in countries with a high internet penetration, such criteria are very useful for online media researchers.

Internet actors and online platforms, meanwhile, have also tried to draft self-regulation guidelines, as a way to respond to criticism from institutions or their audiences. Usually these guidelines are included in their Terms of Service sections. Facebook, for example, dedicates a section to 'Combat harmful conduct and protect and support our community', in which they state[1]:

> We employ dedicated teams around the world and develop advanced technical systems to detect misuse of our Products, harmful conduct towards others, and situations where we may be able to help support or protect our community. If we learn of content or conduct like this, we will take appropriate action – for example, offering help, removing content, removing or restricting access to certain features, disabling an account, or contacting law enforcement.

Online news websites have followed this approach and drafted their own guidelines to content. The extent to which such codes are respected opens a new debate that is beyond the focus of this chapter.

In spite of such phenomena, the goal of this chapter is a twofold. On the one hand it identifies discursive constructions of hate speech related to women that are mostly reiterated in media. On the other hand it provides insights into the role that journalistic choices play in reinforcing such occurrences. By using a combination of qualitative and quantitative analysis, this chapter aims to present a comprehensive inquiry on the role of online news websites in inciting hate speech content targeting women in Albania. Furthermore, as hate speech is reported to be a controversial issue undermining freedom of speech, the chapter aspires to contribute to current and ongoing debates – in Albania and abroad – on online media regulation.

The state of online media in Albania

According to the Postal and Electronic Communications Authority in Albania (AKEP), in 2017 there were around 2.16 million subscribers with access to broadband internet. As reported by the 2011 census, Albania's population was 2.8 million, with 722,262 households.[2] Such high rates of internet access in a small country has fuelled the creation of hundreds of online news websites. According to a report by Media Ownership Monitor for Albania,[3] there are more than 650 online news websites in this country. Only 62 of these media outlets – less than 10% – are led by journalists, which raises questions regarding the quality of content served by these outlets. This high number of media presence online can be a dangerous tool for reiteration of hate speech language, taking into consideration that Albania – and most other countries for that matter – lacks the legislative mechanism for monitoring media content in this regard.

Hate speech, as an explicit term, is not yet part of Albanian legislation. Discrimination, on the other hand, is subject to Law Nr. 10 221 On Protection from Discrimination, adopted in 2010. In this law, the definition on discrimination is as follows:

> 'Discrimination' is every distinction, exclusion, limitation or preference because of any cause mentioned in article 1 of this law [i.e. *gender*, race, colour, ethnicity, language, *gender identity, sexual orientation*, political, religious or phi-losophical beliefs, economic...] that has as a purpose or consequence the hin-dering or making impossible the exercise, in the same manner as with others, of the fundamental rights and freedoms recognized by the Constitution of the Republic of Albania [...].

Additionally, Article 265 of the Criminal Code states:

> Inciting hate or disputes on the grounds of race, ethnicity, religion or sexual orientation, as well as the intentional preparation, dissemination or preserva-tion for purposes of distributing writings with such content, by any means or forms, shall be punishable with two to ten years of imprisonment.

The phrase 'writings with such content, by any means or forms' can be considered inclusive to online media as well, but so far there have been no public cases of use of these articles against the media (Londo 2014).

The most relevant legislation piece to be mentioned here, as it addresses issues of women's discrimination in media, is the Law on Gender Equality in Albania,[4] which was adopted in 2008. Article 26, in this law, refers to gender equality in media:

> Media supports the process of awareness raising on issues regarding gender equality through: a) non-discriminatory reporting on basis of gender b) the use

of neutral terms and language when addressing gender issues c) avoiding gender stereotypes throughout their operations.

2. Broadcasting, publishing and dissemination of materials that include or imply denigrating content, offensive language or limited views on gender basis, are prohibited.[5]

It is not specified either in this law or in any other normative disposition regarding this law what is meant by media and if it is inclusive of online media. Nevertheless, article 26/2 is of immense importance as it addresses hate speech towards women in the media. As most online media content is plagiarised from mainstream media, usually television – as reported in Media Ownership Monitor for Albania (2019), the article in a way addresses this content as well.

As noted in past reports in Albanian media (see Londo 2014, Dizdari, 2013), there is no specific body that deals with hate speech in the media. Furthermore, Londo (2014), in her report provides a description of several cases that were dealt with by the Commissioner for Protection from Discrimination – which is the primary institution entitled to implement and monitor the implementation of the Law on Protection from Discrimination that was mentioned at the beginning of this section. None of these cases is related to women's rights or issues of gender discrimination (see pp. 25–26).

Furthermore, research on hate speech against women in the media in Albania has focused exclusively on audiovisual media[6] – which are subject to law – and has ignored online media. On the other hand, given the prominence that online media has received in Albania in the last years and ongoing debates regarding its regulation, focusing on this medium and shedding light on journalistic practices that fuel hate speech against women could be the best evidence from which to draft effective measures for addressing the issue.

Methodology

The most difficult task when conducting media monitoring on hate speech is the identification of hate speech language. The problem of a single agreed definition and lack of its operationalisation in media research become hindering factors to media monitoring process. Nonetheless, researchers have already approached the issue by considering a list of agreed criteria to be considered when categorising language as hate speech. Several of these criteria were mentioned in the first section of this book chapter ('Research on hate speech'). The same approach was adopted for this research project, to identify hate speech in online media in Albania.

Following Mihajllova et al. (2013) and Ethical Journalism Networks (EJN) instructions on hate speech identification,[7] we compiled a scoring system that comprised the following elements:

1. Targeting of a group, or individual as a member of a group, with a past history of vulnerability
2. Status of speaker

3. Content in the message that expresses hatred
4. The speech causes a harm
5. The speech incites harmful actions
6. The speech is public

The combination of tools and instructions from several resources allows for a wider range of issues to be covered and a better operationalisation of the indicators for online media monitoring. One can argue that such elements – especially points three, four and five – can always be interpreted subjectively. Still, as Bartow (2009, p. 115) states, 'there is no feasible way to measure the quantity of the harassment that women receive online, but the quality, so often rooted in gender-specific opprobrium, is easy to observe'.

Therefore, this project combined qualitative and quantitative techniques for data analysis from media monitoring. Four online news websites were monitored during 1 October–15 December 2018. Media outlets – Panorama.com.al, Balkanweb.com, Lapsi.al and Shqiptarja.com – were selected based on their popularity in Albania[8] and their status. Two of these online media outlets, Panorama and Shqiptarja.com, are also published in print and are part of bigger media conglomerations which include at least one television channel and one radio channel. Balkanweb is only published online but is also part of a bigger media conglomeration. Lapsi.al is a new online medium, created on the initiative of two senior journalists who are also very vocal as analysts on several Albanian political talk shows.

Monitoring format was tailor-designed for this study by taking into consideration several similar studies on monitoring hate speech in the region and beyond (Londo 2014, Mihajllova et al. 2013) and previous studies on media monitoring conducted in Albania (Kaziaj 2016). The goal of this study was to identify hate speech occurrences in Albanian online media by focusing on: forms through which hate speech is articulated; targeted groups; characteristics of hate speech language in media; characteristics of subjects/groups that are a victim for hate speech, and audience reactions in online media in articles that contain hate speech language.

Based on this goal and hate speech's particular characteristics – as targeting a distinctive feature of a group (Mihajllova et al. 2013) – a special focus was put in articles related to any of these groups: women; children; Roma community; Egyptian community; LGBTI community; ethnic minorities; migrants; religious communities; people with disabilities.

The next section builds on an analysis of different facets of hate speech online, and it highlights strategies that online media (i.e. staff employed in these outlets) use to fuel and promote hate speech as a way of directing readers' attention to such news items and have them click them. This element has skipped the attention of researchers so far, but it is of immense investigative importance because journalists' choice of words and titles or their decisions regarding the ways they name subjects in their articles (Richardson 2007) and construct headlines can play a significant role in fuelling hate speech in online media. Several case studies are identified and explored further, using qualitative analysis techniques such as discourse analysis (van

Dijk 2008). Krippendorf's (2004) content analysis framework served as a basis for data administration and analysis. SPSS was used as a way to analyse quantitative data and draw patterns on characteristics of such news items. Additionally, SPSS was very useful for comparative research on approaches that different online media take when it comes to hate speech content, mostly related to user-generated content.

As Gagliardone et al. (2015) underline, it is necessary to not treat the online space as a separate social space, taking into consideration the complexities that the internet has brought to both forms of expression and their regulation. Furthermore, forasmuch as the Albanian context is considered, online content is usually plagiarised from traditional media content, mostly television, as part of general media conglomeration. Therefore, insights provided here could be transposed to wider media content in Albania.

Findings

As shown in Figure 7.1,[9] three categories[10] have the biggest share of news items that contain hate speech/ discriminatory language: Art, Media & Culture – 28.8%; Politics/Governance/Laws – 24.1%; and Crime/Violence – 15.1%.

The category containing the biggest percentage of news items with hate speech content, Art, Media, Culture – 28.8%, is a surprising finding, taking into consideration that such news items are supposed to cover events serving a completely opposite function to that of hate speech language. A closer look at these news

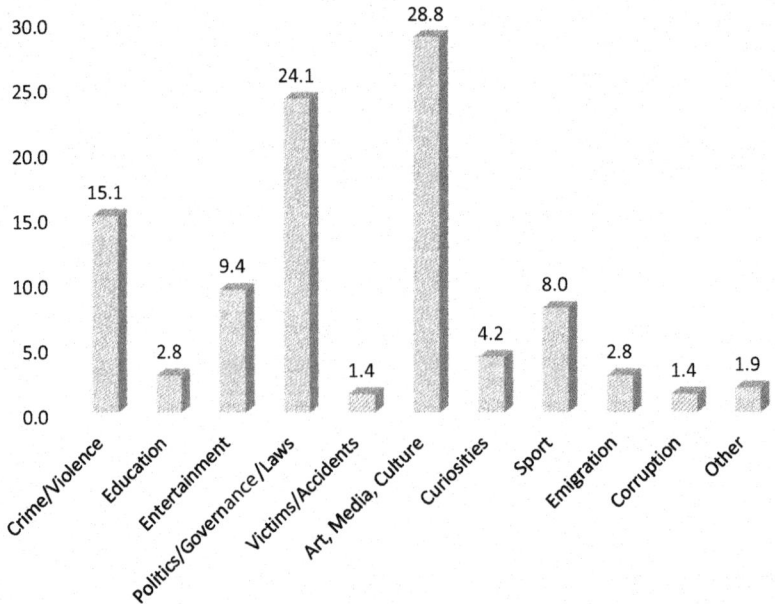

FIGURE 7.1 Percentage of news items with hate speech content based on topic

items shows that most of these articles are 'fabricated' news items that cover stories or events about celebrities. Aiming to attract people's attention to such stories, journalists come up with bombastic titles, often including hate speech content or discriminatory language, as a way to attract more readers, viewers or clicks. This is explained by the fact that many online media outlets rely on clicks for getting financial support from advertisers. As such, coming up with news articles that get those clicks has become a mission for most of these online media outlets.

In many cases these news items comprise social media statuses or comments of celebrities from their own social media platforms, which are just copy-pasted by journalists and offered to the public in the form of a news item. These are some examples of such news items, published in online news websites that were monitored for this research project:

> Fjolla Morina responds to the Iranian billionaire: Homosexual (Lapsi.al, 27 October 2018)
> Fans told her she looked like a transsexual with balls, Ronela responds: they are bigger than yours, assholes (Shqiptarja.com, 25 October 2018)
> Number one bitch, don't give a f.ck (Lapsi.al, 15 October 2018)

These articles can be found in several online news media platforms in Albania, in the exact same form. Additionally, these new items are very easy to 'fabricate' as they are just a simple copy-paste action and in most cases have no author. Such plagiaristic behaviour is also identified in other reports in Albanian media (Media Ownership Monitor Albania 2019).

The second category of news items containing hate speech language is Politics/ Governance/Laws – 24.1 %. This category has been reported as producing more news items in Albania (Kaziaj 2016, 2018). As such there is a bigger chance for this category to contain news items with hate speech content or discriminatory language. These are some examples of such news items:

> Recordings with Nice, Dako[11] same as Rama[12]: There is no son of a bitch (Panorama, 25 October 2018)
> Trump mocks the actress he slept with: that horse-face! (Lapsi.al, 16 October 2018)
> Go after your boss like a dog with your tongue out! (Panorama, 9 October 2018)
> Old piece of sh.t, human failure (Balkanweb, 6 November 2018)

It is not necessarily easy to identify hate speech content from news item titles, but it becomes visible and easily identified in the actual articles, with expressions using denigrating language addressed to people – usually women, as will be elaborated in the next sections – in clear view.

The third category containing a large number of articles with hate speech content is Crime/Violence – 15.1 %. In this category, most news items relate to a specific event, namely the execution of a Greek minority member by Albanian police officers after he opened fire on them. A large number of articles covering this story as it unfolded were published in both Albania and Greece and reported on protests taking place in both countries, after the event, by stating expressions with hate speech content, such as:

Video: Greek extremist opens fire against police, message Greek or Death (Lapsi.al, 29 October 2018)

Racist protest in Athens: 'Kill the Albanian dogs' (Lapsi.al, 28 October 2018)

The death of the Greek soldier, Greeks protest: Let's burn Albanians (Shqiptarja.com, 28 October 2018)

One Greek less – one bastard less, racist banner in the football match (Lapsi.al, 29 October 2018)

Main targets of hate speech in online media

Women comprise the biggest group targeted, the objects of hate speech in almost 35% of all articles. Several studies on online media report that 'hostility toward women generally, and feminists in particular, is rampant' (Bartow 2009).

Even though we cannot draw direct connections between hate speech against women in online media and the increase in violence against women in Albania – which is a pervasive phenomenon (Haarr 2019) – hate speech against women in media can still be considered an indicator for the level of discrimination that exists for this group in society. Naming or referring to certain groups in the media can be taken as an indicator of the shared beliefs among media content producers and their audiences (Richardson 2007). Consequently, the fact that women are the first and major target for hate speech can be taken as an indicator of the realities they face every day in Albania.

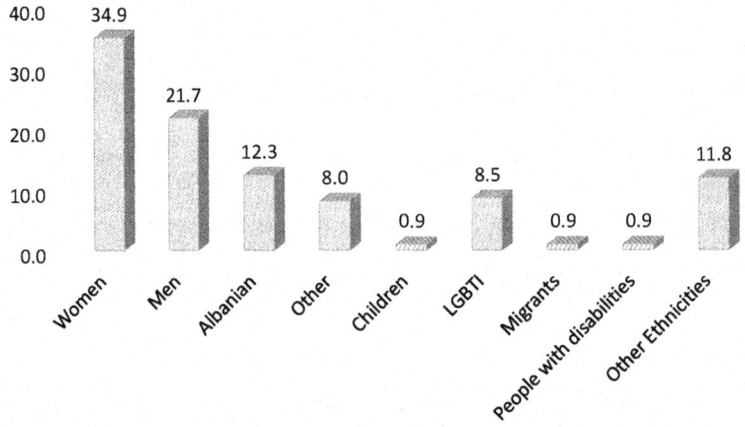

FIGURE 7.2 Percentage breakdown of groups targeted for hate speech

Language used towards women in Albanian online media has several characteristics. In most cases, hate speech/discriminatory language targeting women refers to 'the lack of honesty of women', naming them 'bitches' or using similar denigrating terms:

> Be careful with your style: Alba Hoxha with her legs up (Shqiptarja.com, 13 October 2018)
> You insulted me, bitch, prostitute (Panorama, 18 October 2018)
> Bro's before Hoes: Fjolla Morina replies to the Iranian (Shqiptarja.com, 7 October 2018)
> Mourinho to the fans: Sons of Bitches (Panorama, 8 October 2018)
> Tennis players Stephens – Pavlychenova: The whore wanted to hit me! (Panorama, 3 October 2018)

Another characteristic of hate speech/ discriminatory language directed at women is what we can call implicit or connoted hate speech (Parekh 2012). A typical example of such case can be found in a news item related to the prime minister of Albania, Edi Rama, which was reported in almost all the media outlets monitored for this project:

> Uff, finally a boy, Rama shares the good news (Balkanweb, 25 October 2018)
> Finally a boy – Rama shares the good news (Shqiptarja.com, 24 October 2018)

Such expression refers to a widespread belief among Albanians that baby boys are to be favoured more than baby girls.[13] It is also used as an idiom to signify a positive achievement, as the PM has done in this case. Nonetheless, all idioms reflect, besides their expressive role, certain ideologies that are dominant in society (van Dijk 2008). As such, when stated by people in powerful positions, such as the prime minister, the impact of expressions of this sort that reiterate[14] and reinforce such ideologies is very significant.

Only one reader reacted critically, through a comment on one of these articles:

> On: 25/10/2018 09:39
> What if it was a girl, wouldn't it be a good thing?!!!

Along the same lines, another news item that deserves special attention and analysis is the one referring to an expression that the mayor of Tirana, Erjon Veliaj, used after a woman police officer was harmed during a protest organised by the opposition party. The news item was published under this title in one of the online media we monitored:

> Erjon Veliaj goes crazy: No man is going to marry the police whose fingers were cut off (Lapsi.al, 27 November 2018)

Nonetheless, many other news websites – that were not part of our monitoring – reported the same news item, with titles such as:

Veliaj for the police officer whose fingers were cut off: you destroyed her life, no man will marry her now.[15]

Erion Veliaj: No man will marry Ina, the policewoman whose fingers were cut off/VIDEO.[16]

These expressions that highlight women's civil status and sees them in limited roles – for instance as wives, as in the case of the mayor of Tirana – are reiterated as part of an old mentality.

The impact that such linguistic constructions have on audiences is not just related to language, it is also reflected in social practices and relationships among society members. As stated in the report of Gagliardone et al. (2015) 'the endurance of hate speech materials online is unique due to its low cost and potential for immediate revival, ensuring its continued relevance in particular spheres of discourse'.

An interesting finding from the monitoring process is the characteristics of the hate speech/discriminatory language targeted at men. This category accounts for 21.7% of all news items, but some core characteristics of the language used need to be considered with care before conclusions are drawn.

First, the language used to target men can be categorised more as offensive language rather than hate speech – based on how literature and legislation has defined hate speech language (see introduction). These are some examples of titles of news items monitored in this category:

(Video) Muc Nano[17]- Salianji[18]: You are an idiot, you are accessory, insignificant (Panorama, 10 October 2018)

You were begging for information as a little bastard (Panorama, 15 October 2018)

As far as I'm concerned, you can die: Father does not accept son (Panorama, 15 October 2018)

SP-DP[19] fight in Brussels. Pollo: Balla[20] is a drug patron (Shqiptarja.com, 16 October 2018)

Second, offensive language targeting men in this category does not treat them as a group and does not emphasise group characteristics. It is mostly focused on individuals – that is, it is very personal and does not focus on characteristics that men share with other men but mostly focuses on their public and professional persona. As such, it does not really fall into the category of hate speech. Nonetheless, it was included in the monitoring process and made part of the analysis in order to enable further exploration and be able to draw some comparison with the characteristics of language used for other social groups, such as women.

To better understand differences in the language used by media to target groups rather than individuals, several examples are presented below.

German politician calls Albanians thieves (Panorama, 10 October 2018)

They are gay but they hide it. The well-known businessman outs Albanian politicians (Shqiptarja.com, 13 October 2018)

Racist protests in Athens: Kill the Albanian dogs (Lapsi.al, 28 October 2018)

One of the main findings of this monitoring process is the difference in hate speech/discriminatory language characteristics when women and men are targeted by online media in Albania. In the case of women, the focus is on characteristics that are inclusive to all women. In the case of men, the language used is personal, targeting only one individual and is not inclusive to all men.

Characteristics of subjects who are victims of hate speech/ discriminatory language in online media

According to Figure 7.3, women are the main targets of hate speech, and age is an important variable. Women in the age group 19–25 are subject to more news items with hate speech language. The number of news items on men of the same age group is significantly lower, with only two news items. In contrast, among men, the age group 40+ is the particular target of hate speech/discriminatory language.

If we combine such findings with those presented in Figure 7.1, referring to the topics of news items, we get a better understanding of why women aged 19–25 are particular targets of hate speech language. Figure 7.4 presents a combination of both findings.

As most news items in the category Art, Media, Culture report on women celebrities, it follows that most reporting is dedicated to women in the 19–25 age group. This shows a greater media preference for this age group as subjects for celebrity reporting. In

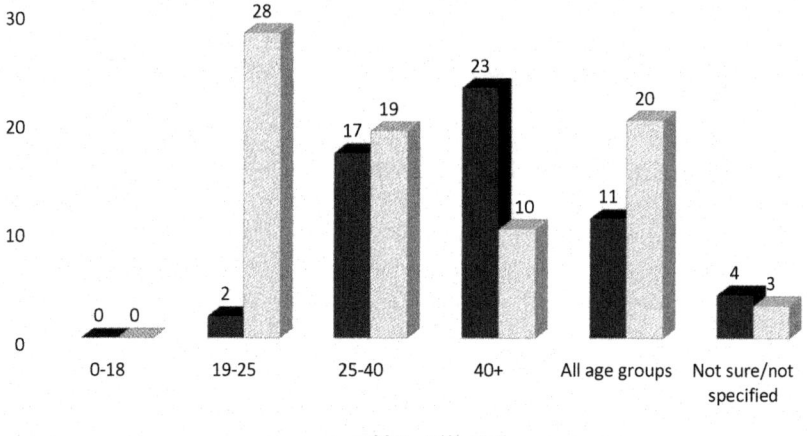

FIGURE 7.3 Age groups targeted for hate speech, showing gender (number of news items)

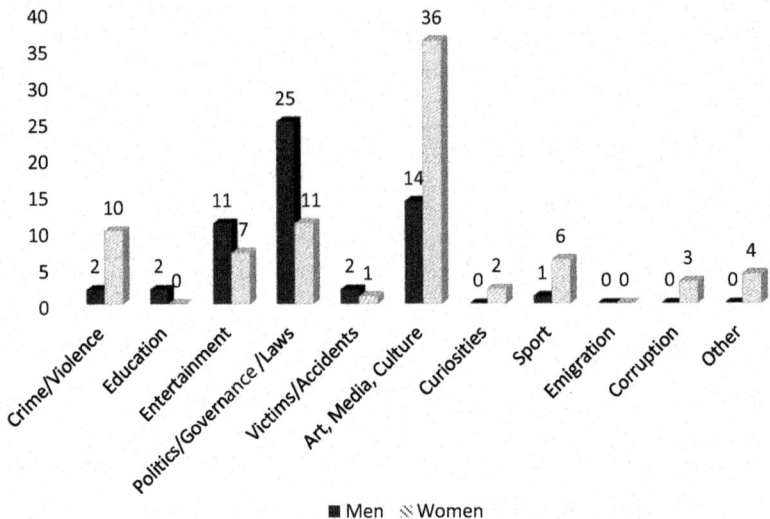

FIGURE 7.4 Topics of articles with hate speech, based on gender of news subjects (number of news items)

contrast, men are mostly covered as part of Politics/Governance and Laws – with 25 news items compared to 11 on women. In this category, most news items revolve around active politicians such as the prime minister, ministers or opposition leaders. Most of these actors belong in the 40 + age category. This explains the large number of news items on men over 40 years old reported in the category Politics/Governance and Laws.

In 45% of news items containing hate speech/discriminatory language, some identity characteristics – such as name, surname, gender, age – of the news subjects who are targets of hate speech are revealed. This can be explained by the fact that most of these news items are fabricated from the social media pages of celebrities and then published as part of the Art, Media, and Culture category on online news websites. As the goal of such news items is to 'sell' by making use of the celebrity's status, all possible details are revealed, even if this goes against the ethical codes governing broadcasting in Albanian media. Although these are clearly stated in the Code of Broadcast, online media is yet not subject to such regulation, so there is effectively no legal instrument to make online media outlets apply ethical and quality principles to their content.

Such a finding supports other research, which states that 'women are identified by name or photo or both, and then savaged' (see Bartow 2009).

Another finding relates to the use of photos in articles containing hate speech/ discriminatory language, as presented in Figure 7.5.

Most articles – 77 more precisely – contain photos of the subject that is a target for hate speech.

On the other hand, it is interesting to note that online media outlets also publish photos of those that voice hate speech/discriminatory language – in 74 news items,

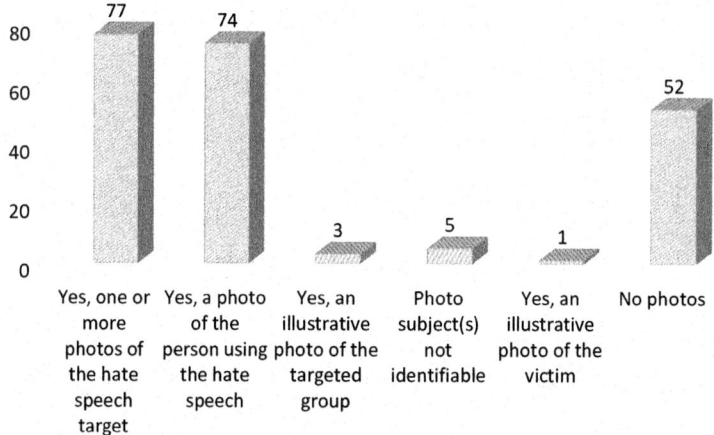

FIGURE 7.5 Articles containing hate speech/discriminatory language: is there a photo?

as shown in the above graph. As a matter of fact, these photos are not used to reveal the identities of people who use hate speech as a way to publicly shame them. No tone of criticism can be found in such news articles and no mention of any legislation or principles related to anti-discrimination. This raises serious questions about the quality of journalism in online media.

Despite the fact that women comprise the biggest group targeted for hate speech/discriminatory language in online media, it is mostly men who are portrayed with photos in news articles online.

According to these findings, photos of women are mostly used when they are a target for hate speech/discriminatory language. Photos of men are mostly used

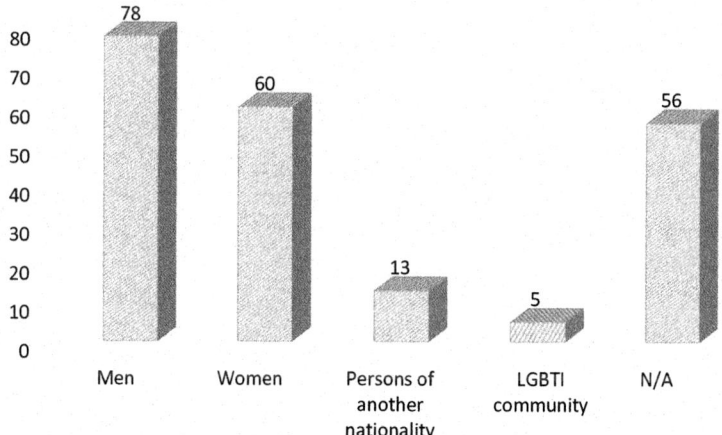

FIGURE 7.6 Subjects of photos by group

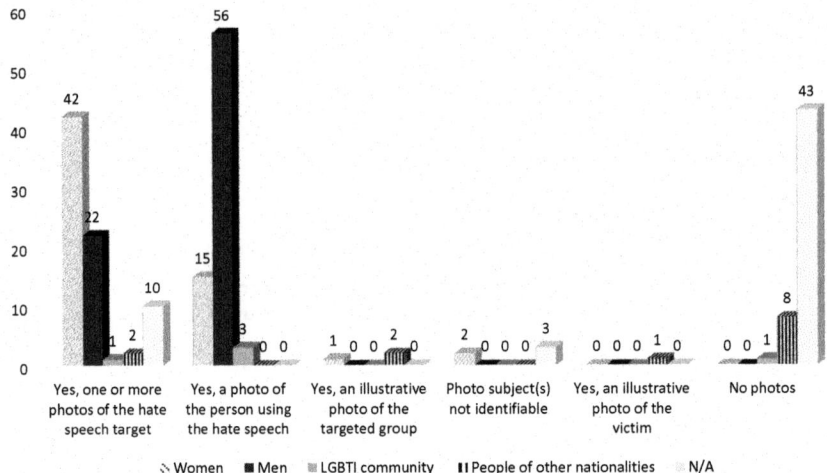

FIGURE 7.7 A deeper understanding of the use of photos

when they are responsible for hate speech/discriminatory language. Additionally, these findings reveal that men comprise the biggest category using hate speech/discriminatory language on online media in Albania. Such findings point to the positions that men and women occupy in Albanian society, with the former being more dominant (Haarr 2019).

The findings also reveal that the two online media that have most news items with hate speech content – Panorama.com.al and Balkanweb – are also the ones that prioritise the categories of Art, Media and Culture, or Showbiz, in their daily reporting. This can be easily assessed by the space that such categories occupy on their websites (central,[21] colourful, etc.) and also by the large number of news articles that are reported every day within such categories.[22]

Conclusion

Five women were killed by their husbands in Albania in January 2020. In 2019, 12 women were reported as killed by their husbands or fathers. News about these events was reported across all media outlets. On online media, such news items were frequently reported next to other news items with hate speech/discriminatory or sexist language against women. We do not want in any way to insinuate that this is a result of hate speech content in media targeting women, but we do want to encourage more critical thinking on hate speech that does not confine it to the online media realm. The culture that is reflected, reinforced and maintained by online media reveals itself in numerous ways in real life situations. For this reason, such phenomenon should be seriously investigated and researched.

This chapter focused on online media content in Albania, aiming to explore practices and trends in journalism that help fuel hate speech and discriminatory language, based on findings from a three-month monitoring process. Additionally, this chapter explored which groups are the main targets of hate speech/discriminatory language in online media and examined different facets and characteristics of such language.

Women were found to be the main target group for hate speech/discriminatory language in Albanian online media, featuring as such in almost 35% of all articles published during the monitored time period. When women are the target, the language employed points to a distinctive characteristic of women as a group, and derogatory terms such as 'bitch' and 'prostitute' are redundantly used. Such findings support previous research conducted on this topic (see Simona et al. 2019, Bartow 2009, Lillian 2007) which call for a greater consideration of sexist language in media and the crucial need to categorise it as hate speech.

Additionally, the biggest age group among women to be a target for hate speech language is 19–25, and this group is mostly portrayed in news items belonging to the category Art, Media and Culture. Furthermore, photos of women are mostly used when they are a target for hate speech/discriminatory language. These two findings reveal that the most common subjects in news articles that contain hate speech are women of a younger age, in a profession related to arts such as singing or performing, and they are redundantly portrayed with photos. Both elements point to a high probability of women being objectified in online news media. As Catharine MacKinnon (1993, p. 17), states in her work on the public portrayal of women:

> In other words, as the human becomes thing and the mutual becomes one-sided and the given becomes stolen and sold, objectification comes to define femininity, and one-sidedness comes to define mutuality, and force comes to define consent as pictures and words become forms of possession and use through which women are actually possessed and used.

Such delineation of consequences from a redundant use and portrayal of women presents a real challenge to Albanian online media. The role that online media professionals play in 'fabricating' news items – frequently by copy-pasting them from social media pages of celebrities and political actors – only reinforces the vulnerabilities of women.

Moreover, the urge online media have to attract viewers' attention, which is then translated into clicks, which in turn are used as the main indicator for attracting advertising to online media – is another important factor that encourages a culture of sensationalistic titles, usually with hate speech content and discriminatory language against women. In addition, the lack of regulations and monitoring institutions for online media content has had its impact on sustaining such phenomena.

Insights provided here are of immense importance for Albania, as – while this book chapter is being finalised – a draft proposal was sent to the Council of

Ministers to amend the existing Law on Audiovisual Media, Nr. 97, 2013 to include online media as subject to this law. This has provoked heated debate amongst the media community as the proposed change is seen as an attempt by the government to control online media.[23]

Notes

1 www.facebook.com/terms.php
2 This the latest census conducted in Albania. Next one was planned for 2020. Results have not been yet published.
3 Report can be accessed here: http://albania.mom-rsf.org/en/
4 www.mod.gov.al/images/PDF/barazia_gjinore_shoqeri.pdf
5 Translated by the author.
6 http://ama.gov.al/wp-content/uploads/2019/09/HATE-SPEECH-1.pdf
7 https://ethicaljournalismnetwork.org/resources/publications/hate-speech
8 www.alexa.com/topsites/countries/AL
9 Figures in this chapter cannot be copied without permission of the author.
10 Categories are named as found in most media outlets in Albania.
11 Vangjel Dako-mayor of Durres – one the major cities in Albania.
12 Edi Rama – the Albanian prime minister.
13 It is a tradition in Albania to wish pregnant women 'a baby boy'.
14 A review of all news items with the PM quote that were published in the exact same form in all online media: www.google.com/search?rlz=1C1CHBF_enAL866AL866&ei=7_CuXZ KXF9H3qwHKs4LoDQ&q=uff+me+ne+fund+me+djale&oq=uff+me+ne+fund+me+ djale&gs_l=psy-ab.3..33i160l4.6341747.6344846..6345930...0.2..0.164.2812.0j23......0.... 1..gws-wiz.......0i71j0j0i131j0i67j0i22i30j0i13j0i13i10j0i13i30j0i13i5i30j0i13i10i30j0i13i5i 10i30j0i8i13i30j33i22i29i30j33i21.uMr6qc4yODc&ved=0ahUKEwjSyoKf6q_lAhXR-yoK HcqZAN0Q4dUDCAs&uact=5
15 www.tpz.al/2018/11/27/veliaj-per-policen-qe-iu-prene-gishtat-i-shkaterruat-jeten-asnje-burre-nuk-do-te-martohet-me-te/
16 www.syri.net/politike/213034/video-cudit-veliaj-asnje-burre-nuk-martohet-me-policen-qe-i-prene-gishtin/
17 Referring to Mustafa Nano, an Albanian analyst.
18 Referring to Ervin Salianji, one of the opposition party members, former member of parliament.
19 SP=Socialist Party, DP=Democratic Party.
20 Pollo – referring to Genc Pollo, DP member; Balla – referring to Taulant Balla, SP member.
21 Check the webpages of Panorama.com.al and Balkanweb.
22 Art and Culture news and Showbiz are refreshed with new articles more often than other sections.
23 A list of media reporting on debates on the new draft law can be found here: www.rep orter.al/?s=ligji+anti+shpifje

Bibliography

Bartow, A. (2009). Internet defamation as profit center: The monetization of online harassment. *Harvard Journal of Law and Gender*, 32(2).

Benesch, S. (2013). Dangerous speech: A proposal to prevent group violence. Dangerous Speech Project. Available at http://dangerousspeech.org/guidelines/.

Bleich, E. (2013). Freedom of expression versus racist hate speech: Explaining differences between high court regulations in the USA and Europe. *Journal of Ethnic and Migration Studies*, 40(2).

Buckels, E.E., Trapnell, P.D. & Paulhus, D.L. (2014). Trolls just want to have fun. *Personality and Individual Differences*, 67, 97–102.

Dizdari, D. (2013). Human rights, discrimination and gender equality issues in the Albanian news media: An analysis. UNDP Albania, Tirane.

Erjavec, K. & Kovačič, M.P. (2012). 'You don't understand. This is a new war!' Analysis of hate speech in news websites' comments. *Mass Communication and Society*, 15(6), 899–920.

Gagliardone, I., Gal, D., Alves, T. & Martinez, G. (2015). Countering online hate speech. UNESCO series on Internet Freedom. UNESCO Publishing. Available at http://unesdoc.unesco.org/images/0023/002332/233231e.pdf.

Haarr, R. (2019). Violence against women and girls in Albania. National population survey. UNDP Albania, Tiran.

Heinze, E. (2009). Cumulative jurisprudence and human rights: The example of sexual minorities and hate speech. *International Journal of Human Rights*, 13(2–3), 193–209.

Human Rights Council (United Nations) (2015). Report of the Special Rapporteur on minority issues, Rita Izsák. A/HRC/28/64.

Kaziaj, E. (2016). 'The adult gaze': Exploring the representation of children in television news in Albania. *Journal of Children and Media*, 10(4), 426–442.

Kaziaj, E. (2018). Journalists' and news editors' views on children as news subjects in Albanian media: Exploring issues of self-censorship, ethics and newsworthiness. *Journal of Applied journalism and media studies*, 7(2), 351–370.

Kaziaj, E. & Van Bauwel, S. (2017). The ignored audience: A multi-method reception study on children and television news in Albania. *Childhood*, 4(2), 230–244.

Krippendorff, K. (2004). *Content Analysis: An Introduction to its Methodology*. Thousand Oaks, CA: Sage.

Lillian, D. (2007). A thorn by any other name: sexist discourse as hate speech. *Discourse & Society*, 18(6), 719–740.

Liperi, O. (2018). Tregu i dobët i reklamave fut median në krizë: Televizionet pa fitime. *monitor.al*. Available online at www.monitor.al/tregu-reklamave-fut-median-ne-krize-te levizionet-pa-fitime-online-mund-print/.

Londo, I. (2014). Hate speech in online media in Albania. In R. Lani (eds), *Hate Speech in Online Media in South East Europe*. Tirane: Albanian Media Institute.

MacKinnon, K.A. (1993). *Only Words*. Cambridge, MA: Harvard University Press.

Marwick, A.E. & Miller, Ross W. (2014). Online harassment, defamation, and hateful speech: A primer of the legal landscape. Fordham Center on Law and Information Policy, Report Nr. 2. Available at https://papers.ssrn.com/sol3/papers.cfm?abstract_id=2447904.

Matsuda, M. (1989). Public response to racist speech: Considering the victim's story. *Michigan Law Review*, 87(8), 2320–2381.

Media Ownership Monitor (2019). Available at https://albania.mom-rsf.org/.

Mihajllova, E., Baçovska, J. & Shekerxhiev, T. (2013). Liria e shprehjes dhe Gjuha e urrejtjes. OSCE, Skopje.

Moran, M. (1994). Talking about hate speech: A rhetorical analysis of American and Canadian approaches to the regulation of hate speech. *Wisconsin Law Review*.

Parekh, B. (2012). Multicultural society and the welfare state. In J. Connelly & J. Hayward (eds), *The Withering of the Welfare State* (pp. 52–68). Basingstoke: Palgrave Macmillan.

Pinto, D. & Singh, V. (eds) (2019). Intelligent and fuzzy systems applied to language and knowledge engineering. *Journal of Intelligent & Fuzzy Systems*, 36(5).

Richardson, J.E. (2007). *Analyzing Newspapers*. New York: Palgrave Macmillan.

Rosenfeld, M. (2012. Hate speech in constitutional jurisprudence. In M. Herz & P. Molnar (eds), *The Content and Context of Hate Speech* (pp. 242–289). Cambridge: Cambridge University Press.

Rozgonyi, K. (2018). A new model for media regulation. *Intermedia*, 416(1).

Sellars, A.F. (2016). Defining hate speech. Berkman Klein Center Research. Available at https://papers.ssrn.com/sol3/papers.cfm?abstract_id=2882244.

Shin, J. (2008). Morality and internet behavior: A study of the internet troll and its relation with morality on the internet. In *Society for Information Technology & Teacher Education International Conference* (pp. 2834–2840). Waynesville, NC: Association for the Advancement of Computing in Education.

Simona, F., Bilal, G., Manuel, M. & Paolo, R. (2019). Online hate speech against women: Automatic identification of misogyny and sexism on Twitter. *Journal of Intelligent & Fuzzy Systems*, 36(5), 4743–4752.

United Nations Population Fund (UNFPA) (2012). Sex imbalances at birth in Albania. World Vision, Tirane.

van Dijk, T.A. (2008). *Discourse and Power*. Houndsmills: Palgrave.

8

'TELL ME HOW OLD I AM'

Cinema, pedagogy, adults and underage trans folks

Magalí Daniela Pérez Riedel and Pablo Ariel Scharagrodsky

Introduction

The aim of this paper is to examine the representation of transgender children in media in Europe and USA through the examination of the relationships of the transgender minors with the adults in their lives. We perform a textual analysis to describe the intergenerational relationships between the characters in three films that feature underage transgender characters. These films are *3 Generations* (2015), *They* (2017) and *Girl* (2018). We observe how the adults' bonds with transgender teens are portrayed in regard to narratives of hormonal and social transition. We identify that transgender kids are depicted as being constantly under the scrutiny and judgement of the adults, especially their parents, relatives and doctors. Critical responses highlight that these productions are sometimes more focused on these medical procedures and on adults' feelings towards their transgender children than the children themselves (Yoshida 2017, Bradshaw 2019, Baker 2019). Thus, the purpose of this study is to understand the cinematic representations of transgender youth through the analysis of the adults' intergenerational relationships and representational practices. Another purpose of this research is to assess the didactic and pedagogical roles of these films.

Findings of this research show that the films reinforce a 'wrong body' discourse, where the goal of transgender people is to 'correct' their bodies through a process of hormonal (and sometimes even surgical) procedures, provided they had received their guardians' consent beforehand. In other words, adults eventually appear to facilitate and endorse their transitioning procedures after the transgender children had struggled to obtain and secure such endorsement. Although the movies disseminate some binary, cisnormative, pathologising and heterosexist assumptions regarding trans identities, we argue that the films make circulate alternative meanings that may educate viewers on specific issues and give room to broader discussions of the rights and needs of transgender minors in a context that fails to recognise their bodily integrity and personal autonomy.

Literature review

In recent years, there has been an increasing visibility of transgender and gender non-conforming people. Trans folks, as well as other non-cisgender and non-heterosexual people, have broken into the mainstream through appearances in scripted and non-scripted television shows that circulate in broadcast television channels, programming services and popular video streaming platforms such as Netflix (GLAAD 2019). LGBTQ characters are also visible in different cinematic circuits, from independent spheres to Hollywood and Cannes Film Festivals, for example, films such as *Tangerine* (2015), *Moonlight* (2016) and *Papi Chulo* (2018). Given the present increasing representation of LGBTQ folks in commercial and independent audio-visual productions, it becomes relevant to study their representational practices and the political and/or educational stands.

A growing body of literature examines media representations of transgender people. One study by Ford (2016) compared mainstream films through the examination of transgender characters in Hollywood. According to Ford, a mainstream film is produced by a major motion picture studio; it is intended to be widely distributed, become a box office success and receive acknowledgements and awards. Ford reported that 'mainstream films continue the hegemonic stereotyping of narratives and characters' (2016: 65). Similarly, Symes (forthcoming) carried out a case study on the independent web series *Her Story* (2016), where a number of the production team and cast were trans and queer. Symes identified the show had a pedagogical function to educate mainstream audiences on the complexities of being trans and to challenge negative representations.

While much of feminist and queer literature since the 1990s has emphasised the subversive and disruptive aspects of the gender performances of transgender and queer subjects (Butler, 1993, Preciado, 2018), recent literature shows the normalising effects on such subversive potential. Mocarski et al. (2013) examined the performance and the portrayals of Chaz Bono in a reality television show. The authors identified the construction of forms of transnormativity that support and simultaneously resist their normalisation. In another study, Lovelock (2017) found that representations of transgender women in television work to reinforce ideals of an 'acceptable' transgender subjectivity. Lovelock also found that trans portrayals in commercial and popular media consolidate the 'wrong body' discourse. According to this trope, transitioning is a way to uncover the 'authentic' self.

Together these studies provide important insights into the analysis of mediated representations of transgender people. However, they focus on representations of transgender adults in commercial media and independent media separately. There remain several aspects of transgender representation about which relatively little is known. This study therefore sets out to examine the didactic and pedagogical roles of these films and seeks to understand how underage transgender folks are portrayed in their relationships with adults both in mainstream and non-mainstream media.

Methodology

Three cinematic productions were selected to be part of this study. Criteria for selecting the films were as follows: a) they feature underage transgender characters in main roles; b) the productions are from different countries and at least one of them must be from Europe; c) they are or have been available in commercial and/or independent theatres, streaming services and film festivals; and d) they are available in English or have subtitles in English. A small sample was chosen: *3 Generations, They* and *Girl*. Hollywood film *3 Generations* focuses on both the experience of Ray (Elle Fanning) as a transgender teenager boy and the journeys of his mother, his grandmother and her partner around Ray's decision to go through a process of social and hormonal transition. The protagonist of the Iranian-American production *They* is called J. (Rhys Fehrenbacher), a pre-adolescent trans child who uses hormonal blockers to stop the arrival of puberty and have time to discover and decide, in their words, whether they feel a girl, a boy or nothing. J.'s preferred pronouns are they/their. Their parents, largely absent from the film, are replaced by J.'s older sister and her Iranian fiancé. The main character of Belgian film *Girl* is Lara (Victor Polster), a 15-year-old transgender girl who is trying to become a professional dancer. She begins her process of hormonal transition with the support of her father as she also begins to inquire about the steps to gender confirmation surgery.

In order to understand the representational practices and intergenerational relationships in these films, a textual analysis was performed. Analysis was based on the conceptual framework proposed by Norman Fairclough (1992), for whom critical discourse analysis (CDA) comprises three dimensions of textual analysis. At the micro level, the 'text/film' dimension, which corresponds to the linguistic analysis of the text/film itself. The second dimension, the 'discursive practice', encompasses the production and interpretation processes of the texts/film that produce the 'interaction'. Finally, the 'social practice' dimension, which refers to the social context where the processes of production and interaction occur and the institutional, social and historical circumstances of that interaction. Thus, it becomes relevant to analyse the text/film in context.

Films as queer pedagogical devices

Beyond the differences in the patterns of meaning and the ways of approaching the different topics, the films analysed here become true pedagogical devices since they produce, transmit, distribute and disseminate meanings that problematise sexual difference, the materiality of bodies, sexualities, desires, pleasures, emotions and relationships between subjects in a disruptive way. Here we use the Foucauldian concept of problematisation (Foucault 1979) to question and reflect on how and why, for example, the body (or sexuality, desire, emotions, pleasure, differences, etc.) has been problematised through a certain institutional practice and certain conceptual devices. We argue that these films act indeed as a dispositive in a Foucauldian sense.

These films make visible new ways of thinking identities, subjectivities, bodies, affective-emotional relationships, forms of empowerment and their relationships with age and different family structures. The films, with their tones, inflections and nuances, project and imagine other possible worlds of meaning on the political-sexual universe, beyond those meanings that are crystallised and instituted in the heterogeneous social world. The films function as pedagogical devices since they deliberately incorporate new ways of problematising sexual, gender, affective and emotional relationships beyond the hermeneutic binarism, sexual dimorphism, heteronormative desire regime and typically modern body hierarchy. With their proposals, claims and desires, Lara, Ray and J. disturb and trouble the tranquillity of the supposed 'normality' of the genders, sexualities and traditional desires that circulate in different social contexts. The various plots constructed in the movies problematise and question the sexual identity considered normal – that is, heterosexuality as the only possible alternative of desire. They move the dimorphic bio-medical conformism, disorganise the supposed 'monstrosity' of the abject bodies. According to Judith Butler (1993), the abject forms the constitutive exterior of the field of the subjects. The abject

designates here precisely those 'unlivable', 'uninhabitable' zones of social life which are nevertheless densely populated by those who do not enjoy the status of subjects, but whose living under the sign of the 'unlivable' is required to circumscribe the domain of the subject. This zone of uninhabitability will constitute the defining limit of the subject's domain; it will constitute that site of dreaded identification against which – and by virtue of which – the domain of the subject will circumscribe its own claim to autonomy and to life.

(1993: 3)

In this sense, the films dilute age as a central component when choosing the sexual object and exercising their personal rights and they undo the idea of a fixed identity that is supposed to be stable and eternal over time.

Girl, 3 Generations and *They* are films that act as a dispositive because, as Agamben argues, a dispositive is 'a heterogeneous set [that] includes virtually everything (…): Discourses and institutions, architecture, laws, police measures, scientific statements, philosophical and moral propositions', configuring a 'network or the web that is established between those elements'. A dispositive has 'a strategic function, it's always inscribed in a power game' as a result of the 'the intersection of power relations and relations of knowledge' (Agamben 2009: 3). The movies become devices that are inscribed in a game of power and a game of truth, linked to a limit or the limits of knowledge, which, as Foucault points out, give birth to it but, above all, condition it. Foucault defines a *dispositif* as 'a set of strategies of the relations of forces supporting, and supported by, certain types of knowledge' (Foucault 2003: 112; Foucault cited in Agamben 2009: 2).

The lives of Lara, Ray and J. become testimonies of resistance, strategies of power and knowledge with a visual, ethical and aesthetic flow that invite us to undo the dominant conventions on social and political relations between sexes and genders. Their personal (and collective) journeys, with their contradictions, ambivalences and paradoxes, force us to consider the unthinkable, what is forbidden to think and feel, instead of simply considering the thinkable, or what it is allowed to think, feel or experience. The films, with different analytics and political positions, invite us to think *queer* – that is, to question, problematise and dispute all forms of good behaviour, adequate knowledge, correct moralities and identity as something crystallised or pre-discursive. The queer epistemology of these films is, in this sense, irreverent, destitute, inconvenient, insolent, daring and reckless. Although the term 'queer' is originally a derogatory term, non-cisgender and non-heterosexual people have appropriated it and made it their own. Today, broadly speaking, it refers to multiple (often contradictory) political movements, educational and cultural approaches and theoretical perspectives whose common goal is to denounce normative structures that oppress people due to their gender and sexuality (and ability, age, size, race/ethnicity, class, nationality, etc.), discriminating and annihilating them both materially and symbolically. In this chapter, we use 'queer' both as a verb and as a noun to make visible our political stand and our critical stance.

The films from this study enhance and stimulate a queer pedagogy since they force the limits of the dominant episteme (Britzman 2016), objecting to those who define 'the regimes of truth' (Foucault 2007) that prevail in society and in the current imaginary as if they were neutral, objective and impartial. The films become true devices because they have 'the capacity to capture, orient, determine, intercept, model or control, or secure the gestures, behaviours, opinions, or discourses of living beings' (Agamben 2009: 14). Beyond the resistance, re-interpretations and questioning from the spectators, the pedagogical orientations put into circulation by the films make visible and denounce not only an unfair, violent, hostile and stigmatiaing situation, but the same semiotic plot configures new objects, issues and problems that restore other senses when thinking about what we are. It is there, where the films find a loophole, an interstitium, a small leak. And they become a *dispositif* (from the Latin *apparatus*, which derives from *apparare*, prepare for), since they configure a particular way of appearing or manifesting the 'sexed reality' where the claim to be oneself is combined with sexual emancipation, ethical political autonomy, equity, dignity, the fight against sameness and the fight to have the right to have rights. In this set of agreements, disputes and conflicts, the three films construct and disseminate an alternative and/or counter-hegemonic political pedagogy of the body, although they do so with certain geopolitical limits since they are narratives of European or North American cases with a particular ethnic-racial bias.

Here we talk about an alternative and/or counter-hegemonic political corporeal pedagogy based on the concept of countersexuality. In the words of Paul Preciado,

> Countersexuality is a critical analysis of gender and sexual difference, the product of the heterocentric social contract, the normative performativities of which have been inscribed onto our bodies as biological truths. (…) Countersexual society is committed to the systematic deconstruction of naturalized sexual practices and the gender system. Countersexual society is therefore a destituting society. (…)

> Countersexual society proclaims the equivalence (not the equality) of all living bodies that commit themselves to the terms of the countersexual contract and are devoted to the search for pleasure-knowledge.
>
> *(Preciado 2018: 20–21)*

It is in this sense that these films expose and put into question sex-gender normativity while they disseminate alternative and counter-hegemonic gender performances, bodies, desires and feelings.

Films as queer didactic devices

Every pedagogical device uses a varied set of didactics or teaching devices. That is, a conglomerate of specific proposals that enhance and amplify the pedagogical sphere in order to improve what is transmitted, distributed and put into circulation. The films analysed here, with more or less intensity, use three types of didactics: an emotional one, a visual one and a sonic one. Although the three operate at different levels, they articulate each other, making a certain illusory sense of coherence in relation to a certain emotional, visual and sonic regime of what is thinkable, possible and correct.

The emotional didactic that circulates in the movies is possibly the most effective in political terms since it enables new emotional forms of empowerment and, at the same time, it denounces the emotional regimes established as 'normal' in most social spaces. Any emotional didactic focuses its attention on the deliberate selection and ranking of certain emotions over others. The three films identify a varied set of emotions that unfairly govern social relationships about queers, such as fear, hate, pain, disgust, anger, rage, apathy or joy. Far from being timeless essences, emotional regimes are transmitted and learned. The didactics of emotions expressed and enhanced in the movies explicitly fight against fear, hatred or disgust generated by the gaze of the 'Other', so common when thinking about differences and building the materiality of bodies and 'different'. The fear, hatred or rejection denounced by Lara, Ray and J. is visible – and questioned – in films as ideological-political constructions in order to ensure an ideal 'us' against other constructions showing them as dangerous and threatening. The films show how fear is manufactured in order to preserve a supposed 'we' against 'Other' imposters that threaten this fictional ideal. Lara, with annoyance and pain, exclaims: 'I'm tired of being an exception.' The adult universe, represented by fathers, mothers and some 'specialists', such as doctors, questions the fear, apathy, resignation, rejection and hatred that is produced ideologically by certain actors and social imagery, betting on visibility and struggling for the recognition of the political rights of trans identities. This bet moves away from the traditional, conservative and historical responses directed towards the trans community, produced by the nuclear and heteronormative families and by the binary and phallogocentric hegemonic medical model. The films, with their nuances and differences, become disruptive pedagogical devices because they not only disseminate new social, emotional, family and medical relationships but also, at the same time, build a new 'reality' on these matters.

The films show that the exception does not exist except in the context of certain social relations crossed by culture, language, power relations and forms of domination. What exists, or rather exists as an invented emotional configuration, is the hostile and violent gaze of the hetero-patriarchy. That is, it is the gaze of the 'Other' that manufactures the category of 'exceptional', deviant, monstrous or sick. The rarity, the grotesque or the 'exceptional' is not in the body of Lara, Ray and J. but in the gaze – never symbolically naked – of the 'Others'. As Sara Ahmed argues, fear creates the very effect of what I am not (Ahmed 2015: 112). She adds: 'Fear does not involve the defence of borders that already exist; rather, fear makes those borders' (Ahmed 2004: 128). The films question the arbitrary and unfair hegemonic construction of these epistemic, legal and ethical boundaries. The production of the transgender subject as an object of fear or rejection depends on past stories of association in the social world: Trans, deviant, sick, ugly, deformed, ridiculous, disgusting, etc. It is this complex operation historically located that is visible and rejected in the films.

Just as the emotional didactic makes visible – and denounces – fear, disgust, hate, pain or anger as effects of violent social and political practices, knowledge and discourses, historically sedimented and ideologically interested; the visual didactic articulates these political-pedagogical operations in order to fix what is possible to show and what is not possible to be shown.

The films make visible the psychic, physical and emotional cost and hardship faced by Lara, Ray and J. for choosing to travel a queer life. They show in a 'stark' and 'embodied' way the symbolic and material cost for being what they wish to be. This cost is materialised in scenes where the body is shown with bleeding feet, curly penises, purple cheekbones, watery eyes, bruised bodies, etc. Bodies that run, cry, groan and suffer. The harassment and violence exerted on the protagonists by their peers and the adults make visible the recurring price that must be paid by those considered by the patriarchal universe as abnormal or abject. Despite this, the films show the different forms of resistance and meaning in the material and symbolic spheres with different degrees of efficiency. In the strategies of resistance, some adult figures such as the father, the mother or the experts are shown and made visible accompanying and defending the dignity of Lara, Ray and J.

The films show and ponder, beyond the pain and stigma produced by the social gaze, the transit of the processes that Lara, Ray and J. are going through. Altogether, in spite of the different types of violence, the films value the image of their 'different' bodies and their changes, as well as the characters' choice and definition of what they are not when talking to other adults in each film: 'Ramona no longer exists. Now there is Ray,' says a protagonist. Or 'Don't call me Victor anymore. I'm Lara,' says another protagonist. 'I am Lauren's sibling,' says J.

The films contribute to build a visual normativity that configures a certain way in which the 'reality' of transgender people, their movements, their bodies, desires and transformations in different social spaces is presented and visually re-presented. The films invite to unveil and de-construct the hegemonic meanings of difference and desire. As Lara points out during her transitioning process: 'I don't know if I like men (…) Maybe I like women.' The films positively ponder – in visual terms – the transition of identities and the contingent crossing of borders.

The role of visual didactic in the different films is to re-educate the eyes, question and displace their oppressive meanings. Where there was pure negativity, fear, disgust and even hatred about the corporeal and sexual difference, the films celebrate the difference of their 'different' characters. They praise their fights and certain emotional bonds. The father tells Lara: 'You are an example to many people.' These situations and their visuality invite us to rethink the gaze as an ideological-political operation and to transit new forms on what to see and on the type of hermeneutical operation that any gaze performs. In this way, rather than becoming the true reflection of trans people, the films contribute with their own visual narrative to performatively construct the objects, problems and themes to which they make reference, demonstrating the built, partial, contingent, interested and perspective aspects of these images, ideas and objects on the heterogeneous trans universe.

It is impossible to think about emotional and visual didactics without a sonic didactic. The films not only transmit and, at the same time, question a certain way of looking and show how to configure and exclude certain types of emotional regimes; they also put into circulation a certain sonic regime. *Girl, 3 Generations* and *They* disseminate and put into circulation rhythms, volumes, patterns and combinations of sounds in certain scenes, situations and moments a particular auditory landscape. The intensities of them are located in certain periods of the films, such as moments of hostility, suffering or resistance by the protagonists. The intensity of a sound, a scream, an exclamation, a groan, a complaint with a sharp voice, a deep breath, a sob or a sigh, shows the impossibility of thinking about the transmission of knowledge only from the visual experience expressed in the movies. In cinematography and communication sciences, the traditional assumption that the visual is the primary site of meaning, identification and pleasure of the viewer has been challenged since the 1990s by the tremendous growth of studies on the role of the sound. It is now a fact that the soundtrack of a movie, together with the dialogue and other sounds, shape the ways the viewer/listener interprets the meaning and perceives the movie (Alter & Koepnick 2004).

The films emphasise the close relationship between certain sounds (with their timbres, tones and intensities) and the construction of more or less empowered subjectivities. The promotion of certain types of agency is always accompanied by a counter-hegemonic or alternative sound regime. Moans, laughter, arguments in a loud voice, pauses, silences and screams are the expression that resists certain unjust, reifying and violent social and sexual conventions. The sound vibrations are articulated with the visual and emotional regimes proposed in the films questioned the sexually civilized sonic landscape or the imperial sonic regimes (Rotter 2010: 11–12).

The protagonists of the films produce types of sound vibration that at the same time as they question certain imperial regimes of sounds, they also stimulate new ways of producing sounds associated with certain objects, themes or situations. Tonal qualities through a word or body movement (Lara dancing, crying or laughing) convey much more meaning than the written word. The 'expressive characteristics' of sound through intensity, tone, interval, rhythm and tempo build new senses on the sexed reality of the protagonists.

Lara, Ray and J. challenge traditional sound landscapes as they install a combination of words with specific intensities and vibrations that evoke the possibility of thinking, acting and feeling, saying and listening in other possible ways. In the case of the transgender universe, sound becomes a way of configuring new forms of power and authority. Shouting, moaning, talking, shutting up, exhaling, breathing or hearing in a certain way is a new possibility of performative expression. It involves not only questioning and (un)doing the normalising gaze, sounds and emotions, but imagining and projecting more dignified and fair sonic, visual and emotional operations and more ethically liveable worlds. This implies thinking and feeling the bodies of transgender people from a space of 'vulnerability and agency' (Butler 2019: 141).

Queering intergenerational relationships

The films focus on the lives of Lara, a teenager transgender girl who aspires to be a professional dancer; Ray, a transgender teen who is at the beginning of his transitioning process; and J., a pre-adolescent who is not yet ready to fully transition. However, the hormonal transition process is at the core of the three plotlines. The films do not centre on 'coming out' experiences stories since the relatives and acquaintances of the young protagonists already know that they are transgender. For example, in *They*, nobody has any conflict with the seemingly non-binary identity of J. Both the character and their gender go unnoticed at times and they are not always central to the film. The opposite happens in *3 Generations* and *Girl*. Ray is going through conflicts with his peers and with his family members, who have difficulty understanding and respecting his gender and his decision to take testosterone. To be able to go on hormone replacement therapy, he has to obtain written consent from the mother and father, who are not part of Ray's life. In *Girl*, Lara's father and brother accompany and support her transition process, but others are not as supportive: her teachers and dance instructors often comment on Lara's difference from other girls and her physical limitations in relation to being a ballet dancer. They state that she must work really hard to practise that activity, although they say they value her perseverance. Her attempts to perfect her dance techniques go hand by hand with her efforts to fulfil a stereotype of femininity and womanhood.

The parents

The role of adults in relation to transgender youth may consist of either enabling or obstructing their paths towards the confirmation of their genders and the right to be themselves. In a global context where discussions about the access of transgender minors to hormonal and/or surgical treatments with or without the consent and authorisation of parents or guardians are still taking place, the films narrate not only the journey of transgender children and young people, their fears, concerns and goals, but also the feelings that overwhelm their family members. Ray's grandmother feels that he is hurrying and she cannot fully understand why he wants to 'mutilate' his body. Ray's mother cries because Ray cut her hair: 'She [sic] promised that she'd never do that. She promised me she'd never shave her head.'

Although the films are said to focus on their transgender characters, cisgender adults and their concerns about the underage trans folks sometimes take over the screen. Regarding *3 Generations*, film critic Emily Yoshida says: 'Each new scene is another combination of characters discussing their opinions and feelings about Ray's gender status' (2017). What is more, the original name of *3 Generations* was *About Ray*. At times the film deals less with the protagonist than with the other characters, as happens in *They* around the immigration status of the Iranian brother-in-law of J. One way or another, to a greater or lesser extent, the personal narratives of young transgender people and their relatives are constructed in line with the transitional narratives of transgender adolescents and infants who are not comfortable and do not identify with the genders they were assigned at birth.

The films reiterate and crystallise some ideas that circulate in the social imaginary: The 'wrong body' trope and the discovery and realisation of an authentic self (Lovelock 2017). The idea that all trans people feel they were born in the wrong body, a body they can't relate to or that they don't feel their own, can be found in the scenes where Ray celebrates that testosterone will reduce his menstrual cycles. A second idea is that all transgender people attempt to modify their body and their gender expression to become a more authentic version of themselves, like when Ray cuts his hair short or when he binds his chest. Thus, transitioning and/or undergoing surgeries seems like a necessary or even a desirable step to have the 'right' body, to 'correct' what is wrong, or to 'reaffirm' the 'true self'. But then there is another discourse that the films expose, which is that the decision-making processes of transgender youth require the intervention and approval of one or more adults, doctors, parents, guardians or tutors. In other words, the films acknowledge the agency of these teens, but they are always subject to the power of their elders. The adults have the final call on what the minors want.

However, in parallel, these productions interrogate the hegemonic, static, aesthetic and cisgender-normative meanings that closet the bodies, identities, subjectivities, sexualities and genders in dichotomous and binary constructs. The films, with their characters, their qualities, their dialogues and particularities, propose alternative meanings that resist these norms. The films invite to rethink the discursive limits of identity to claim for themselves the right to use appropriate personal pronouns (he/him for Ray, they/them for J., she/her for Lara), a fact that translates into a claim for identity, for the right to exist, to be visible and to be named on their own terms, with their own names and preferred personal pronouns.

The goal of the three protagonists is the confirmation of their genders. In all three films, the experiences of transgender people and their family members are closely linked and mediated by the clinic, which results in a symbolic and symbiotic operation that reinforces the idea a transgender underage person needs to be subjected to the scrutiny, judgement and approval of older people, in this case, their family members. For example, in *3 Generations*, Ray's mother, grandmother and her partner go with him to his appointments with the endocrinologist. In *Girl*, the father is present in Lara's meetings with the doctor and the surgeon. The exception is *They*, where J. goes to their appointments and walks down the hospital corridors alone – the parents are mostly absent and the older sister only gives them a ride.

The doctors

The lives of the three protagonists are characterised not only by the acceptance, rejection, support or distance of their parents and relatives but also by the medical gaze. Foucault (2001) argues that the medical gaze is not aseptic, neutral, ahistorical, or disinterested. It does not simply refer to a repertoire of images. It forms a set of historically and ideologically situated visual discourses that construct positions and that are inscribed in social practices, closely associated with certain imaginary and institutions that grant us the right to gaze, regulating and organising a field of the visible and the invisible, of the beautiful and the ugly, of the moral and the immoral, of the true and the false and of the right and the wrong. In other words, the medical gaze in its own operation of gazing is already influenced by a previous notion of difference and identity that conditions what is seen and what is said about the body, sexuality, genders and desire.

In short, the medical gaze not only establishes a 'regime of truth' about bodies, sexualities and sexual difference but also produces the bodily and sexual phenomenon to which it refers, regulates it and, at the same time, constrains it. For example, *They* and *3 Generations* begin and end in a clinic. The characters are interested in receiving testosterone or hormonal blockers to transition and adapt their body image and gender expression to their gender identities. Discussions about surgical interventions are part of their medical appointments as well. In fact, teenagers Ray and Lara often express their desire to remove or surgically modify certain parts of their bodies to have an image according to their gender: Ray wants to remove his breasts and Lara, her penis. The films show how Ray and Lara's strong desire to transition leads them to take drastic measures, sometimes even against the advice of their parents and doctors. For example, one of *Girl*'s first scenes shows Lara trying to pierce her ears on her own; and one of the last scenes shows her trying to cut her penis with a pair of scissors.

The doctors in the film and other health professionals seem to have specialised in transgender studies, as they accompany and support the transition processes of their patients. For example, Lara's psychologist tells her that he sees that she has a woman's body, that she is a woman, with or without hormones. In his words: 'You're a woman, so you have a woman's body already. The only thing we can do is confirm that and support it. But you already are everything you will be then.' But concepts of health and normalcy are evident when doctors and patients discuss hormonal values, bone density figures and other parameters that may have a negative impact on the teens' wellbeing. By the end of *They*, a doctor advises J. to stop taking puberty blockers, suggesting it was about time to make a decision on what would come next, to 'choose' a path.

Conclusions

In this investigation, the aim was to observe how *3 Generations, They* and *Girl* depicted the relationships between the transgender protagonists Ray, J. and Lara and their family members and other social actors such as the 'specialists', particularly doctors. This study has shown that the films focus on the hormonal and social transitioning processes of the young transgender folks and the challenges that they and their relatives face in the way. But one of the more significant findings to emerge from this study is that transgender experiences need the intervention of adults, whether in the form of parents, guardians, tutors or doctors. It is the medical framing that plays a major role in the narratives of these transgender children and their relatives. In these films, doctors and psychologists enable their transitioning processes and are sometimes more supportive than the kids' parents. In spite of portraying the successful journeys of the trans characters in their fight to transition, the films fail to distance themselves from a vast tradition of commercial and independent productions that associate the experience of trans folks with the clinic, contributing to the pathologisation of their identities. Moreover, they reinforce the idea that trans people are born in the 'wrong body' – hence the need to do whatever it takes to 'correct' it to fit within the male/female binary. And they fail to make visible (and intelligible) the wide array of transgender and gender non-conforming identities that inhabit this world.

The films disseminate certain ambiguous and contradictory meanings in a rather traditional or conservative sense. In this sense, no significant differences were found between the commercial and non-commercial films. We did find that the three films fall victim to a white ethnic-racial bias and there is a lack of problematisation of the trans universe from a decolonial perspective (there are trans-Hispanic, African people, etc., in the United States and in Europe), invisibility of the actions of trans political organisations, and certain modes of problematisation that reinforce binary meanings – for example, when Ray's grandmother asks 'why can't she [sic] be a lesbian and period?', or when Lara's family says that she 'looks very pretty'. However, the films operate as devices that propose an alternative and/or counter-hegemonic body politics and pedagogy questioning what is instituted and standardised and, at the same time, they disseminate in an unstable or precarious way new meanings and possibilities in relation to the body, its fluids, its organs, desires, erogenous zones, sexualities, pleasures, erotic-affective relationships, emotional regimes, aesthetics, ages and differences. For this, they use emotional, visual and sonic didactics that operate at different levels, but they articulate each other to manufacture alternative and counter-hegemonic emotional, visual and sonic regimes as they claim sexual emancipation, ethical political autonomy, equity, dignity, the fight against self-control and struggle for the right to have rights.

Overall, this study strengthens the idea that films play a major role in disseminating some affirmative and positive ideas about vulnerable and minoritised groups such as the transgender and gender non-conforming population by educating viewers on their needs and struggles and by showing the changes in their relationships with their family members as they endeavour to embrace and accept their children's changes. This article contributes to identify the significant political-pedagogical power of films about the heterogeneous transgender universe and their possible disruptive or counter-hegemonic functions when producing, transmitting and putting into circulation alternative representations about bodies, desires, emotions and sexual dissidence. Although this study focuses on three European and North American films, the findings may have a bearing on other local productions. What is now needed is a cross-national study involving cinematic productions from other latitudes to understand how trans communities are represented.

References

3 Generations (2015). [film] Directed by G. Dellal. USA: Big Beach Films, InFilm Productions and IM Global.

Agamben, G. (2009). *What Is An Apparatus?* Stanford: Stanford University Press.

Ahmed, S. (2004). Affective economies. *Social Text*, 22(2), 117–139. doi:10.1215/01642472-22-2_79-117.

Ahmed, S. (2015). *La política cultural de las emociones*. Mexico: Programa Universitario de Estudios de Género UNAM.

Alter, N. & Koepnick, L. (2004). Introduction. In N. Alter & L. Koepnick (eds), *Sound Matters: Essays on the Acoustics of Modern German Culture*. New York: Berghahn Books, pp. 3–4.

Baker, A. (2019). *They* (2017). By Anahita Ghazvinizadeh. [online] Cinematary. Available at www.cinematary.com/writing/2019/1/17/they-2017-by-anahita-ghazvinizadeh [accessed 20 April 2020].

Bradshaw, P. (2019). Girl review: Trans teenager dreams of a dancer's life. *The Guardian*, 13 April. Available at www.theguardian.com/film/2019/mar/13/girl-review-lukas-dhont-victor-polster-transgender-ballet [accessed 20 April 2020].

Britzman, D. (2016). ¿Hay una pedagogía queer? O, no leas tan recto. *Revista de Educación*, 9, 13–34. Available at http://fh.mdp.edu.ar/revistas/index.php/r_educ/issue/view/110 [accessed 20 April 2020].

Butler, J. (1993). *Bodies That Matter*. London: Routledge.

Butler, J. (2019). *Cuerpos aliados y lucha política. Hacia una teoría performativa de la asamblea*. Buenos Aires: Paidós.

Fairclough, N. (1992). Approaches to discourse analysis. In *Discourse and Social Change*. Oxford: Polity Press.

Ford, A. (2016). Whose club is it anyway?: The problematic of trans representation in mainstream films – 'Rayon' and *Dallas Buyers Club*. *Screen Bodies*, 1(2), 64–86. doi:10:3167/screen.2016.010205.

Foucault, M. (1979). *La arqueología del saber*. Buenos Aires: Siglo XXI.

Foucault, M. (1999). *Estética, ética y hermenéutica*. Barcelona: Paidós.

Foucault, M. (2001). *El nacimiento de la clínica, una arqueología de la mirada médica*. Buenos Aires: Siglo XXI.

Foucault, M. (2003). *Historia de la sexualidad. La voluntad de saber*. Buenos Aires: Siglo XXI.

Foucault, M. (2007). *Nacimiento de la biopolítica*. Buenos Aires: FCE.

Girl (2018). [film] Directed by L. Dhont. Belgium/Netherlands: Menuet, Frakas Productions and Topkapi Films.

GLAAD (2020). Where we are on TV, 2019–2020. Available at www.glaad.org/wherewea reontv19 [accessed 20 April 2020].

Lovelock, M. (2017). Call me Caitlyn: Making and making over the 'authentic' transgender body in Anglo-American popular culture. *Journal of Gender Studies*, 26(6), 675–687. doi:10.1080/09589236.2016.1155978.

Mocarski, R., Butler, S., Emmons, B. & Smallwood, R. (2013). 'A different kind of man': Mediated transgendered subjectivity, Chaz Bono on Dancing With the Stars . *Journal of Communication Inquiry*, 37(3), 249–264. doi:10.1177/0196859913489572.

Preciado, P. (2018). *Countersexual Manifesto*. New York: Columbia University Press.

Rotter, A.J. (2010). Empires of the senses: How seeing, hearing, smelling, tasting and touching shaped imperial encounters. *Diplomatic History*, 35(1), 3–19. doi:10.1111/j.1467-7709.2010.00909.x.

Symes, K. (forthcoming). *Her Story*: Educating a mainstream audience. In M.D. Pérez Riedel (ed.), *Trans, Out, and in the Public Eye: Representations of Transgender People on Television and Film*. New York: Peter Lang.

They (2017). [film] Directed by A. Ghazvinizadeh. USA/Qatar: Mass Ornament Films.

Yoshida, E. (2017). Movie review: The trans family drama 3 Generations is too cute to be effective. [online] *Vulture*. Available at www.vulture.com/2017/05/the-trans-drama -3-generations-is-too-cute-to-be-effective.html [accessed 20 April 2020].

Elderly have a voice(?): Sexuality, gender and the media across texts and audiences

9

INVISIBLE AGED FEMININITIES IN POPULAR CULTURE

Representational strategies deconstructed

Sofie Van Bauwel

Introduction

In the documentary *Jane Fonda in Five Acts* (Lacy 2018), the paradoxes in representations of ageing femininities are illustrated by the different discourses on ageing women present at the same time. After an appearance at the 2004 Oscar nominations, Fonda was rediscovered and received offers for roles in more than ten feature films and television shows, including *Monster-in-Law* (2005) directed by Robert Luketic, along with *Youth* (Sorrentino 2015) and *Grace and Frankie* (2015–). In the documentary, Fonda points out that this was a turning point in her recent film career as she also became L'Oréal's brand ambassador for older women and it became notable that an older actress was visible in popular media.

The documentary flesh out the paradox of ageing femininities. Fonda's co-actor Sam Waterston states, 'She lived her life in front of us, and if she has grown older, she has shown us what that is like. She is not afraid of being out there. It is about entering back and not quietly in that great goodnight' (*Jane Fonda in Five Acts*, Lacy 2018). He praises her for being who she is and including ageing as part of her. In the same documentary, though, Fonda states, 'I am glad that I look good for my age, but I also had plastic surgery. I am not going to lie about that.' Reflecting on her conflicting position in relation to beauty standards, she says, 'On one level, I hate the fact that I have had the need to alter my psychically. I feel that I am ok. I wish that I was not like that. I love older faces. I wish I was braver, but I am what I am.' These quotes illustrate the difficult, paradoxical position of representations of ageing femininities and pinpoint the core duality of these representations in contemporary visual popular culture.

Although ageing femininities generally remain invisible in popular television fiction, the past decade we have seen a trend of increasing fictional content representing women of age. Some scholars have even argued that the media industry is interested in ageing audiences due to economic factors and the potential of elderly audiences for future television programming (Kubey 1980). Similarly, Imelda Whelehan and Joel Gwynne (2014) highlighted the 'silver tsunami' in advertising and popular discourses in film. Such arguments have been used to explain the interest in the representations of ageing, for example, in *Grace and Frankie* (2015–), an American comedy web television series that has streamed five seasons on Netflix, with one series still running. Actress Lily Tomlin, who plays one of the show's main characters, explains that some crew members are aged, and the show is 'part of our lives in a project where it speaks about what we want to speak about older women, older people' (Lacy 2018). In a study on ageing bodies and faces in contemporary visual culture, Anne Jerslev (2018) found that elderly women have recently appeared 'in beauty and in particular fashion ads, a field from which older people are largely excluded'. Recent years have seen a number of 'not-so-young and elderly celebrities and models figure prominently in campaigns for luxury fashion brands' (Jerslev 2018, 350). For example, celebrities such as Helen Mirren and Joanna Lumley represent 'glamour, fame and accessibility' (Twigg 2018, 345). However, as Whelehan and Gwynne (2014) also pointed out, some representations celebrate ageing, but most highlight decline and deterioration.

In this chapter, we look closely at the representational strategies applied to ageing femininities in popular media content. I examined the representational practices of ageing femininities and bodies in popular visual culture, particularly fiction, and the discourses circulated in many types of popular media texts. By unravelling the discourses on ageing and its intersection with gender, we found three major discourses reflected in representations of ageing femininities, i.e. masked ageing, losing femininity and gaining wisdom with age. In this chapter we will give a theoretical overview of and insights into these limited sets of gender and age-oriented discourses and illustrate them with specific examples.

Representing ageing femininities

As Cecilie Givskov and Line Nybro Petersen (2018) explained in a study on the intersection of ageing and mediatising, the so-called new visibility of ageing is seen as new ageing and results from changing demographics and the global consumer culture of Western welfare states. In the foreword to the World Economic Forum's 2012 report *Global Population Ageing: Peril or Promise?*, Margaret Chan, director-general of the World Health Organization, suggested that populations around the world are rapidly ageing, presenting an important contemporary issue that comes with challenges and opportunities to which we need to adapt:

> Older people are a wonderful resource for their families and communities, and in the formal or informal workforce, they are a repository of knowledge. They can help us avoid making the same mistakes again. [...] The societies that adapt to this changing demographic can reap a sizeable 'longevity dividend'. [...] We need to discard our stereotypes of what it is to be old. We need to consider the

interaction of ageing with other global trends such as technological change, globalization and urbanization. We need to 'reinvent' ageing.

(Chan 2012, 3)

The question is how we can reinvent ageing and how media can play a role in this change. The changes associated with the emergence of new ageing are also giving rise to new lifestyles that media circulate along with discourses about ageing (Givskov and Petersen 2018). Most academic research has focused on representations of ageing in different media outlets and formats, and of these, advertising is one of the most widely researched. For example, in a study on portrayals of older adults in Dutch television commercials, Martine Van Selm, Gerben Westerhof and Bruno de Vos (2007) found some changes in representations of ageing between 1993 and 2007 as the roles of ageing people became more diverse and less stereotypical (i.e. not only as helpless and as victims). Most media representations of ageing, though, remain stereotyped. For example, a study showed that in prime-time television drama series in Taiwan, 'older' characters (beyond the age of 65) are less present and dominant and are often linked to age, while in general, representations of death and ageing people in Chinese TV drama appear as reflections of dominant stereotypes about ageing (e.g. not able to take care of oneself) (Lien, Zhang and Hummert 2009). It seems that older people, particularly women, rarely appear in popular Western media representations (Edström 2018), and the few representations where they appear, usually portray them in supporting roles (e. g. helpless old lady, silly and funny grandmother). For example, Myrna Hant (2007) point out that fictional formats mostly portray women of age as 'others,' pathetic, frail mothers and grandmothers.

As Kristina Wallander (2013) explains, dominant discourses about elders in the past were mostly about 'decline and loss', but some scholars (e.g. Whelehan and Gwynne 2014) have argued that the media industry has recently changed and started targeting seniors. Targeting ageing people includes a visibility of ageing people in the representations the media industry creates. Nonetheless, ageing generally is depicted in a stereotypical way as lacking agency within its otherness or simply not represented (Van Bauwel 2018). For example, Colin Milner, Kay Van Norman and Jenifer Milner (2012, 25–28) argued that media portrayals of ageing often present older adults as 'super seniors' who are healthy, wealthy and age-defying. Milner, Van Norman and Milner (2012) argued that these stereotypes draw on the value of productivity in Western societies, where good citizens are those who are healthy, independent and also economically and socially agentic. These representations seem to include emerging discourses on ageing linked to consumerism pointing at some sort of 'good' ageing and self-care (Featherstone and Hepworth 1995). These representations of good ageing often portrayed idealised cultures of 'agelessness' (Katz 2000), 'successful ageing' (Rozanova 2010, Lövgren 2012) and 'good ageing' in healthy bodies (Cuddy, Norton and Fiske 2005). These new stereotypes indicate the construction of a third age identity (Wearing 2012, 2015), and there seems to be new visibility casted to the concept of 'graceful agers' (Dolan and Tincknell 2012), differing from the very narrow, negative stereotype of ageing as decline and loss.

However, both older and recent representations of ageing people are often gendered, showing men and women in different ways. Rosie White (2014) stated that the intersection of age and gender can result in double discrimination. According to previous studies on TV representations of ageing women (Hant 2007, Ylänne 2012, Wallander 2013, Oró-Piqueras and Wohlmann 2015, Van Bauwel 2018), they mostly appear in daytime soap operas and sitcoms. Most studies on ageing women have found that humour seems to be the key element in representations of ageing femininities (Harwood and Howard 1992); indeed, television content has limited portrayals of intersecting femininities and ageing and rarely depicts them outside the context of humour. For example, in a recent study on portrayals of older women in Finnish contemporary comedy films, Hanna Varjakoski (2019) found more female characters in genres that are centred on humour and use stereotyping as part of their modus operandi. Varjakoski (2019) concluded that comedies discipline ageing women who are non-stereotypical and 'too' non-conforming and independent and represent them as 'out of control' for not conforming to the norms and values linked to ageing women. Similarly, White's (2014) analysis showed that ageing femininities represented as transgressive are disciplined and policed as 'inappropriate'.

In this context, White (2014) highlighted 'cultural ambivalences' in representations of ageing femininities in television comedies that often depict ageing women as 'young-old', healthy, active 'girls'. The representational practice of 'girlification' seems to be very present in representations of femininities in contemporary popular visual cultural. Similar practices such as 'boyification', though, seem to be absent or not as present. Ageing men are more often represented as ageless, healthy, strong and 'still' virile. An older man with a younger woman is an example of this virility discourse on masculinity and, in particular, ageing masculinities. These representations of glamourous ageing femininities can be seen as a fetish against the 'toxicity of decay and decline' and may be described as a 'cultural celebration of physiological exception' (Jennings and Oró-Piqueras 2016, 80–81). Often embodied by celebrities (Marshall and Rahman 2015, Fairclough-Isaacs 2015), this 'successful' ageing accords with representations of postfeminist, non-perfect young girls and their bodies as in the television series *Girls* (2012–; Perkins 2014). This ideology characterises ageing as 'sexy but not sexual' (Jennings and Oró-Piqueras 2016), referring to the fact that ageing could be articulated as 'sexy' but without any active sex life or representation of sexual practices. Stephen Katz and Barbara Marshall (2003) also argued that the neoliberal discourse on ageing does not embrace elders' sex lives as active. Television fiction and lifestyle media focus on the health and fitness of the old body as keys to successful, active ageing (Boudiny 2013) and construct a specific discourse of the ageing body (Gilleard and Higgs 2013). For example, Iolanda Tortajada, Frederik Dhaenens and Cilia Willem (2018, 2) explained that television series such as *Grace and Frankie* successfully

> break[s] with some of the mainstream ageist representations of women as youthful, sexy and desirable [...] and challenges the idea that all women are obsessed with trying to look and act young while being anxious over growing old. [...] Despite some stereotyped portrayals (the hippy and the posh lady)

and certain conventions (not showing the naked mature female body), [it] somehow questions post-feminist popular culture. By putting their finger on the complexities of ageing, the show implicitly makes a point against gendered ageism.

Still, we can say that in contemporary popular cultural texts we can generally distinguish between a limited set of stereotypes about ageing women. In this respect, we may argue that these post-feminist television series do not represent all bodies as equal and do not make the 'beauty-is-everywhere' discourse omnipresent (Van Bauwel 2018). As I showed in my study of the representations of ageing femininities in post-feminist television fiction, representations of ageing femininities have increased in the past five years. However, this visibility in the three series examined (*Sex and the City* 1998–2004, *Desperate Housewives* 2004–2012; *Girls* 2012–) does not translate into bodily representations of ageing (Van Bauwel 2018).

Representations of ageing femininities: limited strategies?

Popular visual culture seems to have represented ageing femininities more often in recent years, but as studies have shown, the contemporary popular media space still lacks diversity and has only a limited set of stereotypes. A discourse on ageing certainly circulates in this space, but it represents the same themes and a limited set of subject positions at the intersection of age and gender, particularly for femininities. Certain stereotypical tropes are reiterated, and in general, the same representational practices seem to be the current strategies for portraying ageing femininities. For example, representations of 'cougars', sexually active ageing women and the 'beauty is everywhere' discourse are omnipresent in popular media texts, but ageing femininities themselves are not very visible. Ageing women occasionally are part of fictional storylines, but globally, such representations seem to be absent or draw on only a limited set of practices of, for example, strong and diverse aged main characters in television fiction. Similar conclusions can be drawn when looking at the ageing bodies in these representations: we don't see as many bodies of aged people as for example we see faces of ageing people, and we do not see their bodies as we do those of young people. Discourses on 'shaming', 'successful ageing' and body modifications due to ageing are present but not visible, and visual representations of these bodies seem to be lacking (Woodward 2006, Whelehan 2013a, Whelehan and Gwynne 2014).

Despite research showing discursive ambiguities in the texts, we generally can distinguish three sets of discourses: masking ageing, losing femininity and gaining wisdom with age (Van Bauwel 2018). The representational practice of articulating ageing femininity as the masking of ageing makes age and ageing very present themes, often embodied by narrative storylines centred on plastic surgery and active sex lives. Similarly, Dafna Burema (2018) concluded that magazines represent 'cougars' as sexually empowered, but at the same time age remains a source of hierarchy. They are less sexy than younger women or sometimes portrayed as desperately trying to remain young.

This masking is often linked to the idealised culture of 'agelessness' (Katz and Marshall 2003) and growing older without ageing (Katz 2001). In fashion advertisements, for example, we can distinguish a change as 'the aesthetic constructions of alternative understandings of beauty may make room for a wider spectrum of female ages in visual culture, as is the case with the recent trend of using elderly women in fashion' (Jerslev 2018, 359). However, at the same time, 'one could ask whether the cool aesthetic expresses a subtle form of ageism, a new way of denouncing the signs of the ageing body and face by masquerading as young and trendy' (Jerslev 2018, 359).

An example of a popular television show in which the masking ageing discourse is omnipresent is *Sex and the City* (1998–2004). This show on the friendships of five young women in Manhattan often presents the notion of agelessness and is seen as part of the celebration of youth in contemporary consumer culture (Woodward 2006, Whelehan and Gwynne 2014). This romantic comedy often thematises this discourse – for example, in the way some main characters do not seem to grow older or even have an age (e.g. Samantha and her non-age). However, the show also problematises agelessness, articulating issues such as denial of ageing. Masking of ageing is linked to the notion of girlification, as mentioned. Meredith Nash and Ruby Grant (2015, 10) explained this girlification of adult women:

> Like *SATC* [*Sex and the City*], *Girls* evokes the post-feminist archetype of the modern 'girls', a term that was made popular in Helen Gurley Brown's (1962) *Sex and the Single Girl*, which introduced the concept of an independent, urban, reflexive, and sexually active, modern woman.

Such girlification is often seen as a post-feminist representational practice of characterising ageing women as acting 'foolishly', 'out of control' and 'out of order', like rebellious teenagers. More positively, studying ageing femininities in the television drama series *Six Feet Under*, Sherryl Wilson (2012) argued that rule-breaking behaviour positions older female characters in 'complex ways' and addresses issues of ageing in non-stereotypical ways.

The second discourse discussed focuses on the theme of losing femininity. For example, at the beginning of the first episode of *Desperate Housewives* season 5, the narrator poses the following question: 'We ask ourselves, "Where did the time go? … How did the woman I saw each day in the mirror become someone I don't even recognise"?' Losing time seems to be equated with losing femininity, and so-called real ageing only emerges when women settle down, marry and have children. This comedy-drama about a group of women living on the same street in a fictional town in the United States has a more parodic undertone than *Sex and the City*, but its representations of ageing femininities seem to be constructed from the same sets of tropes. In particular, having children in different media texts means rapid ageing, and in a recurring frame, losing femininity consists of the surrender of a life of one's own, the end of youth and negative perspectives on bodily changes. Ageing is stressed as inherent to married life and motherhood. The losing femininity discourse is also articulated through the theme of menopause, seen as a deviant marker of ageing

(Cooper 2008). Whelehan (2013b, 89) pointed out the following: 'As Sandra Coney reminds us, "Ageing in men is normal; menopause is not."' A 'sexist double standard of ageing' seems to be at work. According to Rosalind Cooper (2008, 31), 'the negative image of loss of sexuality and youth [...] tend[s] to dominate references to menopause' (Van Bauwel 2018).

The third and final discourse concerns wisdom that comes with age. This discourse is less present in popular fictional media content but can occasionally be found in television content, advertising and fashion media. With the wisdom of age, ageing women are seen as having more knowledge and experience and fewer uncertainties. For example, *Grace and Frankie* often portrays the two main characters as possessing knowledge and experiences, so they know what they want. At the same time, their insecurities are also portrayed. Similarly, the narrator who begins and concludes each episode of *Desperate Housewives* can be interpreted as the 'voice of older women' rather than the traditional voice of God (Van Bauwel 2018). The narrator, Mary Alice Young, is only heard and never seen and is around forty years old when she dies in the pilot. Being represented as 'older' or ageing against the juxtaposition of 'being dead' locates her in this position as the bearer of wisdom. Another *Desperate Housewives* character, Mrs McCluskey, can also be considered a signifying element in the discourse on female ageing and wisdom:

> She is an outcast and does not fit in the nucleus of the other female main characters; furthermore, while she is not part of this specific community that comprises the scope of the narrative, she has knowledge, including secrets. She can be seen as the embodiment of the 'other', or what Wallander (2013) referred to as the 'old-old other'. As the 'other', Mrs McCluskey has more knowledge than anyone else on the show, including insight into all of the main characters' secrets.
>
> *(Van Bauwel 2018, 9)*

Conclusions

In the body of work on ageing femininities in popular culture (e.g. Dolan and Tincknell 2012, Edström 2018), most research has considered representations in television content (e.g. Burema 2018, Van Bauwel 2018, Wallander 2013, Lien, Zhang and Hummert 2009, Hant 2007, Kubey 1980), fiction and advertising (e.g. Jerslev 2018, Lewis, Medvedev and Seponski 2011). Although contemporary media content has recently included ageing people to a larger extent, we can still question the visibility of ageing women and femininities in contemporary visual media. The so-called new visibility of ageing and, more specifically, ageing femininities has been embodied by celebrities represented as embracing their age or ageing. For example, we have discussed Fonda's portrayal in fashion representations, advertising, feature films and television series. These celebrities often endorse products and brands related to their third-age identities such as luxury, health and wellbeing goods.

As Justine Coupland (2009) pointed out, contemporary popular culture has articulated new ideologies and representations of ageing embedded in a commercialised discourse promoting a certain 'look' for ageing. It is stressed that 'looking good' is important and universally desirable, especially for women and those who are not so young. One important finding in Coupland's (2009) study is the discourse on 're-claiming a youthful appearance', which has become visible in fashion magazines and media content more generally. Recently, the changing sociocultural conditions for the ageing body have become fact, as have the media's changing authority and relationship to the ageing body (Givskov and Petersen 2018). These dual and often paradoxical discourses are mediated, but we can question whether these new representations (sometimes described as postfeminist) are disrupting the visual arena (Twigg 2018). Although some scholars (e.g. Healey and Ross 2002, Gilleard and Higgs 2011) have argued that interest in ageing has risen due to audience-driven and economic motives, we must also critique the present discourses on ageing femininities.

We note that popular visual culture has a limited set of available representations of ageing femininities. The rather positive 'beauty is everywhere' discourse is omnipresent (Van Bauwel 2018), but we do not see many visual representations of older women. As Jennings and Oró-Piqueras (2016) argued, a 'cloak of invisibility' still covers ageing women on television. Although some recent television fictional series such as *Grace and Frankie* have drawn on ageing femininities, this visibility does not translate into bodily representations of ageing. Across many types of media outlets, we can see a highly present discourse that often discusses ageing but does not represent it visually. Ageing feminine bodies are especially absent despite the discourse on good or successful ageing. When represented, discourses on ageing femininities are articulated in many ways, and the 'discursive space is used differently' (Van Bauwel 2018), but three representational strategies or practices (i.e. masking of ageing, losing femininity, ageing wisdom) seem to be repeated throughout popular visual culture. The highly present discourse on masking ageing reflects the neo-liberal discourse on successful ageing and can be seen as the glamourous anti-ageing or ageless discourse. As Tordajada, Dhaenens and Willem (2018, 2) stressed, 'mature female bodies are only interesting to media and popular culture insofar as they can be used as a visible proof of a deferred ageing process; otherwise, they remain hidden from the public eye, as they are considered to be abject bodies that do not fit the aforementioned model of successful ageing'.

Representations of ageing femininities in popular culture – particularly visible, embodied representations – have a limited set of articulations. Successful ageing, for example, is discursively constructed through girlification. The second discourse on representations of ageing femininities centres on the theme of losing femininity. Far more negative than the discourse on masking ageing, the losing femininity discourse is often linked to articulations of shame and the theme of menopause. The third and least dominant discourse in contemporary media texts is the wisdom of ageing, which displays a more positive attitude towards ageing. Fictional media programming uses humour as a key element in the construction of representations of femininities, which can be seen as a two-sided, paradoxical representational practice. Ageing femininities are mocked in satire, parody and humour, but at the same time, stereotypical ideas are questioned and sometimes transgressed. This paradoxical duality is present in contemporary representations of ageing femininities. We can thus still question the role of media in the construction of ageing femininities and ask whether the Dove ad campaign tagline 'Withered or wonderful? Will society ever accept old can be beautiful?' will remain relevant in the future. If the contemporary trend of television fiction content targeted at ageing people is further developed, the amount of representation of ageing femininities will expand and hopefully also the diversity within these representations of femininities.

References

Boudiny, K. (2013). 'Active ageing': From empty rhetoric to efficient policy tool. *Ageing and Society* 6, 1077–1098.

Burema, D. (2018). Cougars or kittens? The rpresentation of celebrity cougars and their toyboys in gossip media. *Feminist Media Studies* 18(1), 7–20. doi:10.1080/14680777.2018.1409968.

Chan, M. (2012). Foreword. In J. Beard, S. Biggs, D. Bloom, L. Fried, P. Hogan, A. Kalache and J. Olshansky (eds), *Global Population Ageing: Peril or Promise?* (pp. 3–4). Geneva: World Economic Forum.

Cooper, R. (2008). Prime time: TV menopause, queerly a case for review. *SQS—Suomen Queer—Tutkimuksen Seuran Lehti* 3 (2), 30–37.

Coupland, J. (2009). Time, the body and the reversibility of ageing: Commodifying the decade. *Ageing & Society* 29(6), 953–976.

Cuddy, A., Norton, M. and Fiske, S. (2005). This old stereotype: The pervasiveness and persistence of the elderly stereotype. *Journal of Social Issues* 61(2), 267–285.

Desperate Housewives (2004–2012). Television series. Seasons 1–8. USA: ABC/Cherry Productions.

Dolan, J. and Tincknell, E. (eds) (2012). *Ageing Femininities: Troubling Representations.* Cambridge: Cambridge Scholars Press.

Edström, M. (2018). Visibility patterns of gendered ageism in the media buzz: A study of the representation of gender and age over three decades. *Feminist Media Studies* 18(1), 77–93. doi:10.1080/14680777.2018.1409989.

Fairclough-Isaacs, K. (2015). Celebrity culture and ageing. In J. Twigg and W. Martin (eds), *The Routledge Handbook of Cultural Gerontology* (pp. 361–368). London: Routledge.

Featherstone, M. and Hepworth, M. (1995). Images of positive ageing. In M. Featherstone and A. Wernick (eds), *Images of Ageing: Cultural Representations of Later Life* (pp. 179–190). London and New York: Routledge.

Gilleard, C. and Higgs, P. (2010). Ageing without agency: Theorising the fourth age. *Ageing & Mental Health* 14(2), 121–128.

Gilleard, C. and Higgs, P. (2011). The third age as a cultural field. In D.C. Carr and K. Komp (eds), *Gerontology in the Era of the Third Age: Implications and Next Steps* (pp. 33–49). New York: Springer.

Gilleard, C. and Higgs, P. (2013). The fourth age and the concept of a 'social imaginary': A theoretical excursus. *Journal of aging studies* 27(4), 368–376.

Girls (2012–present). Television series. Seasons 1–4. USA: HBO.

Givskov, C. and Petersen, L.N. (2018). Media and the ageing body: Introduction to the Special Issue. *European Journal of Cultural Studies* 21 (3), 281–289.

Grace and Frankie (2015–present). Television series. Seasons 1–2. USA: Netflix.

Hant, M. (2007). Television's mature women. A changing media archetype: From Bewitched to The Sopranos. http://repositories.cdlib.org/cgi/viewcontent.cgi?article=1021&context=csw.

Harwood, J. and Howard, G. (1992). 'Don't make me laugh': Age representations in a humorous context. *Discourse Society* 3(4), 403–436.

Healey, T. and Ross, K. (2002). Growing old invisibly: Older viewers talk television. *Media Culture Society* 24(1), 105–120.

Lacy, S. (dir.) (2018) *Jane Fonda in Five Acts*. Documentary. USA: HBO.

Jennings, R. and Oró-Piqueras, M. (2016). Heroine and/or caricature? The older woman in Desperate Housewives. In M. Oró-Piqueras and A. Wohlmann (eds), *Serializing Age: Ageing and Old Age in TV Series*, Ageing Studies VII (pp. 71–89). Bielefeld: Transcript.

Jerslev, A. (2018). The elderly female face in beauty and fashion ads: Joan Didion for Céline. *European Journal of Cultural Studies* 21(3), 349–362. https://doi.org/10.1177/1367549417708436.

Katz, S. (2001). Growing older without aging?: Positive aging, anti-ageism, and anti-aging. *Generations* 25, 27–32.

Katz, S. (2000). Busy bodies: Activity, ageing, and the management of everyday life. *Journal of Ageing Studies* 14(2), 135–152.

Katz, S. and Marshall, B. (2003). 'New sex for old: Lifestyle, consumerism, and the ethics of ageing well'. *Journal of Ageing Studies* 17(1), 3–16.

Kubey, R. (1980). Television and ageing: Past, present, and future. *The Gerontologist* 20 (1), 16–35.

Lewis, D.C., Medvedev, K. and Seponski, D.M. (2011). Awakening to the desires of older women: Deconstructing ageism within fashion magazines. *Journal of Ageing Studies* 25(2), 101–109.

Lien, S.C., Zhang, Y.B. and Hummert, M.L. (2009). Older adults in prime-time television dramas in Taiwan: Prevalence, portrayal, and communication. *Journal of Cross-cultural Gerontology* 24(4), 355–372.

Lövgren, K. (2012). 'They see themselves as young': The market addressing the older consumer. In Virpi Ylänne (eds), *Representing Ageing. Images and Identities* (pp. 53–67). Houndsmills: Palgrave Macmillan.

Marshall, B. and Rahman, M. (2015). Celebrity, ageing and the construction of 'Third Age' identities. *International Journal of Cultural Studies* 18(6), 577–593.

Milner, C., Van Norman, K. and Milner, J. (2012). Media's portrayal of ageing. In J. Beard, S. Biggs, D. Bloom, L. Fried, P. Hogan, A. Kalache and J. Olshansky (eds), *Global Population Ageing: Peril or Promise?* (pp. 25–28). Geneva: World Economic Forum.

Monster-in-Law (2005). Feature film directed by Robert Luketic. USA: New Line Cinema.

Nash, M. and Grant, R. (2015). Twenty-something girls v. thirty-something Sex and the City women. Paving the way for 'post? feminism'. *Feminist Media Studies* 15 (6), 976–991.

Oró-Piqueras, M. and Wohlmann, A. (eds) (2015) *Serializing Age: Ageing and Old Age in TV Series*. Bielefeld: Transcript.

Perkins, C. (2014). Dancing on my own: Girls and television of the body critical studies. *Television: The International Journal of Television Studies* 9(3), 33–43.

Rozanova, J. (2010). Discourse of successful ageing in *The Globe & Mail*: Insights from critical gerontology. *Journal of Ageing Studies* 24(4), 213–222.

Sex and the City (1998–2004). Television series. Season 1–6. USA: HBO.

Six Feet Under (2001–2005). Television series. Seasons 1–6. USA: HBO.

Tortajada, Y., Dhaenens, F. and Willem, C. (2018). Gendered ageing bodies in popular media culture. *Feminist Media Studies* 18(1), 1–6. doi:10.1080/14680777.2018.1410313.

Twigg, J. (2018). Fashion, the media and age: How women's magazines use fashion to negotiate age identities. *European Journal of Cultural Studies* 21(3), 334–348. https://doi.org/10.1177/1367549417708432.

Van Bauwel, S. (2018). Invisible golden girls? Post-feminist discourses and female ageing bodies in contemporary television fiction. *Feminist Media Studies* 18(1), 21–33.

Van Selm, M., Westerhof, G.J. and de Vos, B. (2007). Competent and diverse. portrayal of older adults in Dutch television commercials ten years later. *Journal of Geriatrics* 3 (2), 57–65.

Varjakoski, H. (2019). In and out of control: Portraying older women in contemporary Finnish comedy films. *European Journal of Cultural Studies*. https://doi.org/10.1177/1367549419839881.

Wallander, K. (2013). Successful images of successful ageing? Representations of vigorous elderly people in a Swedish educational television programme. *Nordicom Review* 34(1), 91–103.

Wearing, S. (2012). Exemplary or exceptional embodiment?: Discourses of ageing in the case of Helen Mirren and Calendar Girls. In J. Dolan and E. Tincknell (eds), *Ageing Femininities: Troubling Representations* (pp. 145–159). Cambridge: Cambridge Scholars Press.

Wearing, S. (2015). Moms Mabley and Whoopi Goldberg: Age, comedy and celebrity. In D. Jermyn and S. Holmes (eds), *Women, Celebrity and Cultures of Ageing: Freeze Frame* (pp. 59–76). London: Palgrave Macmillan.

Whelehan, I. (2013a). Ageing appropriately: Postfeminist discourses of ageing in contemporary Hollywood. In J. Gwynne and N. Muller (eds), *Postfeminism and Contemporary Hollywood Cinema* (pp. 78–97). Basingstoke: Palgrave Macmillan.

Whelehan, I. (2013b). Fiction or polemic? Transcending the ageing body in popular women's fiction. In I. Whelehan and J. Gwynne (eds), *Ageing, Popular Culture and Contemporary Feminism: Harleys and Hormones* (pp. 29–46). Basingstoke: Palgrave Macmillan.

Whelehan, I. and Gwynne, J. (2014). Introduction: Popular culture's 'silver tsunami'. In I. Whelehan and J. Gwynne (eds), *Ageing, Popular Culture and Contemporary Feminism. Harleys and Hormones* (pp. 1–13). Basingstoke: Palgrave Macmillan.

White, R. (2014). Funny old girls: Representing older women in British television comedy. In I. Whelehan and J. Gwynne (eds), *Ageing, Popular Culture and Contemporary Feminism: Harleys and Hormones* (pp. 155–171). Basingstoke: Palgrave Macmillan.

Wilson, S. (2012). Beyond patriarchy: Six Feet Under and the older woman. In J. Dolan and E. Tincknell (eds), *Ageing Femininities: Troubling Representations* (pp. 123–130). Cambridge: Cambridge Scholars Press.

Woodward, K. (2006). Performing age, performing gender. *National Women's Studies Association Journal* 18(1), 162–189.

Ylänne, V. (ed.) (2012). *Representing Ageing: Images and Identities*. Houndsmills: Palgrave Macmillan.

Youth (2015). Feature film directed by Paulo Sorrentino. Italia: Indigo Film.

10

'OLD DIRTY POPS AND YOUNG HOT CHICKS'

Age differences in pornographic fantasies

Susanna Paasonen

Introduction

In a media culture saturated with depictions of young, or at least youngish, fit and able bodies, the parameters of sexual desirability appear to be very narrowly drawn. For its part, pornography has been perennially accused of having a narrow and stereotypical cast of body types, despite both the factual heterogeneity of sub-categories and fringes that make up the genre, or the high popularity of the search terms such as 'mature', 'stepmom', MILF ('mother I'd like to fuck') or GILF ('grandma I'd like to fuck') connected to female performers. Expanding the scope of inquiry, this chapter sets out to investigate the ageing, older male body as an ambivalent pornographic fantasy figure through a survey made by the Finnish public service broadcasting company YLE in 2017 to chart women's pornographic preferences, likes and dislikes. In what follows, I focus on one survey question in particular, 'Is there a thing that turns you on, even if it feels confusing, gross or weird? Tell more!' Out of some 1,000 responses to the question, 81 specifically mentioned age differences, the overwhelming majority of them addressing the simultaneous attractiveness and repulsiveness of ageing male bodies. Drawing on these responses, this chapter then inquires after older male bodies as sexual fantasy figures, asking what they speak of the dynamics of pornographic representation more generally.

Found data (notes on method)

The survey was set up for collecting background material for a pornography-themed episode of the Finnish lifestyle programme *Jenny+* foregrounding body positivity with a feminist bent. The show's first season run parallel with *Vaakakapina* ('Scale Revolt'), a 2017 online self-acceptance and wellbeing initiative by the same editorial team that made extensive use of social media: vibrant web presence with podcasts, blogs, and information resources was complemented with a Facebook page allowing for peer participation. Targeted at female respondents, the questionnaire on porn preferences could be accessed on Vaakakapina's website where it attracted 2,438 responses, the majority (1,334) being from people aged 20 to 35. The survey consisted of both open-ended and multiple-choice questions charting preferences in body hair, close-ups of genitalia, blowjobs, sex toys, facial cumshots, and much more in the overall spectrum of 'hot or not' (on the scale from 1 to 5). The open-ended questions inquired after the respondent's views of women and men in porn, the kinds of characters they would like to see, the things they would want to change, and the kinds of scenes that they would prefer to see in porn – and, moving into inquiring after experiences of sexuality more broadly, the contributors' perceptions of their own desirability and sex life. The survey was playful yet serious in its aim to chart Finnish women's views on porn performers, preferred scenes, likes and dislikes. Importantly, the volume of these voluntary responses was relatively large (considering the overall national population of 5.5 million).

I literally landed on this trove of data when the show's producer contacted me for a research-based commentary and interview. When reading through the survey, my interest soon clustered on the question cited above (*Is there a thing that turns you on, even if it feels confusing, gross or weird? Tell more!*), which inquired about porn consumption in connection with disgust and shame – partly because these had long been my own themes of scholarly interest, partly because the question was posed in a manner few scholars would or could phrase (McKee 2009), framing porn use in terms of disgust, and partly because the responses were both rich and bountiful. When the producer asked what I found surprising in the material, I identified the responses connected to the pornographic appeal of older men in particular. This is also my focus here.

In the course of my interaction with the editors and producers of *Jenny+*, I was granted research access to the survey. The data was collected fully anonymously and made available to me in formats that did not allow for connecting individual replies to the only background information collected, namely the respondents' ages. The survey participants submitted their replies to be used for journalistic purposes and to be cited in this context: the material was also used in six podcasts enacting the contributors' preferred porn scenarios, available on the YLE website since 2017. While there was no informed consent secured for later scholarly uses, the degree of publicness involved in any academic publishing is of much modest scale than that which the respondents knowingly prepared for their replies to enter. Considered in terms of research ethics, it is unlikely that the respondents could be harmed by the fully anonymous data being repurposed for scholarly ends. Furthermore, academic insight was also part of the journalistic production process that this data was used for: drawing on it for scholarly purposes simply means adding finer granularity to analysis, contributing to existing knowledge formation on women's uses and experiences of pornography, and citing the data in a different context when doing so.

The data comes with obvious limitations in terms of research design, from what themes and questions were raised to how the data was technically collected and stored. I received the responses as PDF, Microsoft Excel and Word files where it is hard to tell where a singular contribution begins or ends. It is not always clear as to what lines are from the same respondent and, indeed, how many responses there are to any singular question. This makes quantitative analysis impossible as other than the simple identifying of terms. For this article, I searched for terms connected to age: 'old' ('vanh★') and age ('ikä'). This resulted in 81 responses mentioning age differences in the context of sexual and pornographic fantasy. In addition, one response specified older men as a turn-off (as 'slimy and disgusting', 'pitiful, desperate old geezer').

While the survey design was beyond my influence or control, it also came with unsuspected benefits as journalists are able to pose the kinds of questions that scholars are trained to veer away from. This also results in replies that scholars most likely would not get. Consider, for example, the question central to this article *(Is there a thing that turns you on, even if it feels confusing, gross or weird? Tell more!)*, which was instrumental in getting to the themes that the journalists wanted to address, and which directly led the respondent on by foregrounding the role of disgust, aversion and shame (the file with the responses was titled 'porn survey shame', 'pornokysely häpeä. doc'). While many respondents critically commented on, and rejected, the association of pornographic and sexual fantasies with grossness, oddity and shame, many more described the ambiguities they felt towards the imageries that aroused them.

Jenny+ was voted the most popular Finnish lifestyle programme in 2017. Its broad following lent the survey call particular visibility and public resonance as people are, understandably, more willing to take time to respond to questionnaires set up by a show that they appreciate than those launched by academic institutions. The replies were often casual in their tone, as in confessional sentences decorated with emojis, and, given the length of some responses, they had taken some time to compose. The data is, in short, rich inasmuch as it is scattered. It should also be noted that the feminist profile of *Jenny+* attracts an audience base well versed in issues of gender equality and social justice: the survey responses examine sexual tastes from a generally non-normative angle and often with considerable analytical skill. All the following translations from the material are mine and aim to communicate its original tone and style.

Fascination and contrast

First of all, nine survey participants simply mentioned older men as turns-on, four others elaborating on their 'unattractive' and 'repugnant' (and hence 'hot') qualities. For some, older men were fascinating and sexually attractive as such:

> Older man attract
> Age difference. Older man. This has always been, and still remains a bizarre obsession. At the moment I have a sex relationship with a man who's almost 60 (we have a 10-year age difference) who's so hot that I can't keep his photo as my phone's wallpaper.

Responses where ageing men were sexual fantasy objects in themselves – as preferred partners, non-normative objects of sexual desire and even possible sexual fetishes – were nevertheless few in comparison to the volume of accounts where titillation emerged from witnessing age differences in sexual scenes on-screen. Most responses merely mentioned 'age differences' and the combinations of 'old man and young woman' as fascinating yet possibly baffling pornographic preferences, without detailing what their appeal was or what affective dynamics they came wrapped in. Meanwhile, others elaborated on their preferred combinations of bodies and scenarios, highlighting the physical contrasts and relations of domination and control between the performers: 'Older men with younger women. Large differences in size (larger man and a small woman), being taken by force, domination.'

Respondents routinely mapped drastic age differences onto a binary gender model and combined these with equally stark juxtapositions in body sizes and types, following the logic of dramatic contrast that clearly marked apart, and separated, the bodies displayed: 'anal sex, much older man (40–65) and a younger woman (20–30). And differences in body types, e.g., muscular (man/woman) x fat (woman/man)'; 'mismatch between the actors, older/rougher man with a younger/innocent woman'. Such juxtapositions are in line with how porn generically accentuates embodied differences and identity categories such as race, social class, nationality, gender and age so that the acts in which such boundaries are transgressed become more pronounced and elaborate. The play with compositions of hard and soft, large and small, dark and light, wrinkly, hairy and smooth cuts across all kinds of scenarios, holding allure and resulting in figures of sexual fantasy: 'Old and fat men with young girls'; 'voyeurism, contrasts e.g. dark and blond or young girl and older man'. As porn tends to play out embodied differences in hyperbole, it is not surprising that the genre has regularly been identified as sexist, racist and ageist in the stereotypes and scenarios that it caters. Displays of embodied differences are regularly set in scenes of power play that draw their attraction from tenacious social hierarchies and power relations (Paasonen 2010a). For half of the survey respondents, age differences mapped onto gender hierarchies in ways leaving older men firmly on top:

> Old men and young women together. Face-slapping. Breast sucking always works, enough for a film as such. A woman dominated, bound, imprisoned, forced, servicing a man. Bdsm
> Old man dominates a young woman.
> Old pervy geezers with a young woman
> Domination, young woman and an old uncle.

Relations of control connected to age were described as titillating yet also something best kept to one's self for the sake of being potentially embarrassing or difficult to explain, possibly even to one's own self:

I'm turned on by older men and authority. But the older man can't be old but older than myself. I'm also turned on by group sex and domination. I'm pretty open about sex but wouldn't perhaps outright admit what porn I watch.

Respondents repetitively associated age differences with the dynamics of domination and submission, yet 24 of them did not specify a preferred gender dynamic and three preferred women on top:

For some reason, a large age difference between porn characters is sometimes attractive. A really old woman and a really young man, or vice versa. It's not disgusting but confusing. Double penetration is also a turn-on when watched, and the insertion of different objects into a vagina. 'Teaching' and 'mentoring' is also a turn-on, so that one of the partners teaches or advices the other one on what to do.

Across age differences, the dominant partner could be male or female as the senior one in the position to teach: 'Teacher student, older man/woman and younger woman. "Forbidden fruit",' although older men remained in clear majority. As discussed below, such scenarios drew much of their attraction from taboos concerning intergenerational sex (combined with a taste for dominance and submission).

The excerpts cited here focus on age, yet many are taken from longer responses giving multiple examples of things that turned people on in porn, age differences being one variable among others. In some instances, this resulted in lengthy, disjointed listings of scenes, characters, motions, settings, and acts. Other listings outlined particular dynamics of interest connected to domination, manly masculinity, awkwardness, and vulnerability alike:

Manly man smelling of testosterone, hairy and robust, with brisk moves and a strong will. In porn, an older man and a younger woman. Multiple cream pies and gangbang scene. Man watching his wife with another. Plumber, etc.

Just awkwardness. E.g., an old dude with the routine of experience caressing a young girl to climax, gruesomeness, ugly people, helpless people, perhaps a little pitiful but pretty people, a beautiful young man with a hand prosthesis and no woman. This is all strange but arousing …

Fisting, Japanese rape porn in public transport. Taking clothes off from another. Age differences.

Older men were described as prop-like placeholders for dominance and authority, yet their desire and pleasure were also foregrounded – as in men using women for their own gratification and their guttural sounds conveying the enjoyment taken: 'A man older than myself 60–70 fucking a younger woman. Enforced sex. Bi-sex. Watching men masturbate. A man would look at me and masturbate. Men making sounds.' In addition to contributing to the power dynamics of a scene, older men stood repeatedly for sexual seniority in the positive sense of experience, mastery, authority and knowledge. For some respondents, they equally stood for realness in ways that support the more general promise of hardcore video porn to authentically show, and to document, the sexual details that have taken place in front of the camera (e.g., Williams 1989): 'Growling, animalism. Old people/oldsters. In these, the realness of the scenes'; 'Older man, younger woman. Brisk, real action, no holding back or pretence.'

Nevertheless, respondents seldom elaborated as to why or how they saw older men as markers of realness, authenticity or the lack of pretence. It can be that some older men perform in semi-amateur productions, or in ones with lower production values indicative of their not fully professional status. In this framework, pornographic displays may be identified as 'labours of love' motivated by sexual pleasure rather than financial reward (Paasonen 2010b). As non- or semi-professional performers, older men stand out from the normative male bodies of commercial porn, which, in responses to another open-ended survey question, were described in negative terms as muscular, big, masculine, dominant, hairless, stiff, machine-like 'fuck machines'. Such hegemonic porn bodies were, in fact, regularly described as 'disgusting' for representing self-centred, sexist and non-communicative masculinity. In this juxtaposition, older men then stood for something more real and relatable, less machine-like, and thereby more human (on porn bodies, see also Rooke and Figueroa 2010, p. 226; Tsaliki and Chronaki 2016, pp. 178, 183). Additionally, respondents may consider older performers to be as if automatically attracted to younger partners, and for the scenes in question to mediate authentic sexual desire. This, again, entails an ageist norm positioning certain bodies as sexually desirable, and others much less so.

Disgusting!

As the survey question inquired after preferences that were simultaneously arousing, confusing and disgusting, responses came with an automatically negative framing. In addition, respondent specifically identified older men as dirty, lewd, ugly, fat, unattractive, slimy and disgusting: 'The thought of old dirty pops and young hot chicks. :-O'; 'Notably older and unattractive men'; 'Old men. Like OLD. This confuses and disgusts.' Here, ageing male bodies became sites of physical and symbolic, or moral, disgust. Scholars have associated sensations of disgust with embodiment of the excessive sort gesturing towards the materiality and mortality of human bodies (e.g., Kolnai 2004, pp. 2, 31–32; Miller 1997, pp. 19, 96–100). In addition to being attached to and drawing boundaries around things or body parts that are considered materially filthy, such as rancid food evoking visceral physical responses of nausea, disgust equally involves the morally objectionable (Cohen 2005, pp. viii, xi; Tomkins 2008, p. 413). Sexuality comprises a particular terrain of disgust, from bodily fluids to the activities producing them, and to sexual preferences deemed 'deviant' for being in conflict with moral (or moralistic) norms (Kelly 2011, p. 31). A disgusting object may simply deviate from that which is socially appropriate, for as affect theorist Silvan S. Tomkins (2008, p. 416) suggests, '[d]epending upon what the society, the parent, peers, or the individual himself has come to regard as true, good, and beautiful, an endless variety of objects and behavior become capable of evoking disgust'.

Sensations of disgust are ones of undesired physical proximity where the offensive object comes too close for comfort, even as this proximity may well be exciting. In the survey responses, such proximities took place in relation to young female bodies: 'Young woman and old/ugly man is a perennial favourite. And huge saggy balls.' The bodies of older men in porn then became sites of nastiness as they entered into close contact with much younger bodies, breaking against cultural norms concerning intergenerational sex:

> Old, fat men fucking young girls. My own orgasm comes for sure if on the video you hear how the old man enjoys immensely and groans and makes sounds. Preferably also so that the girl doesn't moan but perhaps resists, a little frightened by the new situation.

It was both the bodies of older men ('huge saggy balls') and their desires and actions towards younger women that were depicted as revolting yet titillating.

As I argue below, while not necessarily taboo as such, large age differences between sexual partners rub against normative assumptions concerning 'good sex' (Rubin 1989), namely sex that is deemed socially mandated and acceptable. Some respondents seemed to consider the bodies of older men as disgusting and nasty merely due to wrinkles, sagging skin or body weight in a straightforward ageist manner. These unattractive bodies held considerable, albeit ambivalent appeal, as it is not uncommon for sexual desires to be oriented towards the disgusting or shameful (Tomkins 1995, pp. 401–402). Disgust can well amplify sexual desire while the lack thereof can lead to lessened excitement, interest and intensity. If a sense of shame haunts one's sexual explorations, then violations of the taboo can feel particularly magnetic, and fantasies involving 'the most flagrant indecencies or humiliations' may hold particular appeal (Tomkins 2008, p. 183). In porn, that which disgusts then often also arouses, excites and fascinates (see Paasonen 2011). The figure of a disgusting old man encapsulates a broader dynamic where pornographic scenarios play with the forbidden, holding appeal for that reason. The intentionally 'dirty, naughty, debasing and disgusting style or quality of porn' (Attwood 2002, p. 96) affords particular kinds of affective resonance that can lend its products with transgressive appeal. At the same time, disgust both links to and gives shape to boundaries and norms of acceptability, which, in the realm of sexual fantasy, are regularly tried and tested, stretched and exceeded. Fantasies similarly test and help to build hierarchies between different bodies.

In her analysis of Ron Jeremy's porn star image and subsequent semi-mainstream fame, Emily Shelton (2002 p. 199) argues that his popularity is rooted in flamboyant physical undesirability. Contrary to the body standards of contemporary mainstream porn where male performers are fit, muscular, groomed and shaved, Jeremy is 'overweight, unkept, the antiaesthetic of the inferred pornographic fantasy, an atypical pornographic hyperbole that translates into none of the customary prototypes'

(Shelton 2002, p. 118). Shelton (2002, pp. 132, 138) argues that the connection between disgust and desire explains much of Jeremy's cult status, defining him as an unattractive, 'unthreatening everyman' for straight male viewers to comfortably identify with without the risk of homoerotic titillation. In other words, in categorising Jeremy's body as unattractive, even disgusting, Shelton sees him as both a less-than-physically-perfect straight proxy and a distancing device among his straight male fan base. Considered in the light of the survey material focusing on the preferences of female porn consumers, the figure of an unattractive, older male body nevertheless entails more ambiguity and versatility in terms of sexual fantasies than this analysis allows for.

Taboo!

Many respondents directly associated the attraction of age differences with the lure of taboo and the forbidden fruit, framing them as markers of extremity in porn even comparable to rape, necrophilia, and zoophilia:

> Haha, should you ask! I don't like excrement or hurting but many taboo topics are really arousing in the sense of fantasy. With taboos I mean e.g., large age difference, family relations, other special relations of power, enforcing without physical violence, grannies, dwarfs, animals, whatnot.:D The strange and the forbidden are a turn-on!
>
> Rape fantasies, real brutal almost 'animal' sex, blood, necrophilia, psychological manipulation, age difference, most common 'taboos' (e.g. teacher-student, cheating, voyeurism/public spaces) … and other stuff that I don't want to mention

Here, age differences became equated with sexual extremity indicative of 'far out' fetish preferences falling firmly outside the parameters of social acceptability, to the point that some respondents did not feel comfortable anonymously communicating them all. It should, however, be noted that the women involved did not necessarily identify their sexual fantasies as disgusting as such. Rather, the responses gesture toward boundary work in the realm of sexuality where the presumedly bad is a turn-on and where the socially acceptable blends into the kinky, yet where fantasies are recurrently plied apart from the physical fabrics of everyday life: 'Older men (know what they want). Strong men (know what they want). Also, the IDEA of sex with an animal or a relative is arousing (although I really wouldn't do that).'

In 'Thinking Sex', originally published in 1984, Gayle Rubin (1989, p. 281) outlined a sexual hierarchy separating 'good, normal, natural, blessed sexuality' at its heart from the opposite, namely 'bad, abnormal, unnatural, damned sexuality'. Visualised as a circle with inner and outer spheres, Rubin's hierarchy is centred on the 'charmed circle' of good sex involving heterosexual, married, monogamous, procreative, non-commercial exchanges that are practiced in pairs, in a relationship with members of the same generation, in private and without the aid of pornography, props toys or other paraphernalia. Meanwhile, the outer rim of bad sex may be homosexual, unmarried, promiscuous, non-procreative, or commercial. It may be masturbatory or take place in orgies, may be casual, may cross generational lines, and may take place in 'public', or at least in the bushes or the baths. It may involve the use of pornography, fetish objects, sex toys, or unusual roles.

(Rubin 1989, p. 281)

Within this model, which has been influential in feminist and queer studies tracking the value mechanisms through which certain sexual likes are marginalised and others embraced and celebrated (e.g., Warner 2000, pp. 1–5; Kulick 2005, p. 208), inter-generational sex, like pornography, falls to the terrain of 'bad sex'. Inter-generational porn can then be seen as 'doubly bad' in breaking against multiple norms, becoming comparable to incest in its taboo qualities: 'Sex between relatives, sex between young and a considerably older person'; 'Forbidden relations and excitement. E.g., cheating, young&old, stepdad etc.'; 'Porn with a young ('teen') and a clearly older person. Incest porn.'

The division of 'good' and 'less good' sex is firmly social, normative and prescriptive, and its dynamics give rise to a range of fantasies and titillations precisely due to the constant boundary work that it entails. For Tomkins, divisions within sexuality as 'split into a white, pure surface and a black, murky one' is due to the social, religious and private symbolism attached to it. It then follows that sexuality 'becomes a bipolar magnet attracting to itself the wide-eyed wonder, excitement and joy' on the one hand and 'the equally exciting fusion of curiosity, fear and shame' on the other (Tomkins 2008, p. 252). In the realm of sexual fantasies, these two dimensions, or affective registers, fuse together for, despite the seeming clarity of the binary divide, sexual fantasies easily veer towards the taboo and refuse to settle on a singular object.

Ultimately, such boundary work and the affective complexity that it involves help to outline human sexuality as a system of norms and boundaries that hold magnetic appeal by keeping things apart in hierarchical arrangements. Here, the taboo is appealing for the virtue of being forbidden: following Georges Bataille (1986, p. 48), it 'is always a temptation to knock down a barrier; the forbidden action takes on a significance it lacks before fear widens the gap between us and it and invests it with an aura of excitement'. The play with taboo involves transgression which, in the realm of porn, allows for overcoming social convention but also for exceeding the boundaries of self-control and routine presentations of the self through the intensities of bodily sensation:

(Imaginary) domination and precisely so that the man is clearly older. Confusingly many things. I'm attracted by situations where the other partner feels physical sensations so strongly that they lose control over their self and their body. This includes both uninhibited orgasmic moaning or not even being able to stand up, also different situations connected to vomiting, defecation, urination and childbirth.

Taboo, then, calls for the breaching of boundaries, or at least for experimenting with them in the realm of sexual fantasies: in the course of this, boundaries become redrawn, and possibly reinforced.

Porn taxonomies and boundary work

Many survey respondents connected the attractions of age differences and the bodies of older men to long listings of highly specific preferences in pornographic scenes and sub-genres, as in

> Dog/animal licks something from skin or crotch. Teenage + 30+ sex together. Watching animals have sex. Mild domination. Young girl forces a boy or some-one older to lick. Face-sitting. Anime: aliens, tentacles, furry, bara, yuri, yuki. Porn fan fiction. In anime and comics also (step)mom/aunt/cousin + a lonely teenage girl/boy. Blowjobs among men and fucking/chaining a 'tough guy'.

Such listings speak of extensive literacy and cultural capital concerning con-temporary pornography of the kind that scholars have associated with young adults (cf. Albury 2014; Dawson, Gabhainn and MacNeela 2020). They are endemic of a context where pornographic sub-genres seem to be forever diversifying and mul-tiplying on online platforms. This is partly due the centrality of contextual meta-data (such as tags, categories and content descriptions) in and for the searchability of audiovisual content on platforms where the distribution and consumption of porn is centralised. Users are able to search for highly specific terms and markers, many of which might not have been recognisable only two decades ago. The diversifi-cation of categories is further fuelled by the imperative of offering clearly recogni-sable novelties and specialities – from BDSM niches to animated 3D bodies, and beyond – with the aim of reaching new consumers and sparking the curiosity of regular visitors, as it is by the push to incorporate performers of different ages and body types. (see Paasonen 2011, pp. 38–40, 69–70.) Within this framework, age differences feature as specialities and novelties among others.

While the combination of performers of different ages is hardly novel in either heterosexual or gay porn, the category of 'old and young' has gained specific recognisability on video aggregator platforms catering to mass porn audiences (rather than focusing on target groups with niche interests). At the time of writ-ing, a search for 'old and young' produced some 181,000 hits on both Pornhub and xHamster and 558,000 on Xvideos, variations of older women with younger women and men, older men with younger men and women, transgender per-formers and group sex (a.k.a. gangbang) scenes being in ample supply. In the pairing of older men and younger women, video brands such as 'Blue Pill Men' and 'Oldje' feature a homosocial male ensemble enjoying advances in erectile dysfunction medication in order to engage in sex with women 30 to 50 years their junior. All this results in hyperbolic juxtapositions of age, body type and skin texture.

This line of production, or subgenre, may seem targeted at ageing heterosexual male audiences attracted to the spectacle of extended potency and the availability of much younger female partners, yet the survey complicates such assumptions by offering old men as objects of younger female fascination, aversion, disgust and arousal – often simultaneously so: 'I find a slimy slightly dumpy older man with a young woman disgusting but for some reason it's quite a turn-on.' I argue that the survey helps to complicate understandings of pornographic attraction as being based on similarity, proximity and identification with the characters and acts depicted on the screen. According to such a line of thinking, a preference for certain kinds of pornographic sub-genres or sexual fantasies is indicative of a sexual preference, or identity that one may or may not be willing or able to act out (see Paasonen 2011, pp. 181–182). This somewhat causal and narrow view is premised on continuity, or at least contiguity, between sexual interests and desires between scenes watched on a screen and those acted out with partners. The survey responses, again, point to women frequently enjoying scenes premised on distance and detachment. It would be an unwarranted stretch of imagination to argue, for example, that preferences for scenes with older men and teenage women involve identification with any of the characters as such. Rather, their attractions seem to lie in the overall dynamics of the scenes, their power differentials, displays of bodily differences, relations of control and depictions of desire. Many respondents in fact identified scenes and acts that they would most definitely *not* want to act out themselves, or which differed drastically from their own self-understandings as ones that attracted them on the level of fantasy:

> As a straight woman I'm turned on by lesbians in porn, older men.
> Old/young coupling. Does not fascinate me personally but on the screen yes.
> Age difference stuff (young & old) although in real life I'm not turned on by very old men.

Such listed scenarios extended from fisting to extreme humiliation, rape, watersports, anal, lesbian and gay male sex. Respondents emphasised the differences, or indeed the gaps, between their pornographic turn-ons and the kinds of acts and partners they preferred in their sexual relationships. In some cases, this perceived gap in preferences expanded to values and politics underpinning one's very notion of the self:

> Unequal power relations, i.e. young-old, teacher-student, doctor-patient, etc. Especially ones that would be morally dubious in real life.
> Politically completely incorrect and repulsive setting of a young beautiful virgin girl and a lewd 50+ uncle-person that the girl wants to surrender to. Also, a religiously strict frame is arousing – sexual abstinence and saving it for the marital bed, also copious breeding. Really anything that's against all my feminist values in real life.

More than a mere gap, such distinctions between fantasy and real-life cast that which one finds dubious and opposes to on moral and/or political grounds as key pornographic titillations. Given the feminist bent of *Jenny+*, it was not surprising for survey participants to elaborate on disconnections between their personal politics and pornographic likes: this was a recurrent theme in responses addressing scenes of non-consent in particular. The survey question did not specify whether the arousing yet confusing, gross or disgusting preferences addressed were pornographic ones, or ones otherwise connected to one's sexual likes, hence conflating the two. It then follows that some respondents focused on their sexual dreams and intentional daydreams, which they described as being more extreme, bizarre or taboo than the pornography they consume:

> I have lots of sex dreams. In dreams I can be with a woman, with the old gramps next door and sometimes even with my sister. Such things feel disgusting when awake. In dreams they work and I usually even get multiple orgasms during one dream. In porn I don't like anything special, I'm pretty boring with that.

Notably many respondents juxtaposed their sexual fantasies with their lived experiences, interests, attachments and identifications (that is, 'real life'). Scenes of incest and rape, for example, were marked out as ones which, experienced in real life, are purely the stuff of trauma while nevertheless holding strong appeal as fantasies. This also meant that their audiovisual depiction in porn could be experienced as too literal, ethically problematic, or otherwise 'off' in its point of view:

> Slight domination is arousing, perhaps also acted non-consent. I often dream of teenage girls (when hormones rage and desires are easily awoken) with older men in a higher position (teacher). But I don't like seeing that in porn, it's disgusting depicted through someone else's eyes.

Here, pornography is not positioned as a cultural template for extreme sexual fantasies inasmuch as a dissatisfactory rendition thereof. While some respondents described discrepancies between their sexual fantasies and real-life preferences as disconcerting, others highlighted differences between the two, positioning fantasies as sources of self-pleasure, as in this excerpt listing scenarios of non-consent, non-human partners, and unattractive sexual partners, some of these too extreme to really even fantasise about:

> Sex in public is factually so lewd that one wouldn't quite dare to fantasize about it … . Also, animalistic characters are surprisingly hot (i.e. the bear in the fairy tale, Snow-white and Rose-red) and I'm embarrassed to admit to being turned on by e.g. manga where insects and rodents with large cocks fuck tiny fairy girls. Also, repulsive male characters (too old, so-called fat, stupid, too young) are a turn-on. Why? I often see bloody arousing dreams of fucking really horrible types.

Gaps between sexual fantasies, porn use and other sexual preferences are no novelty in scholarship on the topic. Existing studies have shown that women and men both straight and queer consume gay male pornography (Neville 2018; Robards 2018), and that people describe watching things in porn that they like or would want to do, those that they do not want or cannot do, as well as coming across things without much planning or premeditation involved, possibly in search of serendipitous thrills, or merely to alleviate boredom (e.g., McKee et al. 2008; Smith et al. 2015; Paasonen et al. 2015). It follows that no direct correlations should be presumed between a person's sense of sexual identity and her/his/their pornographic preferences. This certainly does not mean that sexual-pornographic fantasies would not matter, or that they would be somehow external to the self: rather, they are spaces for exploration, juxtaposition, play and reflection that animate one's body through positions of proximity and distance alike. Sexual fantasies can simply remain disconnected from practices involving other people, their allure owing precisely to their spectral nature.

Ambivalent disgust

As a sexual and pornographic preference connected to disgust, older male bodies emerged in the survey as objects of desire, aversion and titillation; as figures of sexual seniority and dominance; and as guarantees of representational authenticity and realness. For some respondents, they added to the overall hyperbolic aesthetics of porn where embodied differences are highlighted, exaggerated and juxtaposed; for others, these bodies were extreme in themselves as deviations from generic male porn embodiment. In yet other responses, older bodies were simply marked out as disgusting without further explanation in ways indicative of firmly ageist norms of attractiveness and acceptability. Across the responses, older male bodies in porn were addressed as objects, rather than associated with the personal attributes of any particular performer, role or character. As objects, these representational bodies then held instrumental value in aiding sexual arousal and masturbatory pleasure.

All this points to the multi-faceted nature of sexual fantasies, actions, preferences, and interests that comprise one's sense of sexual self, as itself emerges in encounters in the flesh, through screens and in combinations thereof. The survey responses indicate the tendency of sexual and pornographies fantasies to amalgamate: even while clear distinctions are drawn between what one is (desires and does) and what else turns one on (as in dreams and fantasies), the pornographic cannot easily be pulled apart from the broader realm of turn-ons and taboos contributing to sexual desires, pleasures and attachments. Within these, age is merely one axis of difference through which bodies are brought together in hierarchical arrangements, juxtaposed and enjoyed. From the position of the respondents, the majority of them women in their twenties and thirties, older men – in frequent combination with female teen bodies – stood for familiar otherness encapsulating social relations of power, forms of gendered agency and norms of physical desirability, yet in ways exceeding any singular dynamic or hierarchy. Disgust, the affect inquired after in the survey question, carved out spaces for uneasy enjoyment taken in a hyperbolic theatre of difference and control which, while positioned as belonging to the realm of fantasy, drew its force from social hierarchies and the breaching of norms concerning sexual acceptability and normalcy. Within this realm, the very bad can be very good – or at least very hot.

References

Albury, K. (2014). Porn and sex education, porn as sex education. *Porn Studies*, 1(1–2), 172–181.

Attwood, F. (2002). Reading porn: The paradigmatic shift in pornography research. *Sexualities*, 5(1), 91–105.

Bataille, G. (1986). *Erotism: Death & Sensuality*. Transl. by M. Dalwood. San Francisco: City Lights.

Cohen, W.A. (2005). Introduction: Locating filth. In W.A. Cohen and R. Johnson (eds), *Filth: Dirt, Disgust, and Modern Life* (pp. vii–xxxviii). Minneapolis, MN: University of Minnesota Press.

Dawson, K. Gabhainn, S.N. and MacNeela, P. (2020). Toward a model of porn literacy: Core concepts, rationales, and approaches. *Journal of Sex Research*, 57(1), 1–15.

Kelly, D. (2011). *Yuck! The Nature and Moral Significance of Disgust*. Cambridge, MA: MIT Press.

Kolnai, A. (2004). Disgust. In B. Smith and C. Korsmeyer (eds), *On Disgust*. Chicago: Open Court.

Kulick, D. (2005). Four hundred thousand Swedish perverts. *GLQ: A Journal of Lesbian and Gay Studies*, 1(2), 205–235.

McKee, A. (2009). Social scientists don't say 'Titwank'. *Sexualities*, 12(5), 629–646.

McKee, A., Albury, K. and Lumby. C. (2008). *The Porn Report*. Melbourne: Melbourne University Press.

Miller, W.I. (1997). *The Anatomy of Disgust*. Cambridge, MA: Harvard University Press.

Neville, L. (2018). *Girls Who Like Boys Who Like Boys: Women and Gay Male Pornography and Erotica*. London: Palgrave Macmillan.

Paasonen, S. (2010a). Repetition and hyperbole: The gendered choreographies of heteroporn. In K. Boyle (ed.), *Everyday Pornography* (pp. 63–76). London: Routledge.

Paasonen, S. (2010b). Labors of love: Netporn, Web 2.0, and the meanings of amateurism. *New Media and Society*, 12(8), 1297–1312.

Paasonen, S. (2011). *Carnal Resonance: Affect and Online Pornography*. Cambridge, MA: MIT Press.

Paasonen, S., Kyrölä, K., Nikunen, K. and Saarenmaa, L. (2015). 'We hid porn magazines in the woods': Memory-work and pornography consumption in Finland. *Sexualities*, 18(4), 394–412.

Robards, B. (2018). 'Totally straight': Contested sexual identities on social media site Reddit. *Sexualities*, 21(1–2), 49–67.

Rooke, A. and Moreno Figueroa, M.G. (2010). Beyond 'key parties' and 'wife swapping': The visual culture of online swinging. In F. Attwood (ed.), *Porn.com: Making Sense of Online Pornography* (pp. 217–235). New York: Peter Lang.

Rubin, G. (1989). Thinking sex. In C.S. Vance (ed.), *Pleasure and Danger: Exploring Female Sexuality* (pp. 267–319). London: Pandora.

Shelton, E. (2002). A star is porn: Corpulence, comedy, and the homosocial cult of adult film star Ron Jeremy. *Camera Obscura*, 17(3), 115–146.

Smith, C., Attwood, F. and Barker, M. (2015). Figuring the porn audience. In L. Comella and S. Tarrant (eds), *New Views on Pornography: Sexuality, Politics and the Law* (pp. 267–285). Santa Barbara, CA: Praeger.

Tomkins, S.S. (1995). *Exploring Affect: The Selected Writings of Silvan S. Tomkins*. Ed. by E.V. Demos. Cambridge: Cambridge University Press.

Tomkins, S.S. (2008). *Affect Imaginary Consciousness: The Complete Edition*. New York: Springer.

Tsaliki, L. and Chronaki, D. (2016). Producing the porn self: An introspection of the mainstream Greek porn industry. *Porn Studies*, 3(2), 175–186.

Warner, M. (2000). *The Trouble with Normal: Sex, Politics, and the Ethics of Queer Life*. Cambridge, MA: Harvard University Press.

Williams, L. (1989). *Hard Core: Power, Pleasure, and the 'Frenzy of the Visible'*. Berkeley: University of California Press.

11

HUSTLING AND AGEISM IN THE FILMS EASTERN BOYS AND BRÜDER DER NACHT

Antonio A. Caballero-Gálvez and María Porras Sánchez

Introduction

In general terms, the contemporary gay imaginary has assumed the hetero-normative canons of the hegemonic masculine body determined by the health/fitness imposed parameters, based on youth and hyper-muscularity (Dyer 2002, Bersani 2009, Kimmel 2004). The elderly gay body has been relegated to the margins of the gay scene, inhabited by their peers and hustlers – the only bodies they can access upon payment (Coleman 2009, Callen 1998). Although at an international level male prostitution often involves Hispanic and Asian boys, male prostitutes in Europe are mainly Eastern men (Kuhar & Takács 2007).

This study aims at analysing the abject body of the elderly gay man in contrast with the marginal body of the Eastern Euroepan male hustler. The films in question – *Eastern Boys* (Robin Campillo 2013) and *Brüder der Nacht* (Patric Chiha 2016) – show a stark difference between young marginal bodies – the objects of desire – and older bodies – the agents of such desire. As we argue, the image of a young and callow, strong and healthy body is spreading within the gay community as a new stereotype associated to Eastern Europe, possibly through the emergence of several gay porn companies such as BelAmiOnline and CzechHunter (Brennan 2019). Furthermore, the study addresses invisibility in male prostitution scene, the main topic on both films. While female prostitution is eminently visible, male prostitution is characterised by invisibility and discretion (Guasch & Lizardo 2017). This is why we apply to the films a hermeneutical analysis based on an intersectional approach.

Both films reflect the difficulties male gay community faces when reaching late adulthood. Many gay single men confront loneliness, non-acceptance and marginality when they reach mature age (Berger & Kelly 2001, Slevin & Linneman 2010). Their bodies do not attract young men hooking up at gay bars on weekends, and they do not share the same profiles in online sex and dating apps either (Rodriguez,

Huemmer & Blumell 2016). Both gay bar dance floors and dating apps show a manifest materialisation of the hegemonic masculine beauty (Jönson & Siverskog 2012, Caballero-Gálvez & Herrero-Jiménez 2017). Therefore, they lack a physical or virtual space for finding a sexual partner or boyfriend. To have sex, some mature gay men resort to prostitution or join marginal and/or minority sexual practices around darkrooms or cruising spaces.

The criminalisation of homosexuality is one more among the many human-rights problems that sexual minorities face in Eastern Europe countries. The taboo around sex and gender was breached in 1987, when it became a trending topic in the former communist countries. Prostitution, homosexuality and other gender and sexual subversive identities, which had been considered a symptom of Western degeneracy, were finally acknowledged by the Soviet Union in 1987. Nevertheless, sex and gender issues still face obstacles in present-day Russia, as the governmental opposition to sexual education and different forms of sexual freedom manifest.

At the beginning of the 2000s, Bulgaria and Romania made efforts to avoid decriminalisation through the construction of national identities in which homosexuality was suppressed. However, this identity did not fit within a common European framework that promoted the rights of sexual minorities. The European Union and the Council of Europe effectively pressured Bulgaria and Romania to acknowledge sexual rights in exchange for their participation in the common political space.

In order to analyse the way in which homosexual minorities are represented in the popular culture of post-Soviet Europe and understand the homosexual phenomenon in the complexities of this geopolitical space, Western rhetoric must be avoided. This means looking at homosexuality not as a symptom of a decadent bourgeoisie but as a representation of the critical state of masculinity in Eastern Europe (Baer 2002). Although it is still difficult for the former Soviet republics to accept homosexuality as a legitimate source of pleasure, recent studies (Baer 2009, Nachescu 2005) illustrate examples of gay visibility and sexual experimentation unconstrained by the boundaries of homosexual and heterosexual identities. However, these positions are excluded from the films that we analyse. The young characters in them are not proud of being homosexual or of participating in homosexual practices.

Before carrying out this analysis, we will dissect the definitions and concepts used for the study of the selected films. First, we will discuss the features of gay male bodies in Western contemporary society and the divergent features with the canons of beauty linked to hegemonic masculinity (Connell 2005, Carabí & Armengol 2008). We will also draw a brief outline of male prostitution to understand better the specific context of both films. Such outline will highlight the problems of this type of prostitution, mainly characterised by its invisibility (Ham & Gerard 2014). Lastly, we will address the new stereotype of gay masculinity which has appeared in the gay porn industry in recent years: a young, white and hairless body, mostly associated with Eastern Europe young men (Bunzl 2000). This study will focus on identifying the above-mentioned elements and concepts as represented in both films.

The resulting critical discourse analysis is based on a hermeneutic approach as defined by the visual analysis of audio-visual texts, focusing on narrativity and its visual representation in the films *Eastern Boys* and *Brüder der Nacht*. The hermeneutics of images uses an interdisciplinary interpretation of images through audiovisual analysis. We draw from Paul Ricoeur's definition of hermeneutics as 'the theory of the operations of understanding in their relation to the interpretation of texts' (1981, p. 43). Also, we will follow Gonzalo Abril's 'visual semiotics' (2007, p. 26). For Abril, audiovisual documents must be interpreted in context, in both a reflexive and a discursive way. This double approach allows us to understand the configuration of these two films and describe the power relations portrayed in them.

Brüder der Nacht shows the inside of Romany male prostitution following a group of young Romany men who arrive in Vienna looking for freedom and easy money. If *Brüder der Nacht* portrays Eastern hustlers, *Eastern Boys* describes the loneliness of a mature gay man. The film deals with topics such as prostitution, immigration and commodification, but it also alludes to the transformative power of love. For the purpose of our analysis, it is important to underline that *Eastern Boys* is a fictional film, whereas *Brüder der Nacht* blurs the boundaries between fiction and documentary. Therefore, both the visual and the narrative treatments are completely different.

Old gay male bodies in contemporary Western society: fears and stigmas

From a general perspective, there should not be relevant differences between heterosexual and gay elders. The gay community is a heterogeneous group with the same inner differences of any social group: ethnicity/race, religion/spirituality, education and socioeconomic status. However, with a closer look the dissimilarities become evident. Most Western gay adults have lived within societies and families that have not taken into consideration the peculiarities of their sexuality (Jablonski, Vance & Beattie 2013). Unfortunately, many mature gay men have experienced discrimination, derision and physical and psychological abuse (Whitford 1997). These attacks have been frequently instigated by religious or medical organisations, labelling gays and lesbians as criminals, perverts or sexual deviants (Haber 2009). As Nancy J. Knauer has stated:

> Today, a complex interplay of ageism and homophobia obscures the identities of gay and lesbian elders and keeps their concerns securely removed from public view. Stereotypical ageist and homophobic constructions work in tandem to make the very notion of gay and lesbian elder impossible because seniors are not sexual and homosexual are, by definition, only sexual.
>
> *(2011, p. 55)*

Thus, invisibility and homophobia work hand in hand qith ageism, as both *Brüder der Nacht* and *Eastern Boys* show.

Furthermore, gay and heterosexual mature men enjoy success differently. According to the study 'What Are Older Gay Men Like? An Impossible Question?' (Berger & Kelly 2001), mature success is based on three pillars: health, finances and relationships. A straight man reaching old age with good health, a sound financial situation and a married partner is the example of a successful life. Do gay men meet the same requirements? According to Berger and Kelly, the groups only coincide with regard to the financial factor. In the case of gay men, their health is thwarted by HIV/AIDS, and the majority do not reach old age with a stable partner or married, partly because of the legal problems in many countries. Nevertheless, there is a counterpart: the stigma of ageing that all men share (Adelman 1990) is handled more wisely by the gay community. Like any other vulnerable group, they have learnt to coexist and to overcome the social stigma attached to their sexuality. The same happens with independence or living in solitude. After suffering social and/or family rejection, many homosexuals have learnt to live independently most of their lives.

It is not by chance that the gay community worships the body; there is a clear correlation with the appearance of the HIV/AIDS pandemic. By strengthening the body and building muscle, the homosexual community attempted to leave behind those sick bodies marked by Kaposi's sarcoma. In the end, this tendency was appropriated as a sign of virility – denied to gay men – by heteropatriarchal society, accompanied by the frequent objectification and judgement of gay men bodies through 'body oppression', 'body fascism' or 'lookism' (Signorile 1997, Suen 2017).

In recent years, the subject of ageing and its effects on the body has become an increasingly relevant field of study, approached by different theoretical perspectives. Ageing theories have proved that the body is the site on which identity is built in mature age (Twigg 2004, Katz 2005). The role of the body in the processes of identity construction is a psychological issue but also a social and cultural construct (Twigg 2004). Gay men bodies, as well as women's, are subjected to an objectifying male gaze (Suen 2017). Today's consumer society has created a negative image of old age associated with loss and decline (Marshall & Katz 2002), in contrast to the superior status of youth (Woodward 2003).

In addition, beauty standards associated with gay men's bodies have undergone many changes over time (Wood 2004). The representation of masculine fashion in the film *Orlando* (Sally Potter 1992) is a good example. At present, many people obsess over their bodies. The epitome of male beauty is a young, healthy and muscular man (Bersani 2009, Connell 2005). This ideal of masculine perfection derives from the beauty standards in Ancient Greece, which have re-emerged at different moments in Western history such as the Renaissance (e.g. Michelangelo's *David*) or the social hygiene movement at the turn of the 19th century. The totalitarian regimes of the 20th century saw this ideal of perfection and harmony at its height.

It is through muscles that masculinity has found a way to counteract the weak and effeminate body (Suen 2017). Thus, hyper-muscularity has changed gender hierarchies; at present, the personification of hegemonic masculinity is an urban, white, professional man who is also strong and healthy. As Estrella de Diego has pointed out, this ideal is also connected to class, since muscular bodies were first connected to gay counterculture and the working class and were then appropriated by the middle class as a model of bourgeois homogenisation (2018, pp. 133–135). In terms of representation, masculinity is much more monolithic that femininity because of its connection with power.

In the seventies, effeminate gay bodies – Wilde's lover Lord Alfred Douglas or young Dalí as idealised by Federico García Lorca – were replaced by the he-man ideal – Marlon Brando or Kirk Douglas. This change of identification was motivated not only by hyper-muscularity (Signorile 1997) but also by the subversive attitudes shown by the gay community when dressing and imitating the symbols of hegemonic masculinity. This has been defined by Richard Dyer as 'phallic hysterics' (2002), characterised by a hyperbolic masculinity associated with muscle-building as the sign of the natural power of the phallus, as illustrated by the bodies of Delmas Howe or Tom of Finland.

The tyranny of beauty standards not only oppresses young women but is also present in the imaginary of young gay men. As Brotman, Ryan and Cormier state, 'ageism, beauty and youthfulness are values that reign supreme within most gay and lesbian communities' (2003, p. 198). Facing the supremacy of the beauty of the young male body within gay mainstream culture, the mature gay body becomes 'subject to structural marginalisation of ageism' (Suen 2017, p. 401). A gay man suffers more pressure regarding his physical appearance than a heterosexual man. As a result, an 'accelerated aging' (Bennett & Thompson 1991, p. 61) takes place. This implies that the gay man identifies as old/mature before the heterosexual man. From this stance, the mature gay man feels excluded and marginalised in 'a world in which being old equates to being unattractive and being attractive is a precondition for entry' (Jones & Pugh 2005, p. 258).

In the case of both analysed films, *Brüder der Nacht* and *Eastern Boys*, a new hegemonic gay body emerges, a paradigm based on a young, white and beardless body. For instance, in the first sequence of *Brüder der Nacht*, the director pays homage to one of the queer cinematic icons, *Querelle* (Rainer Wener Fassbinder 1982) by dressing one of the hustlers with a sailor's cap and calling him 'captain'. Both films address the pressure exerted by beauty and aesthetic care, through the facial treatment and hair-styling sessions of the hustlers in *Brüder der Nacht* and the sculptural body of the Boss when he exercises in *Eastern Boys*.

In *Eastern Boys*, the protagonist is Daniel (Olivier Rabourdin), a mature bourgeois man who seeks the sexual services of a boyish Ukrainian hustler, Marek/ Rouslan (Kirill Emelyanov). Marek's gang seizes the opportunity to raid Daniel's apartment, while he is threatened by the Boss (Daniil Vorobyov), an imposing, gym-pumped young man. These three men are the main characters in the film, three men who stand for three antagonistic masculinities: from the innocence and sweetness of Daniel to the violence and ruthlessness of the Boss. He runs a criminal network that exploits vulnerable migrants in need to provide clandestine services for elites. By presenting an older Daniel preying on youth, Campillo highlights certain aspects of the gay experience that reinforce social inequality and are prone to criminalisation (homophobia, homelessness, poverty).

Regardless of the differences in terms of lifestyle and age, a specular loneliness is unveiled through the sexual encounters between Daniel and Marek/Rouslan. Delicately, without any suggestion of pornography, the director shows a simple encounter between two people who need to satisfy their sexual needs, embrace human contact, feel loved during a fleeting moment and experience pleasure with a stranger, something complex and mundane at the same time.

In the case of *Brüder der Nacht*, mature bodies belong to customers seeking sex at the 'Rüdiger' bar. Three older men appear, two overweight and a third concealed behind a hat and sunglasses, highlighting the client's invisibility versus the hustler's visibility. Hustlers refer to these men, ranging from 60 to 65, as 'grandpas', and their shame of having sex with them is evident. The image of mature gays in *Brüder der Nacht* is degrading as they are described as 'perverts' sexually driven by sadomasochism and sodomy.

Young marginal bodies as objects of desire

Although neither of the films falls into the genre category of gay porn, we consider that the masculine stereotypes represented in both audiovisual texts reproduce certain models promoted at present by the gay porn industry. As Rothmann describes: 'The manner in which pornography in films and internet sites alike manifest themes associated reflects the identity construction of certain gay men' (2013, p. 27). Arguably, pornography promotes roles that are reproduced in real life.

Despite the cultural, structural and geographic differences in these kinds of popular assumption assimilated and 'normalised' via the internet, John Mercer (2017) signals the endurance of the multiplicity of male models represented in present-day porn. Gay porn categories such as 'the boy-next door', 'the international', 'daddy', 'the amateur', 'the star', 'twink', 'the 'fooled' straight man' or 'the beautiful boy' are present in both *Eastern Boys* and *Brüder der Nacht*.

Gay pornography has contributed to the generation of a 'saturated masculinity' (Mercer 2017) that functions as a transitional discursive bridge between the heteronormative vision of masculinity and sexuality of the 1980s and 1990s and the current era of hyper-connectivity and virtual globalisation. The development of a saturated masculinity challenges and brings into focus the representation of race within gay porn imaginary. As Ellerson points out: 'Gay masculinity is thus "Americanised" or "Europeanised", rather than encouraged to take on an "Africanised" configuration' (2005, p. 61). Therefore, the hegemonic masculinity remains ethnocentrically white.

Turning to the nationality of the bodies represented in contemporary gay pornography, the fall of the Soviet Union prompted the interest of the pornography industry and prostitution networks in Eastern Europe bodies, exotic and forbidden until then (Bunzl 2000, Štulhofer & Sandfort 2005, Sikes 2010). Although the situation varies from one country to another, from the generalised acceptance of the Czech Republic (Widmer, Treas & Newcomb 1998) to the extreme homophobia of Albania (Van der Veur 2001), sexual minority groups in post-communist societies are more stigmatised than in the West.

Masculine porn shows proliferated in the Czech Republic with the Velvet Revolution in 1989, after the communist government relinquished power in Czechoslovakia, paving the way for a market economy and a multi-party democracy. As Alan W. Sikes in 'Politics and Pornography: Czech Performance in the International Arena' (2010) suggests, the Czech Republic is one of the largest producers of gay pornography at present, promoting platforms as widely known as *BelAmiOnline* and *CzechHunter*. This is a striking difference with other countries of the area such as Bulgaria or Romania, where the gay community is barely visible (Nachescu 2005). Even though the hustlers in both films are mostly Romanian, Bulgarian hustlers also appear in *Brüder der Nacht*, while in *Eastern Boys* there are also Russian and Chechen characters.

The differences between Romanian and Bulgarian hustlers are evident in *Brüder der Nacht*, since Romanians complain of the Bulgarians charging low prices and they are divided into differentiated groups. The rates are explained in the film and prices vary depending on the sexual practices and the duration of their services. Usually, there is more supply than demand. According to the film, there are 20 hustlers for two clients, and most of the boys share ties as family and friends. Comradeship and mutual support makes their existence more endurable. The newcomers usually enjoy a success that quickly diminishes. In the film, one of the protagonists tells how he had arrived in Austria to help his family five years before and was then fired for not speaking the language. He then became a beggar and, finally, a sex worker. All the characters complain of the lack of work in their home countries and the exploitation they suffer in Austria. That is why many of them turn to prostitution since they believe it is an easy and fast way of making money. Even though pornography is absent from the film, most of the characters fit within the described profile: dark-haired white boys, beardless and lean.

In *Eastern Boys* different languages mingle – Russian, Ukrainian, Chechen, French and English – not for communication but rather for watching, exploiting, capturing and annulling each other. Youths do not work as hustlers for money in this film, but prostitution is their last resort in moments of despair, after fleeing some of the ongoing armed conflicts in Europe. Except for Marek/Rouslan, the boys' nationalities remain undistinguished.

Bodies in *Eastern Boys* range from the slender, dark-eyed Marek/Rouslan to the blue-eyed, blond-haired and muscular Boss. They both share the characteristics of gay porn actors participating in audiovisual porn production companies such as BelAmiOnline or CzechHunter. Several boys in *Brüder der Nacht* fit within the same spectrum as well.

Invisibility on the male prostitution scene

Considering that male prostitution is fundamentally a hidden industry in any part of the world, sex workers and clients alike tend to hide their identity. Nevertheless, while clients remain anonymous, sex workers frequently need to expose themselves and they transfer their image rights to their firm. This representation, mostly based on gender – even racial – stereotypes, has had a great impact on the perception and public awareness of prostitution. As a matter of fact, invisibility reflects power, with the customer occupying a higher status while the sexual worker remains vulnerable; both films show the power of the older man versus the insecurity of the youth; the supremacy of the buyer versus the subjection of the one who sells his body. Rather than a privilege, the invisibility of those involved in street sex work has become a recurrent tradition that enables the client to identify the sex worker through a series of distinctive features for their 'consumption' (Keeler & Jyrkinen 1999). This way, customers can easily find and identify specific hustlers.

Male prostitution involves more than genitalia, it relates to the whole body. Therefore, sexual experience becomes a vehicle, a work tool. Men who work as prostitutes are a reduced minority (Mendieta-Izquierdo 2018), displaced to a hidden, invisible and clandestine space. The spaces where male prostitution is practised are generally connected to the gay scene, or to places related to gay sexual practices. First, there are closed spaces such as saunas, adult film theatres, clubs or bars, as in *Brüder der Nacht*. They can be also virtual spaces such as sex and dating apps. Lastly, there are public spaces – squares, parks or stations, such as the train station in *Eastern Boys*.

In prostitution – whether practised by male, female or transgender sex workers – the experiences featured in a sexual encounter depend on when and where the economic transaction takes place and who is involved in it. Furthermore, in the case of gay male prostitutes, the homosexual stigma adds to the prostitution stigma, which also goes together with the ethnic/racial stigma since it is common belief that prostitution goes hand in hand with illegal immigration (Stenvoll 2002). As Anne-Maria Marttila points out: 'Sex industry as a whole and prostitution in particular can be seen as an ethnospace' (2005, p. 38) because Western men satisfy their sexual needs through the sexualized bodies of 'exotic' men. Racism seems to play a fundamental part in the sex business. However, the attraction to the exotic, the foreign and the unknown seems to be at the heart of the obsession for 'Eastern' bodies. From this perspective, the line between xenophobia and xenophilia may be easy to cross for clients. One of the main motivations behind preserving the sex workers' invisibility has been a strategy to allow and retain certain social and class privileges. Some groups, marginalised by the dominant social and legal narratives through a 'strategic invisibility' (Mountz 2010), have turned against this tendency, used against undocumented migrants.

Clients of male prostitutes are perfectly integrated in what Patricia Hill Collins (2002) defines as 'the matrix of domination', marked by the global stigma that victimises the non-wealthy, non-heterosexual and non-Christian. In this sense,

Ruth Frankenberg argues: 'Whiteness signals the production and reproduction of dominance rather than subordination, normativity rather than marginality, and privilege rather than disadvantage' (1993, p. 237). In the case of *Eastern Boys*, Daniel, the client, is a single gay man: a white Frenchman in his late forties or early fifties, he is he is a businessman living in a residential neighbourhood in an elegant apartment full of modern appliances tended by an East Asian cleaning lady. His privilege contrasts with the hustler, Marek/Rouslan, a young Ukrainian prostitute, possibly an unaccompanied minor awaiting refugee status, exploited by the gang's boss. Within the context of male prostitution, sexuality is determined by its marginality within society. Sex becomes a merchandise, a trading object, a transaction (Weeks 2017). In turn, it is a sexuality marked by hegemony and dominant masculinity, and therefore a phallocentric sexuality based on penetration and the immediate and urgent satisfaction of sexual needs. Hustlers selling their bodies are considered immoral (Lancaster 2006). In addition, they need to carry this social stigma, a burden and a dishonour that, together with the traditional stigmas associated to the gay community, prompt their silence and concealment, perpetuating its invisibility.

In *Brüder der Nacht*, their bodies are the protagonists' sole possession, the only thing they can sell. They try to ease their restlessness at being far away from their countries, creating ties with their comrades to alleviate their sense of homelessness. Most of them are lonely men who live in council houses and spend their nights doing 'services' for the clients of the 'Rüdiger' bar. They call this activity 'business' to distinguish it from pleasure. When night falls, their second life begins, their family and kids oblivious.

Focusing on the invisibility of prostitution, *Brüder der Nacht* portrays the reality in which young hustlers live. They are not invisible in the film – on the contrary, it is the client, the elderly gay man, who occupies the background as a simple spectator of the hustlers' lives. Most of these young men are heterosexual, many of them are married and have children, but they make a living as sex workers. This subject is seldom studied and rarely broached by Romanian communities, much less by families. At home they follow the policy of 'don't ask, don't tell'. Although their environment knows the origin of this livelihood, they prefer not to ask where the money comes from.

The film does not approach the subject with a moral intention; rather, it presents an empathic but harsh portrayal of the lives of some people who have been forced to do something they never imagined they would do. Most of them consider 'gays' those who kiss and do 'everything', whereas active fellatio and penetration are not considered a 'gay activity'. Some of the characters innocently declare that, before migrating to Vienna, they thought the only gays were transvestites, and they were subsequently surprised that their clients were older 'normal' men.

Eastern Boys begins at the Parisian train station Gare du Nord with a group of boys hanging out, seeking potential targets. They are Eastern European boys, ranging from 25 to teenagers, migrants from the poorest regions of the ex-Soviet republics. They are possibly working as hustlers, but this is not clarified in the film. In turn, Daniel, the French character, shows an insecurity that betrays the fact that it is possibly his first time approaching a hustler. When he starts the conversation, he seems to be suggesting a romance rather than casual sex.

In this case, the power Daniel holds as a customer who pays disappears the moment he realises that what he has done is illegal. Marek/Rouslan seizes this opportunity, calling the entire gang to ransack Daniel's elegant apartment. While they plunder, their boss threatens the older man by showing his athletic figure and physical prowess, even dancing flirtatiously to the rhythm of electronic music. The long burglary sequence unveils the power dynamics within the gang as seen through the eyes of Daniel, who is terrified and possibly aroused by the boss's advances.

As the film moves forward, Daniel's sexual interest in Marek/Rouslan is replaced by paternal feelings as he gradually empathises with Marek's homelessness and alienation. While Daniel stands for generosity and the boss remains an abuser and a pimp throughout the film, the character of Marek/Rouslan moves from that of an impulsive rogue who takes advantage of an older man to someone who yearns for freedom.

The invisibility of prostitution is ever-present in both films, with the exception of the 'Rüdiger' in *Brüder der Nacht*, where everything is possible and the prostitution is obvious. Outside this space, the characters' behaviour radically changes. In the case of *Eastern Boys*, prostitution is only manifest when Marek/Rouslan and Daniel have sex and money changes hands.

Conclusions

The intention behind this work is to expose a problem that has an impact on society but also affects individuals. In fact, ageing affects everyone, but at the same time we must acknowledge that its consequences have a strong impact on the gay community. Ageism has been described as 'a threat to 'aging-well' in the 21st century' (Angus & Reeve 2006, p. 137). In this chapter, we have documented how internalised ageism may cause low sexual self-esteem among elderly gay men and low self-esteem in general. It is necessary to change the parameters for approaching old age, especially among homosexual men. Growing old, with its associated body image, is one of the most pressing issues confronted by homosexual men at present.

Both films reflect the insecurities and low self-esteem of elderly gay men, who find themselves in a subordinate position and seek in young bodies something they have lost. This situation has been reinforced by gay media, which show a disproportionate number of young bodies when they should present a wider range of body types. A wider variety could help eliminate or at least alleviate ageism within the gay community as well as the internalised ageism of elderly gay men.

The three main sections of the analysis converge in the representation of 'whiteness' and the absence/misrepresentation of the remaining ethnicities/races regarding the representation of hegemonic gay bodies and the visibility of gay prostitution or gay pornography. The overexposure to 'whiteness' is latent in both *Eastern Boys* and *Brüder der Nacht*. Even though 'whiteness' is not the main focus of this study, the analysis reveals that it is an unavoidable subject in the films. First, because of the absence of other races and ethnicities and the supremacy of whiteness in gay audiovisual representation; second, because clients are mostly attracted to white young men; and last, because of the narrative of a white European man as the 'saviour' of marginal sex workers in both films.

Even though these male prostitutes all come from Eastern Europe, their reasons for becoming sex workers are different in each film. In *Brüder der Nacht*, the first motive is easy money, and the second, the obligation to maintain their families in their home countries. In the case of *Eastern Boys*, none of them seems to have sex with their potential clients with the exception of Marek/Rouslan, but they pass as hustlers in cheating and stealing from their clients. In addition, in neither of the films the hustlers are openly gay, although Marek/Rouslan's sexuality remains obscure because of the increasingly paternal – or parent-child – bond with Daniel.

As a result, the image of the gay community portrayed in both films and the depiction of East European characters as migrants and gay young men struggling with marginality and ostracism does not cast a hopeful light on the homosexual community in this geopolitical context. Nevertheless, we must acknowledge that foreign political pressure, intensified during the accession process to the European Union, has fuelled the existence of a new generation of sexual minorities activists whose political and social visibility has grown since the development of social society in post-1989 Eastern Europe. A possible consequence is that these young Eastern men do not consider prostitution something forbidden or repulsive but a way of surviving and, above all, supporting their families. Such conclusions are strictly related to these films, although other contemporary productions do deal with similar topics. Only future research might show whether the new stereotype of the Eastern hustler is a temporary fad or if his presence is a political sign of contemporary sexual and LGBTQ+ liberation.

References

Abril, G. (2007). *Análisis crítico de textos visuales*. Madrid: Síntesis.

Adam, B.D. (2000). Age preferences among gay and bisexual men. *GLQ: A Journal of Lesbian and Gay Studies*, 6(3), 413–433.

Adelman, M. (1990). Stigma, gay lifestyles, and adjustment to aging: A study of later-life gay men and lesbians. *Journal of Homosexuality*, 20(3–4), 7–32.

Angus, J. & Reeve, P. (2006). Ageism: A threat to 'aging well' in the 21st century. *Journal of Applied Gerontology*, 25(2), 137–152.

Baer, B. (2009). *Other Russias: Homosexuality and the crisis of post-Soviet identity*. New York: Springer.

Baer, B. (2002). Russian gays/western gaze: Mapping (homo) sexual desire in post-Soviet Russia. *GLQ: A Journal of Lesbian and Gay Studies*, 8(4), 499–521.

Bennett, K.C. & Thompson, N.L. (1991). Accelerated aging and male homosexuality: Australian evidence in a continuing debate. *Journal of Homosexuality*, 20(3–4), 65–76.

Berger, R.M. & Kelly, J.J. (2001). What are older gay men like? An impossible question? *Journal of Gay & Lesbian Social Services*, 13(4), 55–64.

Bersani, L. (2009). *Homos*. Cambridge, MA: Harvard University Press.

Brennan, J. (2019). Exploitation in all-male pornography set in the Czech Republic. *European Journal of Cultural Studies* 22(1), 18–36.

Brotman, S., Ryan, B. & Cormier, R. (2003). The health and social service needs of gay and lesbian elders and their families in Canada. *The Gerontologist*, 43(2),192–202.

Bunzl, M. (2000). The Prague experience: Gay male sex tourism and the neocolonial invention of an embodied border. In D. Berdhal, M. Bunzl & M. Lampland (eds), *Altering States: Ethnographies of Transition in Eastern Europe and the Former Soviet Union* (pp. 70–95). Ann Arbor, MI: University of Michigan Press.

Caballero-Gálvez, A.A. and Herrero-Jiménez, B. (2017). Representaciones de género en las redes móviles de contactos cuerpo e identidad en 'Adopta un tío'. *Revista Prisma Social*, 2, 31–56.

Callen, A. (1998). Ideal masculinities: An anatomy of power. In N. Mirzoeff (ed.), *The Visual Culture Reader* (pp. 603–616). London: Routledge.

Carabí, À. & Armengol, J.M. (eds) (2008). *Debating Masculinity*. Barcelona: Icaria Editorial.

Coleman, R. (2009). *The Becoming of Bodies: Girls, Images, Experience*. Manchester: Manchester University Press.

Collins, P.H. (2002). *Black Feminist Thought: Knowledge, Consciousness, and the Politics of Empowerment*. London and New York: Routledge.

Connell, R.W. (2005). *Masculinities*. Cambridge: Polity.

de Diego, E. (2018). *El andrógino sexuado: eternos ideales, nuevas estrategias de género*. Madrid: Antonio Machado Libros.

Dyer, R. (2002). *The Matter of Images: Essays on Representations*. London and New York: Routledge.

Ellerson B. (2005). Visualizing homosexualities in Africa *Dakan*: An interview with filmmaker Mohamed Camara. In L. Ouzgane & R. Morrell (eds), *African Masculinities* (pp. 61–73). Basingstoke: Palgrave Macmillan.

Frankenberg, R. (1993). Growing up white: Feminism, racism and the social geography of childhood. *Feminist Review*, 45(1), 51–84.

Guasch, O. & Lizardo, E. (2017). *Chaperos: Precariado y prostitución homosexual*. Barcelona: Edicions Bellaterra.

Haber, D. (2009). Gay aging. *Gerontology & Geriatrics Education*, 30(3), 267–280.

Ham, J. & Gerard, A. (2014). Strategic in/visibility: Does agency make sex workers invisible? *Criminology & Criminal Justice*, 14(3), 298–313.

Hayes, B.C. (1995). Religious identification and moral attitudes: The British case. *British Journal of Sociology*, 46(3), 457–474.

Heaphy, B. (2007). Sexualities, gender and ageing: Resources and social change. *Current Sociology*, 55(2), 193–210.

Jablonski, R.A., Vance, D.E. & Beattie, E. (2013). The invisible elderly: Lesbian, gay, bisexual, and transgender older adults. *Journal of Gerontological Nursing*, 39(11), 46–52.

Jones, J. & Pugh, S. (2005). Ageing gay men: Lessons from the sociology of embodiment. *Men and Masculinities*, 7(3), 248–260.

Jönson, H. & Siverskog, A. (2012). Turning vinegar into wine: humorous self-presentations among older GLBTQ online daters. *Journal of Aging Studies*, 26(1), 55–64.

Katz, S. (2005). *Cultural Aging: Life Course, Lifestyle, and Senior Worlds*. Canada: Broadview Press.

Kaufman, G. & Phua, V. C. (2003). Is ageism alive in date selection among men? Age requests among gay and straight men in Internet personal ads. *Journal of Men's Studies*, 11(2), 225–235.

Keeler, L. & Jyrkinen, M. (1999). On the invisibility of the buyers in the sex trade. In L. Keeler & M. Jyrkinen (eds), *Who's Buying? The Clients of Prostitution*. Helsinki: Ministry of Social Affairs, Council for Equality, 4: 6–12.

Kimmel, M.S. (2004). Masculinity as homophobia: Fear, shame, and silence in the construction of gender identity. *Race, Class, and Gender in the United States: An Integrated Study*, 81, 93.

Kimmel, M.S. & Aronson, A.B. (2003). *Men and Masculinities: A Social, Cultural, and Historical Encyclopedia.* Santa Barbara, CA: ABC-CLIO.

Knauer, N.J. (2011). *Gay and Lesbian Elders: History, Law, and Identity Politics in the United States.* London and New York: Routledge.

Kuhar, R. and J. Takács (2007). *Beyond the Pink Curtain: Everyday Life of LGBT People in Eastern Europe.* Ljubliana: Peace Institute.

Lancaster, R.N. (2006). 'That we should all turn queer?' Homosexual stigma in the making of manhood and the breaking of a revolution in Nicaragua. In *Culture, Society and Sexuality* (pp. 120–138). London and New York: Routledge.

Marshall, B.L. & Katz, S. (2002). Forever functional: Sexual fitness and the ageing male body. *Body & Society*, 8(4), 43–70.

Marttila, A.M. (2005). The hiding men in prostitution. *NIKK Magasin*, (1), 36–39.

Mendieta-Izquierdo, G. (2018). Percepción de cuerpo y corporalidad en hombres que ejercen prostitución viril en Guadalajara, México. *Ciência & Saúde Coletiva*, 23, 1541–1549.

Mercer, J. (2017). *Gay Pornography: Representations of Sex and Masculinity.* London: Bloomsbury Publishing.

Mountz, A. (2010). *Seeking Asylum: Human Smuggling and Bureaucracy at the Border.* Minneapolis, MN: University of Minnesota Press.

Nachescu, V. (2005). Hierarchies of difference: National identity, gay and lesbian rights, and the church in postcommunist Romania. In A. Stulhofer & T. Sandfort (eds), *Sexuality and Gender in Postcommunist Eastern Europe and Russia* (pp. 57–78). New York and London: Howarth Press.

Ricoeur, P. (1981). *Hermeneutics and the Human Sciences: Essays on Language, Action and Interpretation.* Cambridge: Cambridge University Press.

Rodriguez, N.S., Huemmer, J. & Blumell, L.E. (2016). Mobile masculinities: An investigation of networked masculinities in gay dating apps.' *Masculinities & Social Change*, 5(3), 241–267.

Rothmann, J. (2013). 'Doing'and 'using'sexual orientation: The role of gay male pornographic film in the identity construction of gay men. *South African Review of Sociology*, 44(3), 22–41.

Signorile, M. (1997). *Life Outside: The Signorile Report on Gay Men: Sex, Drugs, Muscles, and the Passages of Life.* New York: Harper.

Sikes, A.W. (2010). Politics and pornography: Czech performance in the international arena. *Theatre Journal*, 62(3), 373–387.

Slevin, K.F. & Linneman, T.J. (2010). Old gay men's bodies and masculinities. *Men and Masculinities*, 12(4), 483–507.

Stenvoll, D. (2002). From Russia with love? Newspaper coverage of cross-border prostitution in Northern Norway, 1990–2001. *European Journal of Women's Studies*, 9(2), 143–162.

Štulhofer, A. & Sandfort, T. (2005). Introduction. In *Sexuality and Gender in Postcommunist Eastern Europe and Russia* (pp. 1–25). Binghamton: Haworth Press.

Suen, Y.T. (2017). Older single gay men's body talk: Resisting and rigidifying the aging discourse in the gay community. *Journal of homosexuality*, 64(3), 397–414.

Twigg, J. (2004). The body, gender, and age: Feminist insights in social gerontology. *Journal of Aging Studies*, 18(1), 59–73.

Van der Veur, D. (2001). *Caught between Fear and Isolation: Lesbian Women and Homosexual Men in Albania.* Amsterdam: COC Netherlands.

Weeks, J. (2017). *Sex, Politics and Society: The Regulation of Sexuality since 1800.* Basingstoke: Routledge.

Whitford, Gary S. (1997). Realities and hopes for older gay males. *Journal of Gay & Lesbian Social Services*, 6(1), 79–95.

Widmer, E.D., Treas, J. & Newcomb, R. (1998). Attitudes toward nonmarital sex in 24 countries. *Journal of Sex Research*, 35(4), 349–358.

Wood, M.J. (2004). The gay male gaze: Body image disturbance and gender oppression among gay men. *Journal of Gay & Lesbian Social Services*, 17(2), 43–62.

Woodward, K. (2003). Against wisdom: The social politics of anger and aging. *Journal of Aging Studies*, 17(1), 55–67.

Films

Campillo, R. (2013). *Eastern Boys*. France: Les Films de Pierre.

Chiha, P. (2016). *Brüder der Nacht*. Austria: Wildart Film

12

AGEING WOMEN ON SCREEN
Disgust, disdain and the Time's Up pushback

Karen Ross

Introduction

> Being powerful is so much more interesting than being beautiful.
> *(Helen Mirren,* The Wrap *Power Women Breakfast, 16 June 2015, New York)*

Twenty years ago, a research team I led was commissioned by a British commercial TV company (Carlton TV) and its digital sister (Ondigital) to find out what older viewers thought about the ways they were represented on TV and to determine their interest in themed programming for the silver generation (Healy & Ross 2002). We conducted 24 focus groups in which 228 people took part, the majority of them being women, and we were not surprised to find that most people disliked the characterisations of older age on TV, which often seemed stereotypical and rather negative. There was almost zero interest in an 'oldies' channel, not least because older people's interests are as varied as any other demographic but also because 'old age' does not have an agreed starting point and could include anyone from their late forties onwards, potentially incorporating at least two and possibly three generations. Why would a fifty-something have anything in common with a ninety-something? But the overwhelming criticism from older audiences was about their absence rather than presence on the small (and indeed the big) screen, an odd omission given the global trend over at least the past three decades of an ageing population. In the UK, there are more people aged 65+ than under 18, but this reality is not reflected in popular culture which remains a landscape largely populated by the young and the beautiful. I was in my early forties when I led that project and now, twenty years later, some things have changed but something that remains extremely troubling is not just the continuation of stereotypes of older age but gender-based differences which see older women being considerably less visible and valued than older men and more negatively represented, a theme to which we return later.

Popular culture is inextricably linked with social mores and practices and plays a significant role in both perpetuating and challenging stereotypes, be they age-related or focused on any other characteristic such as sex, gender, disability or class. Older people themselves believe that how they are represented in popular culture influences how they are treated in the real world and how they are regarded more generally by society (Healy & Ross 2002, Butler et al. 2006). It is exactly this presumed relationship between 'mediaworld' and 'realworld' which attracts so much scholarship in an effort to explore content, reception and the conditions of production, and to suggest strategies for change. Understanding the media logic of ageing and its visual and narrative construction helps us to unpack the underlying assumptions which drive both fictional and fact-based content in producing stereotypical or emancipatory renditions of the ageing body. This chapter therefore begins with a short synopsis of key trends in researching older age and the media before moving to consider the contemporary scene.

First, a very short skip through history

Analysing the way(s) in which older people are portrayed in moving image media, including TV and film, has been a research focus for at least the past fifty years, especially in the US and the UK, although age-related studies have been significantly less popular than research focused on gender more generally. Most of the studies which were conducted in the latter half of the twentieth century tended to look at volume, determining the extent to which older characters were visible in relation to their preponderance in the population and thus mostly demonstrating their under-representation, so that the problem of representation is both one of volume and of type. Nearly fifty years ago, Petersen (1973) identified that women over the age of 65 represented nearly 6 per cent of the US population but accounted for less than 2 per cent of TV characters compared with 4 per cent and 14 per cent for men. Other studies demonstrated that the ratio of male to female characters was 3:1 (Levinson 1973), a finding replicated by a number of later studies. Gerbner et al.'s (1980) study found that although there were more women than men characters in their twenties, the ratio fell to less than one in five across the life course. Women characters were significantly younger than men, rarely had an occupation outside the home and were most commonly portrayed as housewives. In terms of character content, Vernon et al. (1991) suggested that older male characters embodied more desirable and positive traits than older women. Robinson and Skill (1995) suggested that in general terms, all these studies, across several decades, shared the same analysis, that older people were under-represented both in relation to their actual number and in relation to all other age groups. Finally, in one of very few longitudinal studies, Edström (2018, p. 77) analysed how popular media in Sweden represented older people, sampling content from news, feature stories, fiction and advertising in each of 1994, 2004 and 2014. She argued that across this time period, the 'structures of visibility and the clusters of gender-age representation in the media foster stereotyping. The media buzz not only contributes to ageism, but is also still distinctly gendered'.

Representing the older woman

So much for history, but what about now? Has anything really changed? Well, yes and no. On the negative side, a woman's value to the media continues to depreciate as she ages so that, for example, although nearly half the female population of the US is now over 40, they only account for a quarter of TV characters (Miss Representation, 2011). Walker (2012) showed that in print and TV advertisements, and in TV shows, older adults are depicted as posing a financial burden on society, reflecting the work of Kessler et al. (2010) who noted the under-representation of the older-old in the television programmes they analysed, although their findings were more positive about the visibility of the younger-old. Edström's (2018) analysis of Swedish media in 2014 found that older women were rarely seen in fashion-based content or enjoying sexual relationships and although there were some positive representations of the older woman, she was nearly always affluent, well-groomed and exhibiting the bodily credentials of normative femininity. More positively, a few studies have found a steady increase in visibility of older people in the media and a move towards more positive portrayals (Ylänne 2015).

But, as ever, context is everything and different nations have taken different approaches in responding to the global ageing of the population and different researchers use more or less nuanced categories of older age, such as younger-old compared with older-old, all of which serve to make generalised statements and international comparisons somewhat tricky. Certainly in the UK and the US, the last twenty years have seen a shift in portrayal, in both TV and film, with more (and more diverse) roles being written for older women, not least because more women are entering and staying in the industry as writers, producers and directors and because the digital revolution has enabled new online services such as Amazon Prime and Netflix to both distribute and also produce original content (see Bobolt & Williams 2016, Smith et. al. 2018). However, one woman's feisty grandmother is another's grumbling old crone so we at least need to acknowledge our own subjectivity when analysing media texts. Arguably, part of the reason that we see a more positive inflection to older age is the discourse of 'successful ageing' or 'ageing well', exemplified by the idea of a healthy third age and promoted by the baby-boomer generation who now consider themselves to be precisely these active third-agers, but this notion of 'positive' ageing is not without its problems, a concern to which we return later.

For most contemporary feminist moving image researchers, representations of the older woman in both fictional and fact-based media forms are seen to inhabit one of two primary corporeal forms, either as an ageing well or an ageing poorly body (Jermyn 2016, MacGregor et al. 2018). Both these positions resist identification by many older women who either can't afford to buy themselves out of an inexorable decline or fear the prospect of incipient decrepitude, or both. Located at the extremes of all the possible ageing experiences, both positions prompt concern in the older female imaginary and their sense of self-identity (Grist & Jennings 2017). This unrealistic positioning of ageing femininity as either wonderful or horrifying casually elides the significant differences in life course experiences between women in their fifties and women in their nineties, cloistering everyone in a grey-lined ghetto of shame, ridiculed for having had too much botox or not enough.

Much scholarship has been dedicated to interrogating specific films and TV content in terms of characterisation and plotlines, in order to understand exactly how narratives of the ageing woman are constructed and delivered (Dolan 2016, Marshall & Rahman 2015). While individual film scholars have identified a number of both positive and negative trends through mostly small-scale, interpretive studies, quantitative analyses regularly conducted by US-based institutes and focused on Hollywood have revealed the slow pace of change in terms of visibility. For example, the University of Southern California's Annenberg Inclusion Initiative Research Team regularly conduct surveys of both content and production elements of the highest-grossing films, and in their longitudinal analysis of more than 1,000 films released between 2007 and 2017, less than a quarter of the women on screen were judged to be aged 40+ (Smith et al. 2018). The Center for the Study of Women in Television and Film at San Diego State University has tracked the location of women in the movie industry since 1998 through their *The Celluloid Ceiling* reports and is the longest-running and most comprehensive study of women's behind-the-scenes employment in film. In the 2019 report written by Martha Lauzen, women accounted for 20 per cent (up 2 per cent on the 2017 study) of all directors, writers, executive producers, producers, editors and cinematographers working on the top 250 films, and films with at least one female director employed a greater percentage of women working in all aspects of production than those with exclusively male directors. However, women accounted for only 8 per cent of directors working on the top 250 films in 2018, down three percentage points from 2017 and below (by one percentage point) their number in 1998, which is rather disappointing. This is important because, as demonstrated, women directors are more likely to employ other women and who is behind the camera has a significant impact on who is in front of it and whose stories get to be told. Nicole Kidman made exactly this point in her acceptance speech in 2018 at the Screen Actors Guild awards. While these data are not disaggregated by age, the majority of high-profile women directors such as Andrea Arnold, Kathryn Bigelow, Jane Campion, Sofia Coppola, Nora Ephron, Gurinder Chadha, Deepa Mehta and Nancy Meyers would all be considered older women. While these data draw on Hollywood, there are very similar findings when we look at the European film industry. The European Women's Audiovisual Network's (2015) report on women directors in Europe found that in its study of seven European countries (Austria, Croatia, France, Germany, Italy, Sweden, UK), only 21 per cent had a woman director. In the European Parliament's 2019 briefing which looked at the same issue, it reports that the weighted average of films directed by women in the 2012–2016 period was <20%, although there were considerable national variations, with country results varying from 5 per cent (Latvia) to 30 per cent (Sweden). The briefing also shows that the industry remains stubbornly horizontally and vertically sex-segregated, with more women working in costume design and editing and more men working with sound, music and image (Katsarova 2019).

Silver and still sexy, but not always in a good way

One of the more enduring stereotypes, indeed myths, of the older woman is her disinterest in sex, a state of affairs which apparently does not befall ageing men, perhaps because of the mostly negative connotations of the menopause, where the inability to procreate is tied to the new status of no-longer-a-real-woman. When the older woman demonstrably challenges this stereotype, she is then subjected to another stereotype, that of the 'cougar'. Arguably, the first and most infamous cougar to grace our screens was Mrs Robinson played by Anne Bancroft in the 1967 movie, *The Graduate* (dir. Mike Nicols), who seduces 21-year-old Benjamin Braddock (played by Dustin Hoffman). Since then, any older woman who has a partner younger than herself, or even just expresses interest in a younger man, is routinely described as a cougar as if it is only by her stealthy and predatory behaviour that an older woman can somehow trap a younger man into having sex with her. In 2007, the cougar went mainstream in a new US TV sitcom called *Cougar Town* (2009–2015), starring Courtney Cox as the uber cougar, seeking constant validation through the sexual attention of younger men. The series prompted highly contradictory responses, some commentators arguing that it was a positive and empowering portrayal of an older woman being happily sexual and challenging the orthodoxies of a sexless life. Others suggested that the show was simply another male fantasy tale since Cox's character was so superficial, one-dimensional and unlikeable (Harris & Asthana 2009). Burema (2018) argues that media coverage of 'celebrity' cougars such as Demi Moore and Madonna is often quite positive, stressing their financial independence and sexual power while portraying their junior love interests as largely 'interchangeable', although she also found contradictory examples of 'cougars' being cast in the more traditional role of the caring and nurturing mother figure, albeit wearing a sexy apron.

Pointing to the contradictions inherent in many portrayals of the older, sexually interested woman in British films such as *Last Orders* (2011) and *The Best Exotic Marigold Hotel* and its sequel (2012, 2015), Dolan (2016) suggests that plotlines and characters work to both productively engage with discourses of romance and agency which challenge conventional (for which read *negative*) stereotypes about older women, but at the same time mostly insist on a heteronormative relationship script, which does not. But as she points out elsewhere (Dolan 2020), Hollywood's recent embrace of the older women as still sexually desirable and indeed desiring, is to be welcomed, especially in roles where she is 'allowed' both a fully developed character and also to be the protagonist rather than the victim. While many such 'positive' renditions of the ageing woman can simultaneously be criticised for the characteristics which they lack, they nonetheless serve as important reminders that casting an older woman in the lead is a lot less risky than it was once imagined, not to mention providing points of identification and pleasure for older women audiences. As Jermyn (2012, p. 10) wryly observes, 'Assessing the representation of ageing and 'older' female celebrities is by turns seemingly hopeful and newly affirming one moment, and destructive and retrograde the next.'

Riding the wave of the newly discovered sexually adventurous older woman and eager to monetise the grey dollar, the dating industry has established several sites and apps dedicated to catering to the romantic ideals of the silver surfer who could also be interested in swiping left. Most of them are the silvered versions of mainstream parents such as eHarmony, Match and Elite Singles, but some are entirely original including Silver Singles. One British newcomer to the scene, Lumen, takes inspiration from dating apps such as Tinder and is based on 'the swipe' but where a fuller profile is required in order to promote 'quality conversations and connections'.

Full disclosure: I have downloaded this app and have never once swiped left. I remain disappointed. The primary problem for older women seeking love over the internet is that despite what men say in their profiles in terms of the age-range of women in which they could be interested, they inevitably default to women under 35, no matter how old they are.

'Successful ageing' for good and for ill

As discussed above, any number of contemporary representations of older women in both fictional and fact-based media such as advertising and magazines are oriented towards showing women ageing well and enjoying a third age, a tendency which both serves to frame ageing as something over which we can exert control and sets up a standard against which older women are measured and often found wanting. Subscribing to the paradigm of successful ageing means obeying and conforming to the normative expectations of 'appropriate' femininity, and women's magazines in particular provide the tools for doing that through a focus on fashion (style for the over-fifties), face (keep those wrinkles at bay) and food (retain that youthful figure), all of which require the purchase of products and place us firmly back in the corset of consumption. While the postfeminist mantra of choice and empowerment is a repeated refrain, it cleverly glosses the delivery of citizens into the arms of capital. Over the past decade, the fashion industry in particular has promoted the older woman as, ironically, a newly emerged fashionista who, via the endorsement of a range of celebrities, have featured in numerous campaigns for high-end brands such as Kate Spade (Iris Apfel, aged 93), Céline (Joan Didion, aged 80) and Yves St Laurent (Joni Mitchell, aged 71), suggesting that real style is truly ageless (Jermyn 2016). What is equally obvious is that real style also costs real money.

Jane Fonda perhaps epitomises the kind of 'ageing well' woman with whom luxury brands like to work, but where mother nature has had a helping hand from the surgeon's knife, something which Fonda now says she regrets.

> On one level, I hate the fact that I've had the need to alter myself physically to feel that I'm OK … I wish I wasn't like that. I love older faces … I wish I was braver, but I am what I am.
>
> *(Fonda quoted in Telling 2018, n.p.)*

As with Helen Mirren, Fonda has been the 'face' of L'Oreal, a poster girl for the older woman who looks after her skin because she's worth it and can afford it, although in Mirren's case, she insisted that L'Oreal be forbidden to digitally enhance her photos in post-production. While it's heartening to see brand leaders featuring older women in their campaigns, using beautiful ageing celebrities is not so brave, and using them to sell products targeted at older women is just good business sense and more cynical than courageous. The ageing-well celebrity provides an aspirational role model for the older consumer, promising a healthy and positive life – you too can look like me if you buy product X – while avoiding popular discourses of dependency and decrepitude which are also part of the ageing process for so many people.

But in case of any embarrassed reluctance to seem overly interested in banishing wrinkles, Searing & Zeilig (2017) detect a subtle and interesting shift in the language of advertising targeting the older woman consumer, where pseudoscience is increasingly used to suggest the medical benefits of this or that moisturiser, cleverly allowing women to justify the expense on the grounds of health rather than vanity. This faux scientific discourse is also heavily used in the promotion of 'superfoods' such as goji berries and turmeric which allegedly contain anti-ageing properties to sustain a healthy life, a promise which has no basis in empirical evidence but owes much to our desire to believe in magic. This consumerist turn to the grey dollar epitomises the neoliberal project of the self as a constant work in progress, setting up an interesting contradiction wherein the historical disavowal of the older woman as worthless is pitched against her value as a consumer with money to spend on delaying the ageing process.

There is thus a particular older-woman script – the three Fs which I suggest above, fashion, face, food – to which we must adhere and implement in order to both avoid the social opprobrium which otherwise attends the ageing female body and as a means by which to halt the descent into the fourth age hell of dependency and death (see also Pack et al. 2019). Not only is that script entirely normative in terms of prescribing the most 'appropriate' form of femininity, it is explicitly heteronormative in its insistence on what Marshall (2018, p. 363) calls the pursuit of 'hetero-happiness'. The flipside of discourses of ageing well is, of course, its opposite, and the primary targets of this counter-discourse tend to be figures in public life and especially ageing celebrities – and here we see the classic double-bind of gender and age. If women celebrities attempt to maintain the beauty standards expected of them by artificial means, they are condemned for their vanity, but if they ignore the advancing years and remain happy in their ageing bodies, they are ridiculed for 'letting themselves go'.

But what about those of us who don't want to conform, who celebrate our laughter lines and our curves, or who simply can't afford to purchase that elusive elixir of youth? As Twigg (2018) argues, the media's template for ageing well disavows those other ways of ageing which focus on aspects of the self which do not require fixing, which are oriented towards inner resilience and contentment and not outward appearance. Undoubtedly, the idea of successful ageing – that 70 is the new 50 or 60 is the new 40 – is immensely attractive, but creating a new 'norm' for the older person who is 'fit, fashionable, functional and flexible' (Marshall & Rahman 2015, p. 577) sets up an ideal which is impossible to achieve for all those people who are ill, poor, disabled or simply living life on their own terms. Media which are specifically oriented towards the older consumer, especially lifestyle magazines, are often at the centre of such third-age-positive discourses (see Lumme-Sandt 2011). Promoting a positive message about the benefits of older age is obviously a good thing to do but such messages can have contradictory effects, prompting more positive characterisations of a healthy and liberated older age but at the same time implying that those whose lives are not so rich and fulfilling are somehow to blame for their own failures. While a proportion of older people are indeed retiring younger and embracing a third age which is exciting and fulfilling, another group are living an unwell fourth age in isolated poverty: all these experiences are part of the reality of ageing and should also be part of the media mix, showing the diversity of older age in all our glorious grumpiness, wild frivolity and frustrating frailty.

A tiny nod to intersectionality

The vast majority of studies of ageing, gender and the media privilege the former two aspects without any further intersectional analysis so that most work centres on a white, heterosexual subject even as this limitation is acknowledged. In the few studies that move beyond this paradigm, some Asian and Black women characters and images can be observed positively moving against ageist and racial stereotypes. For example, Tincknell (2019) suggests that while the work of director Gurinder Chadha was (and still is) significant in offering a range of fully formed and multi-dimensional older Asian woman characters (for example, *Bhaji on the Beach*, 1993, and *Bend It Like Beckham,* 2000), two British TV series – *Goodness, Gracious Me* (BBC 1998–2001, 2015), and *The Kumars at Number 42* (BBC 2001–2005) were particularly subversive in their portrayal of older Asian women characters who displayed a 'Rabelaisian rambunctiousness' which was both refreshing and nuanced our understanding of how age and gender and race can be productively re-considered. In similar vein, Crawford Mondé (2018) analysed images of older Black women on Tumblr and suggests that many of the images she sampled present narratives of age, gender and race which run counter to mainstream depictions of the ageing female body since they focus on Black women's ageless beauty in explicit comparison to White women. At the same time, however, the author recognises the danger inherent in this kind of reverse biological essentialism since it is the very basis on which racism has flourished.

Women viewing women

Older people are under no illusion about how they are regarded by media professionals and indeed by members of the wider (younger) society among whom they live, and one of the interviewees in my own earlier study made a comment which typified the sentiments of so many people who participated: 'you're not important anymore, you're finished!' However, older people do not escape the watchful gaze of the canny advertiser who is looking to monetise any demographic, so that programmes which are perceived to attract older viewers have advertising breaks which feature funeral plans and mobility aids. Again, older viewers themselves feel patronised by such blatant targeting with its focus on infirmity and death at a time when they are just as likely to be enjoying their retirement and interested in buying a new car rather than needing a motorised wheelchair or incontinence pads. On the other hand, older audiences appreciate shows that eschew such negative themes and are particularly enthusiastic about those which are humorous and relatable. For example, Jerslev (2018) undertook an analysis of comments posted up on Jane Fonda's Facebook page about the US sitcom, *Grace and Frankie* (Fonda plays the character of Grace), suggesting that older women viewers understand the show as a real show with real older women. A significant aspect of what viewers enjoy about the show is the presentation of two very different but equally valid ways of being an older woman, with Grace's relentless pursuit of lost youth countered by Frankie's indifference to her sags and wrinkles. But both women are vital, entrepreneurial and sensual, none of which attributes commonly feature in most portrayals of older women but all of which endear the audience to the characters:

> this is the best show I've seen in years – something I very much relate to at age 64. You take serious and sensitive issues of the Baby Boom generation and handle it honestly and with a sense of humour. What did Bette Davis say – getting old ain't for sissies … .
>
> *(participant quoted in Jerslev 2018, p. 197)*

Grace's desire to hold back the ravages of time is echoed in so many other contemporary shows which feature all-women ensemble casts. In her analysis of three popular series which also featured groups of women at different points in the life course – *Sex and the City* (1998–2004), *Desperate Housewives* (2004–2012) and *Girls* (2012–), Van Bauwel (2018) suggests that while there was some acceptance of the ageing process, the predominant themes which focused on ageing were mostly framed around attempts to stop it happening.

Speaking truth to the things that power already knows: actors speak out

In response to the low visibility of older women on screen, a number of high-profile women actors have used platforms such as their acceptance speeches at different international award ceremonies to both lament the dearth of roles for the older woman and praise those actors who do get to play those roles for their talent, simultaneously calling out the industry and showing how the studios who buck the trend reap the rewards. Of course, casting an A-list celebrity is scarcely courageous as she has already established her box office potential, but it is still noteworthy when an older woman has the principal role in a mainstream Hollywood film which is not explicitly about ageing.

> How wonderful it is that our [women's] careers can go beyond 40 years old because 20 years ago, we were pretty washed up by this stage in our lives ... we have proven that we are potent and powerful and viable. I beg that the industry stays behind us because our stories are finally being told.
> *(Nicole Kidman, acceptance speech for winning outstanding performance by a female actor in a television movie or miniseries, for her role in* Big Little Lies, *24th Screen Actors Guild Awards, 21 January 2018)*

In the same year, Jane Fonda (then aged 80) stated that ageism in Hollywood was 'alive and well' after studio executives wanted younger stars to front *The Book Club* (dir. Bill Holderman 2018) instead of her and fellow Oscar-winner Diane Keaton (then aged 72). Fellow co-star Mary Steenburgen (then aged 65) said about the film that 'It's kind of a miracle, actually, that it ever occurred because Holly-wood does kind of ask you in some ways to rather disappear as you get older' (Steenburgen quoted in the *Daily Telegraph*, 17 May, 2018, n.p.). Several years earlier, at *The Wrap*'s first Power Women Breakfast in New York in 2015, Helen Mirren said that Hollywood's sexism was 'ridiculous. And 'twas ever thus. We all watched James Bond as he got more and more geriatric and his girlfriends got younger and younger. It's so annoying' (Mirren quoted in Goldsmith 2015, n.p.). However, as actor Anne Hathaway acknowledges,

> I can't complain about it because I benefitted from it. When I was in my early twenties, parts would be written for women in their fifties and I would get them. And now I'm in my early thirties and I'm like, 'Why did that 24-year old get that part?' I *was* that 24-year-old once, I can't be upset about it, it's the way things are.
> *(Hathaway quoted in Whitaker 2015, n.p.)*

Fortunately, there are plenty of older actors who are not only upset about it but calling it out and doing something about it. Jessica Lange (then aged 70) sees the problem but is also seeking solutions:

> Ageism is pervasive in this industry ... . It's not a level playing field. You don't often see women in their 60s playing romantic leads, yet you will see men in their 60s playing romantic leads with co-stars who are decades younger [so] you go to television. You go to the stage. You do whatever you can because you want to keep working.
> *(Lange quoted in Miller 2017, n.p.)*

And of course, 2018 kicked off with the launch of the Time's Up movement, following on from #MeToo, and supported by 300 women actors, agents, writers, directors and other women in Hollywood banding together. The Time's Up website describes the movement as a 'unified call for change from women in entertainment for women everywhere. From movie sets to farm fields to board-rooms alike, we envision nationwide leadership that reflects the world in which we live.' One of their first missions is what they call the 4 Percent Challenge, 4 per cent being the percentage of the top 1,200 films between 2007 and 2018 that were directed by a woman. The 4 Percent Challenge is a pledge that industry members can take to produce a feature film project with a female director in the 18 months following the launch in January 2018. By the end of the inaugural month, the website stated that the campaign had received pledges from 100 major players in the entertainment industry including both individuals and studios. Time will tell if those pledges turn into action.

Decades of research into the relationship between gender, age and screen-based media shows the complex ways in which those elements work together and influence each other to produce different renditions of the ageing woman which go through a continuum from sexist ageist stereotype to positive, realistic agency and a few stops in between. But what is surprising is that across the contemporary landscape there is so little in between those polar positions that the ageing woman on screen is mostly framed as ageing well or ageing badly, and remains mostly white, mostly hetero. At a time when the population is ageing all over the world and young people are turning away from traditional media such as film in favour of streaming services, ignoring the very generation who were brought up on film and television could turn out to be a rather expensive and potentially disastrous mistake.

Last thoughts

In 2018, the Royal Society for Public Health and the Calouste Gulbenkian Foundation published the findings of research they commissioned into attitudes towards ageing and their impact on the health and wellbeing of older people. Among the report's recommendations were several relating to the media since the research demonstrated the importance of that industry in being both part of the problem and, potentially, part of the solution:

> An independent review of the representation of older people in the media; the Independent Press Standards Organisation (IPSO) to include 'age' in the Editors' Code of Practice as a characteristic by which journalists must not discriminate; Facebook to include 'age' as a protected characteristic in its community standards on hate speech.
>
> *(2018, p. 5)*

As with all analyses, media texts are endlessly polysemic, as is obvious from even a cursory look at the variability of film criticism of this or that film or TV show, and evaluations of the ageing female actor seem to move backwards and forwards through an arc from disdain to delight. As actors such as Judi Dench and Helen Mirren are praised for their positive role modelling with characters who exude confidence, agency and not a little sexual appetite, those characters are simultaneously criticised for their frailties and the heteronormative scripts of femininity which proscribe their behaviour (Pua 2018, Dolan 2016). Perhaps this is inevitable, that those (relatively) few ageing women celebrities who grace our screens and devices carry the impossible burden of representing our hopes and dreams of a realistic rendition of an *olderwoman* personhood, precisely because they are all we have. We recognise the socially constructed nature of femininity and its ageing aspect and yearn for representations which show the diversity of our experiences, not simply replacing one set of (negative) stereotypes with more positive ones. Where is the humanity of women's lived experiences, in all its colours and hues? But in positive mode, I join Nicole Kidman in toasting all those women actors, directors and other industry folks whose creativity, bravery, sheer hard work and resilience has built a foundation upon which generations of younger women can thrive, and I drink from the half full rather than the half empty glass of their talents. Viva Judi and Helen!

References

Applewhite, A. (2016). *This Chair Rocks: A Manifesto Against Ageism.* Waterville, ME: Thorndike Press.

Bobolt, S. and Williams, B. (2016). If you want to see diversity onscreen, watch Netflix. And Amazon. And Hulu. Celebrtate diversity and chill. *Huffington Post*, 26 February. Accessed 16. 3. 2020. Available at: www.huffingtonpost.co.uk/entry/streaming-sites-di versity_n_56c61240e4b0b40245c96783?ri18n=true.

Bosch, V.J. (2016). Playing with ageism. *The Gerontologist*, 15 April. Available at: https://aca demic.oup.com/gerontologist/article/56/3/592/2605657/Playing-With-Ageism.

Brunsdon, C. (2001). *The Feminist, the Housewife, and the Soap Opera.* London: Clarendon Press.

Burema, D. (2018). 'Cougars or kittens? The representation of celebrity cougars and their toyboys in gossip media, *Feminist Media Studies*, 18(1), 7–20. doi:10.1080/14680777.2018.1409968.

Butler, R., Etcoff, N., Orbach, S. and D'Agostino, H. (2006). 'Beauty comes of age': Findings of the 2006 Dove global study on aging, beauty and well-being. Available at: https://sta tic1.squarespace.com/static/55f45174e4b0fb5d95b07f39/55f45539e4b09d46d4847b60/55f4 5539e4b09d46d4847c93/1255277563001/Beauty+Comes+of+Age+2006+Dove+Global+ Study+on+Aging+Beauty+and+Well-being.pdf.

Calouste Gulbenkian Foundation UK Branch and the Royal Society for Public Health (RSPH) (2018). That age old question: How attitudes to ageing affect our health and wellbeing. RSPH, London.

Christensen, C.L. (2019). Visualising old age: Photographs of older people on the website of the DaneAge Association. *Nordicom Review*, 40(2), 111–127. doi:10.2478/nor-2019–0036.

Communications Research Group (1999). Too old for TV? The portrayal of older people on television. Age Concern England, London

Crawford Mondé, G. (2018). #BlackDontCrack: a content analysis of the aging Black woman in social media. *Feminist Media Studies*, 18(1), 47–60. doi:10.1080/ 14680777.2018.1409972.

Daily Telegraph (2018). 'Ageism in Hollywood 'alive and well': Jane Fonda reveals bosses wanted younger stars to front her film. 17 May. Available at: www.telegraph.co.uk/news/2018/05/16/ageism-hollywood-alive-jane-fonda-reveals-bosses-wanted-younger/.

Dolan, J. (2016). 'Old age' films: Golden retirement, dispossession and disturbance. *Journal of British Cinema and Television*, 13(4), 571–589.

Dolan, J. (2020). Older women and cinema: Audiences, stories, and stars. In K. Ross, I. Bachmann, V. Cardo, S. Moorti and M. Scarcelli (eds), *The International Encyclopedia of Gender, Media, and Communication*. Available at: https://doi.org/10.1002/9781119429128. iegmc191.

Edström, M. (2018). Visibility patterns of gendered ageism in the media buzz: A study of the representation of gender and age over three decades. *Feminist Media Studies*, 18(1), 77–93. doi:10.1080/14680777.2018.1409989.

European Women's Audiovisual Network (EWA)(2015). Where are the women directors? Report on gender equality for directors in the European film industry. EWA, Strasbourg. Available at: www.ewawomen.com/wp-content/uploads/2018/09/Complete-report_compressed.pdf.

Geraghty, C. (1990). *Women and Soap Opera: A Study of Prime Time Soaps*. Oxford: Polity Press.

Gerbner, G., Gross, L., Signorielli, N. and Morgan, M. (1980). 'Ageing with television: Images on television dramas and conceptions of social reality', *Journal of Communication*, 30, 37–47.

Goldsmith, J. (2015). Helen Mirren calls Hollywood ageism 'f–king outrageous' at Wrap's 1st Power Women Breakfast in NYC. Available at: www.thewrap.com/helen-mirren-calls-hollywood-ageism-f-cking-outrageous-at-wraps-1st-power-women-breakfast-in-nyc/. Accessed 1. 1. 2020.

Gracie, C. (2019). *Equal: A Story of Women, Pay and the BBC*. London: Virago.

Grist, H. and Jennings, R. (2017). Future and present imaginaries: The politics of the ageing female body in Lena Dunham's *Girls* (HB0, 2012–present). In C. McGlynn, M. O'Neil and M. Schrage-Früh (eds), *Ageing Women in Literature and Visual Culture: Reflections, Refractions, Reimaginings* (pp. 195–216). London, New York, Shanghai: Palgrave Macmillan.

Harrington, Lee C. and Brothers, D. (2010). A life course built for two: Acting, aging, and soap operas. *Journal of Aging Studies*, 24, 20–29.

Harris, P. and Asthana, A. (2009). Female 'cougars' are on the prowl. Or are they just a male fantasy? *The Observer*, 27 September. Available at: www.theguardian.com/lifeandstyle/2009/sep/27/cougar-courtney-cox-older-women. Accessed 31. 12. 2019.

Healy, T. and Ross, K. (2002). Growing old invisibly: Older viewers talk television. *Media, Culture & Society*, 24, 105–120.

Hobson, D. (2002). *Soap Opera*. Oxford: Polity Press.

Holland, P. (1987). When a woman reads the news. In H. Baehr and G. Dyer (eds), *Boxed in: Women and Television* (pp. 133–150). New York: Pandora Press.

Jenkins, J. and Finneman, T. (2018). Gender trouble in the workplace: Applying Judith Butler's theory of performativity to news organizations. *Feminist Media Studies*, 18(2), 157–172. doi:10.1080/14680777.2017.1308412.

Jermyn, D. (2012). 'Get a life, ladies. Your old one is not coming back': Ageing, ageism and the lifespan of female celebrity. *Celebrity Studies*, 3(1), 1–12.

Jermyn, D. (2016). Pretty past it? Interrogating the post-feminist makeover of ageing, style, and fashion, *Feminist Media Studies*, 16(4), 573–589. doi:10.1080/14680777.2016.1193371.

Jerslev, A. (2018). A real show for mature women ageing along with ageing stars: *Grace and Frankie* fandom on Facebook. *Celebrity Studies*, 9(2), 186–201. doi:10.1080/19392397.2018.1465298.

Katsarova, I. (2019). The place of women in European film productions: Fighting the celluloid ceiling. European Parliament, Brussels. Available at: www.europarl.europa.eu/RegData/etudes/BRIE/2019/633145/EPRS_BRI(2019)633145_EN.pdf.

Kessler, E.M., Schwender, C. and Bowen, C.E. (2010). The portrayal of older people's social participation on German prime-time TV advertisements. *Journal of Gerontology Series B: Psychological Sciences and Social Sciences*, 65B(1), 97–106. Available at: https://doi.org/10.1093/geronb/gbp084.

Lauzen, M.M. (2019). The Celluloid Ceiling: Behind-the-scenes employment of women on the top 100, 250, and 500 films of 2018. San Diego State University, San Diego.

Lee, J. (2014). Male TV host wears same suit for year: No one notices. *USA Today*, 17 November. Available at: www.usatoday.com/story/news/nation-now/2014/11/17/tv-host-same-suit-sexism/19161031/.

Levinson, R. (1973). From Olive Oyle to Sweet Polly Purebread: Sex role stereotypes and televised cartoons. *Journal of Popular Culture*, 9, 561–572.

Loos, E.F. and Ekström, M. (2014) Visually representing the generation of older consumers as a diverse audience: Towards a multidimensional market segmentation typology. *Participations*, 11(2), 258–273.

Lumme-Sandt, K. (2011). Images of ageing in a 50+ magazine. *Journal of Aging Studies*, 25, 45–51.

MacGregor, C., Petersen, A. and Parker, C. (2018). Promoting a healthier, younger you: The media marketing of anti-ageing superfoods. *Journal of Consumer Culture*. doi:10.1177/1469540518773825.

Makita, M., Mas-Bleda, A., Stuart, E. and Thelwall, M. (2019). Ageing, old age and older adults: A social media analysis of dominant topics and discourses. *Ageing & Society*. doi:10.1017/S0144686X19001016.

Marshall, B.L. (2018). Happily ever after? 'Successful ageing' and the heterosexual imaginary. *European Journal of Cultural Studies*, 21(3), 363–381.

Marshall, B.L. and Rahman, M. (2015). Celebrity, ageing and the construction of 'third age' identities. *International Journal of Cultural Studies*, 18(6), 577–593.

Miller, K. (2017). Jessica Lange can finally relax. *AARP Magazine*, 18 July. Available at: www.aarp.org/entertainment/television/info-2017/jessica-lange-news-interview.html. Accessed 1. 1. 2020.

Miss Representation (2011). DVD directed by Jennifer Newsom. San Francisco, CA: Girl Club Entertainment.

Pack, R., Hand, C., Laliberte Rudman, D. and Huot, S. (2019). Governing the ageing body: Explicating the negotiation of 'positive' ageing in daily life. *Ageing & Society*, 39, 2058–2108.

Petersen, M. (1973). The visibility and image of old people on television. *Journalism Quarterly*, 50, 569–573.

Pua P. (2018). Iron lady to old lady: The neutering of James Bond's M. *Feminist Media Studies*, 18(1), 94–107. doi:10.1080/14680777.2018.1409991.

Robinson, J.D. and T. Skill (1995). The invisible generation: Portrayals of the elderly on prime-time television. *Communication Reports*, 8, 111–119.

Searing, C. and Zeilig, H. (2017). Fine lines: Cosmetic advertising and the perception of ageing beauty. *International Journal of Ageing and Later Life*, 11(1), 1–30.

Smith, S.L., Choueiti, M., Pieper, K., Case, A. and Choi, A. (2018). Inequality in 1,100 popular films: Examining portrayals of gender, race/ethnicity, LGBT & disability from 2007 to 2017. Inclusion Initiative, USC Annenberg.

Telling, G. (2018). Jane Fonda is not proud of her plastic surgery and wishes she was 'braver': 'but I am what I am'. *People*, 20 September. Available at: https://people.com/movies/jane-fonda-says-she-isnt-proud-plastic-surgery/. Accessed 29. 12. 2019.

Tincknell, E. (2019). Monstrous aunties: The Rabelaisian older Asian woman in British cinema and television comedy. *Feminist Media Studies*, 20(1), 135–150. doi:10.1080/14680777.2019.1599038.

Twigg, J. (2018). Fashion, the media and age: How women's magazines use fashion to negotiate age. *European Journal of Cultural Studies*, 21(3), 334–348.

Van Bauwel, S. (2018). Invisible golden girls? Post-feminist discourses and female ageing bodies in contemporary television fiction. *Feminist Media Studies*, 18(1), 21–33. doi:10.1080/14680777.2018.1409969.

Varjakoski, H. (2019). In and out of control: Portraying older women in contemporary Finnish comedy films. *European Journal of Cultural Studies*, 22(5–6), 684–699.

Vernon, J.A., Williams, J.A., Jr., Phillips, T. and Wilson, J. (1991). Media stereotyping: A comparison of the way elderly women and men are portrayed on prime-time television. *Journal of Women & Ageing*, 2(4), 55–68.

Walker, A. (2012). The new ageism, *The Political Quarterly*, 83(4), 812–819. doi:10.1111/j.1467–1923X.2012.02360.x.

Wardrop, M. (2012). Mark Thompson: 'Not enough older women on the BBC'. *Telegraph*, 9 February. Available at: www.telegraph.co.uk/culture/tvandradio/bbc/9070685/Mark-Thompson-not-enough-older-women-on-the-BBC.html. Accessed 30. 12. 2019.

Whitaker, H. (2015). 'So you think you know Anne?' *Glamour*, October. Available at: www.glamourmagazine.co.uk/article/so-you-think-you-know-anne-october. Accessed 1. 1. 2020.

World Association for Christian Communication (WACC) (2015) Who makes the news? Global Media Monitoring Project 2015. WACC, Toronto.

Ylänne, V. (2015) Representations of ageing in the media. In J. Twigg and W. Martin (eds), *Routledge Handbook of Cultural Gerontology* (pp. 369–375). London: Routledge.

13

NO COUNTRY FOR OLD MEN?

Representations of the ageing body in contemporary pornography

Federico Zecca

Introduction

Historically, ageing has not sat well with pornography. At its emergence in the early 1970s as a legitimate cinematic genre (Williams 1999), in fact, pornography has built a universe mainly inhabited by young, beautiful, 'permatanned, waxed, bleached' (Härmä & Stolpe 2010, p. 113) bodies. Even more dramatically than other fields of cultural production (Van den Bulck 2014), Golden Age pornography has prized 'the beauty, energy, grace, moral fortitude and optimism of youthful bodies' (Bond and Cabrero 2007, p. 116) – therefore embracing very strict 'standards of youthfulness' (Rosow 1974, p. 146). However, forms of exploitation of the ageing (mainly female) body started to emerge during the so-called video era of the 1980s and early 1990s (Williams 1999, Alilunas 2016), when new pornographic sub-genres such as 'mature' were originally developed within the broader context of burgeoning amateur porn.

It is only thanks to the spreading of digital technologies and the advent of the internet over the last two decades, though, that the ageing body has found a wider discursive and commercial visibility within the area of adult entertainment. As stated by Peter Lehman, in fact, the digital revolution 'has opened the sexual representation of male and female bodies to a much wider variety of age, race, body types, and range of features [...] than previous forms of porn' (2006, p.13). As a consequence, the pornographic depiction of the ageing body has originated particular typologies of products and market niches, as well as specific taste communities. In order to understand the extent of the phenomenon, it suffices to take a look at today's most important distribution platform for online adult content, Pornhub: among its more than a hundred default categories, for instance, at least three are explicitly dedicated to age-themed material – 'mature' (around 30,500 videos as I write), 'MILF' (around 140,000), and 'old/young' (around 18,000); moreover, the platform hosts more than 200 channels directly ascribable to the above-mentioned categories.

Notwithstanding the progressive importance acquired by the ageing body in pornography, this subject has suffered so far from academic neglect, with very few exceptions (Paasonen 2011). The objective of this chapter is therefore to provide a first investigation of the meanings and uses of the ageing body in contemporary pornography. In the first part I try to position the ageing body within the sphere of contemporary pornography, at the crossroads between two different dynamics: a socioeconomic dynamic related to the current state of the adult industry, and an epistemic dynamic related to the formation of the pornographic subject. In the second and third parts I try to outline some ideas for the analysis of the strategies informing the pornographic representation of the ageing body; more precisely, drawing on age studies, as well as media and cultural studies, I investigate the 'codes and conventions of the available cultural forms of presentation' (Dyer 1993, p. 2) through which pornography (re)presents the ageing body.

In order to do so I have surveyed the offer provided by the most popular (generalist) porn aggregators (Pornhub and Xvideos) and extensively analysed some of the most important specialised websites (21sextreme, Oldje, Moms Teach Sex). From this survey, I have identified four main types of pornographic materials, each of them related to different representational strategies. The first three types include sub-genres and categories ascribable to so-called corporate pornography, while the last one exists most exclusively within the multifaceted galaxy of amateur pornography (Biasin, Maina, Zecca 2014). These materials are analysed keeping in mind two fundamental underlying issues. First, age is to be understood as a cultural construct that operates within certain biological limits, that is, as both a biological and a cultural process articulated in 'firmly coded [...] stages which include childhood, middle age and old age' (Featherstone, Hepworth 1991, p. 372). And second, the cultural construction of age interacts with the cultural construction of gender: as we will see in the next parts, in fact, the pornographic representations of age, and the social meanings they convey, differ largely according to the performers' gender and sexuality.[1]

Contemporary pornography and the ageing body

Contemporary pornography is to be understood as a field of tensions, in which the ageing body itself is deeply involved. The first of these tensions is represented by the socioeconomic dialectic – typical of so-called 'convergence culture' as described by Henry Jenkins (2006) – between corporate and grassroots practices. As is well known, Jenkins has developed the term 'convergence culture' to describe the 'technological, industrial, cultural, social changes in the ways media circulates within our culture' (282), as occurred after the digital revolution. More specifically, according to Jenkins convergence culture is characterised by two opposite processes: corporate convergence and grassroots convergence. Corporate convergence is a top-down corporate-driven process in which 'media companies are learning how to accelerate the flow of media contents across delivery channels in different media to expand revenue opportunity, broaden markets and reinforce viewer commitments' (18). On the contrary, grassroots convergence is a bottom-up consumer-driven process in which 'consumers are learning how to use different media technologies to bring the flow of media more fully under their control and to interact with other consumers' (18).

The dialectic between corporate and grassroots convergence has deeply informed the production and consumption practices within contemporary pornography as well. On the one hand, porn companies try to accelerate the media flow and broaden their markets by differentiating their production and reaching new audiences and niches; on the other, a new breed of porn 'prosumers' has started to use the new digital means of production and distribution to create and control their own pornography and to interact with other users (Attwood 2010). The joint effect of these two processes has brought to a quantitative exasperation and a qualitative differentiation of the pornographic production, in other words to a multiplication of products and audiences that Linda Williams has described through the paradigm of 'proliferating pornographies' (2004, p. 1).

As we will see in the following paragraphs, the ageing body in contemporary pornography perfectly fits into this scheme. For instance, porn corporations such as MindGeek, Gamma Entertainment or International Media Company BV create specific age-themed subsidiaries, websites or video series in order to capitalise on this particular market sector. At the same time, middle-aged or older performers can circulate their own works through 'solo' websites they fully own and operate, while amateur and pro-am (professional-amateurs) models can upload their DIY videos on their personal accounts on porn aggregators such as Pornhub or Xvideos – thus opening 'independent' spaces for the expression of their bodies and subjectivities (Jacobs 2007; Attwood 2012; Biasin, Maina, Zecca 2014).

The second dialectic inherent in contemporary pornography is epistemic and closely related to the construction of the pornographic subject – and, as a consequence, to the structuration of the pornographic body. Drawing loosely on Jacques Derrida's philosophical reflections, we could say that the sphere of contemporary pornography is informed by a carno-phallogocentric logic – that is, by 'the scheme that governs the production of the subject in Western culture' (1992, p. 294). As noted by Laura Odello, through the category of 'carno-phallogocentric' Derrida had described 'the structure itself of sovereignty, that is of the metaphysical subject who organizes around him the ethic and political-juridical space' (2005, p. 298). According to Derrida, this subject is produced by means of a process of exclusion (of other subjects) and through the construction of a structural Otherness.

Pornography has always established complex and contradictory relations with this scheme, especially after the digital turn and the advent of the above-mentioned regime of proliferating pornographies. On the one hand, in fact, pornography (or, specific kinds of pornography) seems to reiterate (and reinforce) the logic of carno-phallogocentrism as defined by Derrida, in that it seems to create the quintessential sovereign subject. Even literally, since the sovereign subject is, as Odello would say, a 'virile character, possessing the phallus' (2005, p. 208). This pornographic subject is white, male, heterosexual, able-bodied and young. His sexual identity is centripetal; he is able to dominate the narrative space as well as the space of vision. He is a subject around which and in opposition to which other subjectivities construct themselves and develop. On the other, pornography (or, other kinds of pornography) seems to undermine the carno-phallogocentric scheme from the inside, deconstructing the system of oppositions on which it is based (or, at least, some of its central nodes). Pornography can build, in fact, heterotopic spaces in which subjects take on centrifugal and decentralised identities, driven towards the 'care of the self', as Foucault would say (1986), rather than the domination of others.

In this sense, the ageing body in pornography seems to be involved in a sort of contradictory process, being both an Otherness and an Identity. It is, in fact, constructed as Other or, that is to say, as one of the Others in opposition to which the pornographic sovereign subject defines himself and his identity. In other words, the ageing body is always seen as a 'marked body' in a context where youth is the norm embodied by the sovereign pornographic subject, as happens for instance in so-called granny porn (as we will see later). But at the same time, pornography may build the ageing body as a legitimate new subject that is no longer totally informed by the carno-phallogocentric logic. In other words, the opposition between norm and Otherness may be blurred or even erased, as happens in some instances of alternative, queer and amateur pornography.

To sum up, the pornographic representation of the ageing body is positioned at the crossroad of different tensions that involve both the productive process (in terms of cultural production) and the epistemic dimension (in terms of subject formation). For these reasons, the ageing body in contemporary pornography is not a single, monolithic entity; on the contrary, it is a plural category, which occupies different positions in the contemporary pornographic landscape, acquires different meanings and establishes multifaceted relations.

'Enfreaked' women and 'divine' men

The first type of materials I have identified is closely related to a specific sub-genre, so-called 'granny porn'. A very representative website dedicated to this sub-genre is 21sextreme – part of the European network 21sextury, in turn owned by the porn conglomerate Gamma Entertainment – which features (as I write) 770 videos in which elderly women are shown while performing a wide range of sexual acts with younger partners. The materials available on this website employ – and exacerbate – the same construction of the commonly accepted image of old age generally seen in 'legitimate' media representations, grounded in widespread visual stereotypes and cultural conventions.

According to Bill Bytheway and Julia Johnson (1998), such construction is based on three main discursive strategies: the first is to focus attention upon, and therefore to stress, the bodily signifiers of age, such as wrinkles and flaccidity; the second is to attach to the person a set of hairstyles, clothes and 'appendages' that immediately represent and recall age; the third is 'to portray the person in a relationship with others, a relation which reflects an age difference and a state of dependency' (254). This image of age is directly related to what Kathleen Woodward has defined as the 'youthful structure of the look' – that is, 'the cultural tendency [...] to reduce an older person to the prejudicial category of old age' (2006, p. 164). For Woodward, through this look older people tend to be equated with, and conflated into, their age – as if agedness was the very (and only) essence of their true selves.

In order to make sense of the ways in which these strategies function in the granny sub-genre, I briefly discuss a specific video among the many available on 21sextreme, *Norma is back* (2015). At the beginning of the video, an old woman dressed in an outmoded flower-print dress sits on a bed, smiling and fondling herself. The camera explores the woman's body and face in extreme close-up, highlighting her varicose veins, saggy breasts, sunken eyes, the wrinkles around her mouth and her flaccid skin. After this short presentation she is joined by a young man, who immediately engages with her sexually. Throughout the scene the woman lies almost motionless, while the young man guides her during each phase of the intercourse, moving her body and changing her positions – thus reinforcing the idea that she is totally dependent on him.

However, in the granny sub-genre this stereotypical construction of old age is usually associated with a further strategy. According to Clarissa Smith (2014), in fact, corporate pornography usually implements a process of 'enfreakment' to represent non-normative bodies and identities (including female ageing bodies). For Smith, 'enfreakment' is a

> process by which representations draw attention to the exotic and erotic elements of bodies which signify outside the realm of normativity [...] through very conscious restaging of 'difference' to render these bodies aggrandised freaks or exoticised (eroticised) freaks [...]. In the freak show, the 'abnormal' is not shown in 'normal' states but in ways which draw particular visual attention to the 'abnormality' that offers potential 'entertainment' to its audiences.
>
> *(81)*

In this sense, by focusing excessively on the elements of their bodies that exceed the standards of youthfulness, granny porn exoticises/eroticises the abnormality of the female ageing body, turning it into a grotesque spectacle that caters to specific market niches.

But why the female ageing body is so directly associated in the granny sub-genre with the exoticisation/eroticisation of abnormality? One possible suggestion is that this sub-genre takes to the extreme level the system of 'durable, transposable dispositions' (Bourdieu 1990, p. 53) – that is, the habitus in a Bourdieusian sense – through which old age and the ageing body are culturally interpreted and appraised. For instance, feminist writers have noted that in our society older women are not allowed to be sexual, and are generally 'exhorted to leave their 'sexiness' at the door' (Whelehan 2013, p. 9). Women not complying with this ageist and sexist norm – as is the case with the performers in granny videos – are deemed 'at best laughable and at worst disgusting' (Featherstone, Hepworth 1991, p. 380). More generally, according to many scholars in Western culture old age signifies a 'pathological process' (Katz and Marshall 2002, p. 46) or a 'disease' (Barrett, Raphael, Gunderson 2014, p. 39), since it is considered as a 'deep signifier of incipient disability or closeness to death' (Gilleard, Higgs 2000, p. 133). As observed by Mike Featherstone and Andrew Wernick (1995), in fact, the ageing body is subjected to constant stigmatisation and disempowerment, and is regarded as producing shame and disgust, especially when placed in sexual contexts.

In this sense, granny porn sexualises precisely the laughable, disgusting and pathologic elements of the female older body – as it is commonly perceived in mainstream culture – by positioning it as a physical and symbolic excess, outside (and against) age-appropriate behaviours and representations regulated by society. Through the strategy of enfreakment discussed above, therefore, the female ageing body is offered to the entertainment of the viewers potentially interested in the sexual fetishisation of difference and abnormality. It is also worth noting that the representational strategies that characterises this sub-genre can be understood as part of a more general tendency of contemporary pornography. As stated by Susanna Paasonen, in fact, contemporary pornographies tend to 'veer toward the extreme, the shocking, and the generally gross' with the aim of 'evoking visceral reactions in their consumers' (2011, p. 229), and therefore increasing their affective intensity.

These strategies are partly replicated in the second type of materials I take into consideration here, related to the corporate pornography sub-genre known as 'grandpa', which shows older men having sex with much younger women, often characterised as teenagers. In this case, I have chosen to focus on one of the oldest and most popular grandpa porn websites, Oldje, established in 1995 and now part of the Netherland-based pornographic company Class Media. At first glance, the videos available on this website (759 as I write) tend to construct a certain image of age through the same discursive strategies described above: not differently from what happens to the female body in granny porn, the male ageing body is here represented by explicitly stressing the signifiers of old age – white hair, baldness, pronounced wrinkles, lacking teeth, flaccid abdomen, limp muscles, etc. – at the same time giving emphasis to the age difference through the juxtaposition with younger female bodies.

However, in these videos the very same image of age is totally re-signified and acquires a completely different meaning. While the first type of materials – as I have shown – represents the female ageing body through a strategy of enfreakment and of eroticization of abnormality, in this case the representation of the male ageing body is centred on the eroticisation of power.

This strategy is articulated on two different though interrelated levels. On a first level, Oldje's videos display the 'perpetuation of men's [sexual] power in representations of older men' (Hearn 1995, p. 107). Their male protagonists are in fact characterised by an unquenchable sexual drive, capable of defying not only the possible 'bodily betrayals' related to old age (Barrett, Raphael, Gunderson 2014, p. 41) – and therefore of exorcising the ghost of impotence – but also of challenging the habitus itself that constructs old people as physically and sexually disabled, or even asexual (Barrow, Smith 1979). On a second level, these videos exhibit the sexual domination of old men over younger women. As mentioned before, these younger women are first of all constructed as teenagers: they are thin and petite, have small breasts, wear no (or childish) makeup, they frequently have ponytails and braids, etc. Moreover, they are represented as horny and impudent brats who challenge the older men to measure up to their youthful bodies and satisfy their hunger for sex. In the typical Oldje narrative the old man out-matches this challenge, taming the younger woman thanks to his sexual power.

To exemplify the strategy of eroticization of power employed by Oldje, I briefly examine one of the many videos available on the website, entitled *The Little Bitch* (2011). The video starts with an old man sitting on a sofa and reading a newspaper. He has a rugged face, grey hair, a three-day beard and is probably lacking some upper teeth. The man is immediately joined by a cheerful teenager, who asks him what he is doing in her house. The man is an old family friend, and tells the girl that he remembers her as a little baby. Initially, the girl is crouched behind the sofa and the man can only see her face. After a while, the girl stands up – she is wearing tiny shorts and a low-cut top that exposes part of her breasts – and starts teasing the man by moving her body, with a slightly mocking attitude. The man is taken aback at first. But after a second, he stands up, gets close to the girl, and towers over her. When the woman asks him if 'she can be his girl', the man grabs her and starts kissing her lips. Sexual intercourse follows right after.

In a sense, Oldje's videos – and grandpa porn more in general – seem to stage a revanchist scenario, in which old and ugly men reaffirm their masculinity, taking their revenge on young and beautiful women. In other words, the male ageing body is here presented as a sort of 'divine' body, infused with hyperbolic masculinity and capable of exerting an absolute power over female performers characterised as childish and passive. According to Lauren Langman (2004), 'grotesque and exaggerated elements of male fantasy demonstrat[e] and celebrat[e] phallic power as compensatory masculinity' (207). These elements function, in fact, as 'a fallback position of agentic power verses [sic] castration and impotence' (207). Drawing on Langman's reflections, then, the grandpa sub-genre can be analysed as a compensatory fantasy for male viewers socially undermined in their masculinity by negative cultural assumptions about age.

'Wise' women and 'perverse' amateurs

I have focused so far on two different types of pornographic materials depicting ageing bodies. Both of them construct the image of age through similar visual stereotypes, stressing its physicality and embodiment. Besides, they are both closely related to the cultural understanding of age (Gullette 1997) as a process of loss and decline (of power, of beauty, of ability, etc.), although with opposite outcomes. In the first type, this understanding underlies and informs the construction of the female ageing body as an exoticised and eroticised 'sexual freak': age is therefore spectacularised and offered as entertainment in its excess and abnormality. In the second type, on the contrary, the representation of the ageing man as hyperbolically masculine seems to challenge this cultural stigmatization of age through the construction of a functioning, sexually able, and dominant ageing body: age seems here to be exorcised and offered as a fantasy of power.

These two types of pornographic materials are also characterised by a similar socioeconomic positioning: although they are part of the offer provided by corporate pornographic conglomerates, they nonetheless represent two very specialised niches that cater to well-defined target audiences. From this point of view, the third type of materials I take into consideration differs substantially from the other two, since it caters instead to a non-specialised porn audience. I am referring here to products related to the mainstream sub-genre 'stepmom', in which midlife women engage in sexual acts with young men (usually fictionalised as their stepsons or as their daughters' boyfriends) or young women (generally stepdaughters), and teach them how to perform and enjoy good sex. Alongside other popular sub-genres (such as 'anal', 'teen', 'blow job', 'big tits', and so on), the stepmom sub-genre represents in fact a large share of the generalist porn market. The reason of this commercial centrality, as we will see, is inherent in the modalities through which age and the female ageing body are conceptualised in this specific type of materials.

For the sake of this analysis, among the hundreds of websites dedicated to this sub-genre I have chosen to examine Moms Teach Sex (part of the Nubiles Porn Network, owned by US company XFC INC). The rationale behind my choice resides in the popularity of this website's official channel on the most relevant porn aggregator in the world, Pornhub: with its 1,706,401 subscribers and 1,283,454,119 video views (as I write), in fact, Moms Teach Sex's channel is ranked the tenth most popular channel on the platform, thus being the first step-mom website in Pornhub's chart. As an example of the kind of materials shown on this website, I examine a video titled *So Much to Teach You* (2014), starring acclaimed MILF porn star Brandi Love. The vignette starts with a gorgeous middle-aged woman (Love) who invites her young and beautiful new neighbour (Aidra Fox) to join her and her shy stepson (Tyler Nixon) for a swim in their pool. After undressing, the two women catch the boy sitting on a sofa with a huge erection. Instead of scolding him, though, the stepmom decides that it is time for him to lose his virginity with the help of the charming neighbour. What follows is a threesome characterised by the fact that the older woman to some extent 'directs' the sexual intercourse, by giving her stepson and her neighbour precious advice on how to perform specific sexual acts (fellatio and cunnilingus, among others), at the same time taking her fair share of pleasure from both of them.

This video – but the same applies to the whole sub-genre with no significant exceptions – shows a common trait with the second type of materials I have identified (grandpa porn), since it seems to counter (at least partially) the negative social perceptions of age by presenting the ageing body as sexually powerful. Drawing on Joel Gwynne, we can say that stepmom videos can be considered as part of a broader 'cougar discourse' (2014, p. 49), in which midlife women are constructed as sexually agentic. As Sharron Hinchliff writes, in fact, cougar is 'a label which is part of, and at the same time reinforces, the sexualisation of "older" women' (Hinchliff 2014, pp. 67–68).

However, compared to the grandpa sub-genre, a website such as Moms Teach Sex shows an important difference in the construction of the image of age. Even though age difference is still pivotal in the representation of the ageing body, in fact, in this instance the representation of mature women totally avoids the stress on physicality previously seen at play. No signifier of age is here particularly highlighted. On the contrary, in videos like *So Much to Teach You* the traces of age seem to be at least partially removed from the surface of the representation – Brandi Love's body is fit, her breasts surgically remodelled, her wrinkles erased, and so on. In other words, the female ageing bodies portrayed in stepmom videos are to some extent constructed as ageless: certainly not young, but definitely not framed as old as in the other classes of materials I have analysed.

It is interesting to note that this process is consistent with what Hinchliff writes about midlife women in mainstream media. 'The sexy midlife woman expresses her sexual agency; she does not hide her sexual desire [...]. However, while the taboo around sexuality in middle adulthood is slowly breaking down, there remains clear disdain of "older" bodies' (2014, p. 71). According to Hinchliff, midlife women can be represented in media culture (pornography included, I would say) only if they meet very strict criteria of youthfulness and bodily perfection. That is, only if they appear young, or at least not old.

While somehow virtualised at a physical level, though, in the stepmom sub-genre age is emphasised and valorised at a symbolic level through a narrative of sexual initiation. Just like in *So Much to Teach You*, in fact, in most of the videos belonging to the subgenre, the stepmoms are seen helping their younger (male or female) counterparts solve the problems they endure in their sexual life. In this case, therefore, to be older means to be 'better': in other words, the ageless-ageing body is here signified in a positive way as the bearer of sexual experience and wisdom.

A unique example of this double process of virtualisation and valorisation of age can be found in the discursive construction of the body of the universally acclaimed porn veteran Nina Hartley. With a more than thirty-year career in the porn industry, the American performer born in 1959 is still active in several sub-genres of both corporate and indie pornography, including 'mature' and 'BDSM'. The focus on experience and knowledge rather than on physicality is clearly demonstrated, for instance, by the contents of her official website. While words such as 'experience', 'teaching' and 'lesson' recur very frequently in the titles and comments associated with the videos, Hartley's body is constructed as still attractive and not-so-different from the bodies of her younger sexual partners. In a sense, Hartley is an emblematic model of what has been called 'youthful aging' (Dolan 2011), a notion that opposes the pathologised understanding of old age, focusing instead on ageing as a 'joyous, energetic, and vibrant' (Van den Bulck 2014, p. 68) process in which an active sexuality is emphasised and promoted (Katz, Marshall 2003).

Differently from the first three, the fourth and last type of age-themed pornography I analyse here is composed of grassroots, consumer-driven materials that circulate primarily inside 'micro-porn spaces' (Jacobs 2007, p. 2) governed by bottom-up production modes and informal sharing economy. Specific sectors belonging to the complex and multifarious sphere of amateur porn tend, in fact, to construct a representation of the older person as a legitimately desirable and desiring sexual subject, for (and from) a niche of consumers or existing subcultures and communities (if not the general public). These materials show a clear paradigm shift in the understanding, and therefore in the representation, of the ageing body. While in the other types – as I have shown – age is enfreaked, exorcised or virtualised, this production submits the ageing body to a process of legitimisation and inclusion. In other words, in this case age is represented neither as an abnormality to exoticise/eroticise nor as a disability to exorcise, and not even as something to be 'effaced', but as an integral part of a 'reflexive' project of self-expression.

In order to select a representative example, I rely on the existing literature on amateur pornographies. More specifically, drawing on Sergio Messina's analysis of what he terms 'realcore' (2010), I examine the case of Sissy Babette, an overweight middle-aged submissive exhibitionist from Berlin with a very small penis, renowned and appreciated within a narrow community of aficionados.

Sissy Babette shows his pictures and a few short clips (three to four minutes long on average) for free on the pornographic tube Xvideos.[2] In his videos he is always alone, wearing a white bra and grandma-style knickers, masturbating in his room or outdoors, often while penetrating himself with a butt plug. These scenes are set in a variety of 'regressive' scenarios: Sissy holding a Barbie doll, or sucking a pacifier, or ejaculating on pictures of naked women, and so on. This pornographic self-exhibition is explicitly posed by the author himself as part of a sexual ritual of digital public submission. Not surprisingly, he comments his own images with this invitation to the viewer: 'This file is published for Sissy Babette's public humiliation. Please distribute and share this file on the web as you like' (Messina 2010, p. 107).

Differently from the other three types discussed above, Sissy Babette's 'social masochist' (Reik 2011) cross-dressing performances are not related to a specific corporate sub-genre, but comply instead with a style that I have defined elsewhere as porn 'home movie' (Zecca 2014, p. 324). On the one hand, these materials are in fact characterized by a 'heightened sense of mundane reality' (Klein 2006, p. 255) – wherein the bedroom where he sets his performances is messy, the bed unmade, the clothes abandoned carelessly on the sheets, and so on. On the other, they exceed and transgress the most common representation of the male ageing body in pornography (simultaneously abject and powerful, as we have seen in the second part), in that they exhibit an old, overweight and sexually unfit body that unapologetically offers itself to the small group of individuals who share similar sexual penchants.[3]

Being first and foremost tools for self-expression and exhibitionism, the videos filmed by the Berliner cross-dresser can therefore be considered as part of the new 'collective discourse on sex' (Stella 2011, p. 96) that boomed with the advent of new digital technologies and the internet. To some extent, this collective discourse sets individuals free from the role of sick (and freak) that sexology attributes to them, and helps them to (re)construct their own sexual identity inside 'a community of people who share the [same] predilections' (Lehman 2006, p. 13). As Renato Stella contends, through such discourse (even) the 'perverse' (in sexological terms) are able to 'showcase their own pleasure without concealing it anymore' (2011, p. 96). Therefore, in Sissy Babette's case, the representation of the ageing body is to be interpreted as part of a larger project of (sexual) self-expression. In his videos, age is not enfreaked or exorcised; on the contrary, it is simply exhibited for what it is, a central aspect of the man's physical and sexual self. Drawing on Chris Gilleard and Paul Higgs, age can be viewed here more as a position of difference than as a deviation from a youthful self – a state of being 'not youthful' rather than 'full of age' (2013, p. 99).

Conclusion

In this chapter I have tried to demonstrate how contemporary pornography is permeated by different and at times antithetical tensions related to age, which mirror, in some instances intensify, and sometimes even challenge widespread social perceptions and schemes at play in Western culture at large. In order to do so, I have outlined four representational strategies through which contemporary pornography (re)presents and signifies the ageing body. The first strategy constructs older women as sexual freaks, turning their body (and their sexual desire) into a grotesque spectacle; the second stages a chauvinist fantasy, glorifying the phallic power of older men against young girls; the third represents midlife women as hypereroticised 'sexperts' through a double process of virtualisation and valorisation of age; and finally, the fourth strategy understands age as part of a wider project of (self)expression of non-normative bodies and desires.

For reasons of space, I have focused mainly on the relationship between sexuality, age and gender. Of course, further research should be done in an intersectional perspective – that is, taking into account the role played by elements such as race and class in the construction of the pornographic ageing body. For instance, in grandpa porn age difference and class difference often conflate since the male protagonist's social status is usually visibly marked as lower than that of his female younger companion – and therefore his exertion of sexual power over her can be considered as a white working-class male revanchist fantasy against upper-middle-class women. Or, in some examples of interracial granny porn the racial difference between the old white woman and the young African American performer may be exploited in order to exaggerate the strategy of enfreakment enacted on the female ageing body. Embracing this intersectional perspective is certainly a necessary step in order to add a further layer of complexity to the study of the pornographic representation of the ageing body.

Notes

1 Due to space limitations, I will focus mainly on heterosexual pornography, leaving the analysis of the ageing body in gay pornographies to further explorations.
2 Sissy Babette started sharing his pictures on alt porn newsgroups as early as the 1990s, and then moved to Xvideos in the early 2010s. His Xvideos channel is now closed and retrievable only on the Internet Archive at the address: https://web.archive.org/web/20150930052100/https://.xvideos.com/profiles/sissy-babette (last seen 15 January 2020). He still has an active profile on the old school picture-based adult hoster Image Fap.

3 His Image Fap profile lists around 440 fans, who comment his pics and videos, generally expressing appreciation and discussing sexual fantasies.

References

Alilunas, P. (2016). *Smutty Little Movies: The Creation and Regulation of Adult Video*. Oakland, CA: University of California Press.

Attwood, F. (2010). Younger, paler, decidedly less straight: The new porn professionals. In F. Attwood (ed.), *Porn.com: Making Sense of Online Pornography* (pp.88–106). New York: Peter Lang.

Attwood, F. (2012). Art school sluts: Authenticity and the aesthetics of altporn. In C. Hines and D. Kerr (eds), *Hard to Swallow: Hard-Core Pornography on Screen* (pp. 42–56). London: Wallflower Press.

Barrett, A.E., Raphael, A. and Gunderson, J. (2014). Reflections of old age, constructions of aging selves: Drawing links between media images and views of aging. In C.L. Harrington, D.D. Bielby and A.R. Bardo (eds), *Aging, Media, and Culture* (pp. 39–50). Lanham, MD: Lexington Books.

Barrow, G.M. and Smith, P.A. (1979). *Aging, Ageism, and Society*. New York: West Publishing.

Biasin, E., Maina, G. Zecca, F. (eds) (2014). *Porn After Porn: Contemporary Alternative Pornographies*. Milan: Mimesis International.

Bond, J. and Cabrero, G. Z. (2007). Health and dependency in later life. In J. Bond, S.M. Peace, F. Dittmann-Kohli and G. Westerhof (eds), *Ageing in Society: European Perspectives on Gerontology* (pp. 113–141). London: Sage.

Bourdieu, P. (1990). *The Logic of Practice*. Stanford: Stanford University Press.

Bytheway, B. and Johnson, J. (1998). The Sight of Age. In S. Nettleton and J. Watson (eds), *The Body in Everyday Life* (pp. 243–256). London: Routledge.

Derrida, J. (1992). *Il faut bien manger, ou le calcul du sujet: Entretien (avec J.-L. Nancy)*. In E. Weber (ed.), *Points de suspension* (pp. 91–114). Paris: Galilée.

Dolan, J. (2011). Firm and hard: Old age, the 'youthful' body and essentialist Discourses. In *Actas del IV Congreso de la SELICUP: Pasado, Presente y Future de la Cultura Popular: Espacios y Contextos*. Palma de Mallorca: Edicions UIB.

Dyer, R. (1993). *The Matter of Images: Essays on Representations*. London: Routledge.

Featherstone, M. and Hepworth, M. (1991). The mask of ageing and the postmodern life course. In M. Featherstone, M. Hepworth and B.S. Turner (eds), *The Body: Social Processes and Cultural Theory* (pp. 371–389). London: Sage.

Featherstone, M. and Wernick, A. (1995). Introduction. In M. Featherstone and A. Wernick (eds), *Images of Aging: Cultural Representations of Later Life* (pp. 1–15). London: Routledge.

Foucault, M. (1986). *The History of Sexuality, Vol. 3: The Care of the Self*. New York: Pantheon.

Gilleard, C. and Higgs, P. (2000). *Cultures of Ageing: Self, Citizen, and the Body*. Harlow, UK: Pearson Education.

Gilleard, C. and Higgs, P. (2013). *Ageing, Corporeality and Embodiment*. London: Anthem Press.

Gullette, M.M. (1997). *Declining to Decline: Cultural Combat and the Politics of the Midlife*. Charlottesville, CA: University Press of Virginia.

Gwynne, J. (2014). 'Mrs Robinson seeks Benjamin': Cougars, popular memoirs and the quest for fulfilment in midlife and beyond. In I. Whelehan and J. Gwynne (eds), *Ageing, Popular Culture and Contemporary Feminism: Harleys and Hormones* (pp. 47–62). Basingstoke: Palgrave McMillan.

Härmä, S. and Stolpe, J. (2010). Behind the scenes of straight pleasures. In F. Attwood (ed.), *Porn.com: Making Sense of Online Pornography* (pp. 107–122). New York: Peter Lang.

Hearn, J. (1995). Imaging the aging of men. In M. Featherstone and A. Wernick (eds), *Images of Aging: Cultural Representations of Later Life* (pp. 97–115). London: Routledge.

Hinchliff, S. (2014). Sexing up the midlife woman: Cultural representations of ageing, femininity and the sexy body. In I. Whelehan and J. Gwynne (eds), *Ageing, Popular Culture and Contemporary Feminism: Harleys and Hormones* (pp. 63–77). Basingstoke: Palgrave McMillan.

Jacobs, K. (2007). *Netporn: DIY Webculture and Sexual Politics*. New York: Rowman & Littlefield.

Jenkins, H. (2006). *Convergence Culture: Where Old and New Media Collide*. Cambridge, MA: MIT Press.

Katz, S., Marshall, B. (2002). Forever functional: Sexual fitness and the ageing male body. *Body & Society*, 8(4): 43–70.

Katz, S., Marshall, B. (2003). New sex for old: Lifestyle, consumerism, and the ethics of aging well. *Journal of Aging Studies*, 17(1), 3–16.

Klein, M. (2006). Pornography: What men see when they watch. In P. Lehman (ed.), *Pornography: Film and Culture* (pp. 244–257). New Brunswick: Rutgers University Press.

Langman, L. (2004). Grotesque degradation: Globalization, carnivalization, and cyberporn. In D.D. Waskul (ed.), *Net.seXXX: Readings on Sex, Pornography and the Internet* (pp. 180–206). New York: Peter Lang.

Lehman, P. (2006). 'A dirty little secret': Why teach and study pornography? In P. Lehman (ed.), *Pornography: Film and Culture* (pp. 1–24). New Brunswick: Rutgers University Press.

Messina, S. (2010). *Real Sex: Il porno alternativo è il nuovo rock'n'roll*. Latina: Tunué.

Odello, Laura (2005). Divorazione. *Aut Aut*, 327, 206–223.

Paasonen, S. (2011). *Carnal Resonance: Affect and Online Pornography*. Cambridge, MA: MIT Press.

Reik, T. (2011). *Masochism in Modern Man*. New York: Farrar, Strauss & Co.

Rosow, I. (1974). *Socialization to Old Age*. Berkeley, CA: University of California Press.

Smith, C. (2014). It's important that you don't smell a suit on this stuff. In E. Biasin, G. Maina and F. Zecca (eds), *Porn After Porn: Contemporary Alternative Pornographies* (pp. 57–83). Milan: Mimesis International.

Stella, R. (2011). *Eros, Cybersex, Neoporn: Nuovi scenari e nuovi usi in Rete*. Milan: Franco Angeli.

Van den Bulck, H. (2014). Growing old in celebrity culture. In C.L. Harrington, D.D. Bielby and A.R. Bardo (eds), *Aging, Media, and Culture* (pp. 65–76). Lanham, MD: Lexington Books.

Whelehan, I. (2013). Ageing appropriately: Postfeminist discourses of ageing in contemporary Hollywood. In J. Gwynne and N. Muller (eds), *Postfeminism and Contemporary Hollywood Cinema* (pp. 78–95). Basingstoke: Palgrave McMillan.

Williams, L. (1999). *Hard Core: Power, Pleasure, and the 'Frenzy of the Visible'*. Berkeley: University of California Press.

Williams, L. (2004). Porn studies: Proliferating pornographies on/scene: An Iitroduction. In L. Williams (ed.), *Porn Studies* (pp. 1–23). Durham, NC: Duke University Press.

Woodward, K. (2006). Performing age, performing gender. *NWSA Journal*, 18(1), 162–189.

Zecca, F. (2014). Porn sweet home: A survey of amateur pornography. In E. Biasin, G. Maina and F. Zecca (eds), *Porn After Porn: Contemporary Alternative Pornographies* (pp. 321–337). Milan: Mimesis International.

INDEX

Note: Page numbers in *italics* indicate figures and page numbers in **bold** indicate tables on the corresponding pages.

Abidin, C. 18
ableism 89, 96
Abril, G. 163
abstinence 156
abuse 30; child sex 63–7; online media 101; psychological 163; sexual 5, 58
accessibility 41, 54, 90, 136
activism: feminist 4, 12–20
addiction to pornography 62
Adelman, M. 164
adolescence 46–7
adulthood 4, 53, 61–2, 76, 79, 82, 96, 161, 198; adults 119–31
advertising 13, 31, 87, 90, 96, 107, 115, 136–7, 140–1, 176–7, 180–1, 183
African American performers 200
African people 130
Agamben, G. 122–3
age: actors' opinions 183–5; ageing body in contemporary pornography 191–3; ageing body, pornographic representations of 190–201; ageing femininities 136–41; ageing women on screen 175–86; differences in pornographic fantasies 146–59; divine men 193–6; 'enfreaked' women 193–6; history of women on screen 176; intersectionality 182; invisible ageing femininities 136–9; old gay male bodies

163–6; perverse amateurs 196–200; porn taxonomies and boundary work 155–8; representing the older woman 177–8; sex toys and 86–97; 'silver and sexy' 179–80; 'successful' ageing 180–2; taboo and 153–5; valorisation of 198, 200; virtualisation of 198–200; 'wise' women 196–200; women viewing women 182–3; young marginal bodies as objects of desire 166–7; *see also* adulthood; anti-ageing discourse; childhood; disgust; elderly people; wrinkles; youth ageism 2, 7, 96, 138–40, 149, 151–2, 158, 161–71, 176, 182, 184–5, 194; hustling and 161, 71
'agelessless' 138, 142, 180, 182, 198; cultures of 137, 140
Ahmed, S. 125
Albania 3, 6, 100–16, 167; age groups targeted for hate speech *111*; articles containing hate speech/discriminatory language *113*; characteristics of subjects who are victims of hate speech/discriminatory language in online media 111–14; hate speech towards women in online news websites 100–16; main targets of hate speech in online media 108–11; percentage breakdown of groups targeted for hate speech *108*; percentage of news items with hate speech content

106; photos, use of *114*; research on
hate speech 101–2; state of online
media 103–4; subjects of photos
113; topics of articles with hate
speech *112*
Albury, K. 155
Alexander, J. C. 80
alienation 170
Alilunas, P. 190
'A-list' celebrities 183
Álvarez, A. 19
amateur porn 166, 190–3, 196, 199;
perverse amateurs 196–200
anal sex 149, 156, 197
Anderson, T. L. 95, 97
Andreassen, R. 1
animalism 151, 157
anime 155
Ann Summers 90
Annenberg Inclusion Initiative Research
Team 178, 188
anonymity 41, 52–3
anthropology 1
anti-ageing discourse 142, 181; *see also* age
anti-discrimination 113; *see also*
discrimination
anti-feminism 13–19; protests and laughs to
combat 15–18 *see also* feminism
anti-porn arguments 67
anti-Semitism 100–1
Araüna, N. 4, 11–14, 16, 18, 20, 22
Argentina 3
Armengol, J. M. 162
Arnold, Andrea 178
art 88
artists 81, 91
arts, the 28, 115
Asadaf, A. 12, 14–16
asexuality 62, 195
Ashton, Mark 81–2
Asia 67; Asian origin, people of 67, 93, 161,
169, 182
Aslinger, B. 24
Asthana, A. 179
Attinelo, P. 76
attractiveness 97, 146, 158
Attwood, F. 1, 3, 59, 60, 68, 90, 93–4,
152, 192
audience reception studies 4
audio-visual media 12–13, 104, 116, 120,
155, 157, 163, 166, 167, 171, 178
Australia 25, 35, 37
Austria 167, 178
authenticity 7, 16, 50, 151, 158
Avila-Saavedra, G. 24

award ceremonies 183; *see also* BAFTA
awards; Oscar award ceremonies

Babette, Sissy 199–200
'Baby Boom' generation 177, 183
Baer, H. 18, 162
BAFTA awards 81
Baker, A. 119
Bale, C. 51
Balkanweb 105, 107, 109, 114, 116
Banet-Weiser, S. 13, 17
Barbagli, M. 44
Bardzell, J. 90
Bardzell, S. 90
Barrett, A. E. 195
Barrow, G. M. 195
Barry, C. L. 78
Bartow, A. 101, 105, 108, 112, 115
Bataille, G. 154
BBC (British Broadcasting Corporation) 27,
35, 182
BDSM equipment 88, 90, 94, 149, 155, 198
Beattie, E. 163
Becker, R. 37
BelAmiOnline 161, 167
Belgium 3
Benesch, S. 102
Bennett, K. C. 165
Berger, R. M. 161, 164
Bersani, L. 161, 164
Biasin, E. 191–2
Bigelow, Kathryn 178
bigotry 19
biochemistry 75
biology 47, 88–9, 122–3, 182, 191
biomedical science 43, 47
bisexuality 31
'bitches': use of the derogatory term 109
black females 182
Blackman, S. 61, 69
blogs 147
'blow jobs' 147, 155, 197
Blumell, L. E. 162
Bobolt, S. 177
bodily integrity 6, 120
body fascism 164
body positivity 146
body weight 152
Bono, Chaz 120, 132
Borghs, P. 29, 31, 38
Boudiny, K. 138
Bourdieu, P. 194
bourgeoisie 162, 165
boybands 30
'boyification' 138

Bradshaw, P. 119
Bragg, S. 41, 60
Bramham, P. 62
Brando, Marlon 165
brands 94, 135–6, 141, 155, 180–1
breasts 129, 194, 196, 198
Brennan, J. 161
Britzman, D. 123
Broll, W. 91
Brotman, S. 165
browsing history 41, 46
BRT 29
Bruns, A. 12–13
Buckels, E. E. 101
Buckingham, D. 2, 26, 41, 59, 60, 62
Bulgaria 162, 167
Bunzl, M. 162, 167
Burema, D. 139, 141, 179
Butler, J. 89, 120, 122, 127
Butler, R. 176

Caballero-Gálvez, A. 7, 13, 15, 161–2, 164, 166, 168, 170
Cabrero, G. Z. 190
Çakirlar, C. 79, 83
Calouste Gulbenkian Foundation 185
Campillo, R. 7, 11, 161, 166, 174
Campion, Jane 178
Cannes Film Festival 120
Carabí, A. 162
Cardoso, D. 5, 41–2, 44, 46, 48–52, 54
caricature 18
Carlton TV 175
carno-phallogocentrism 192–3
castration 196
Castro-Martínez, A. 11
Catholic Church 43
Cavalli, A. 43, 54
celebrities 14, 107, 111–12, 115, 136, 138, 141, 179–81, 186; celebrity culture 12, 111, 179, 181, 183
Celluloid Ceiling 178
census data 103, 116
Chadha, Gurinder 178, 182
Chambers, S. A. 24
'charmed circle' of good sex 88, 153
Chechen language 167
Chewning, L. V. 2
Chiha, P. 7, 161
childbirth 154
childhood 5, 29, 58–65, 67–71, 191; sexuality and digital spaces 58–70; sociotemporal invention of 65
China 63, 67, 137
Chronaki, D. 1, 5, 52, 59, 61–9

cinema 2, 5, 6, 14, 75–9, 81–3, 119–31; cinematic representations 6, 119–21, 131, 165, 190; HIV-related stigma in European cinema see HIV/AIDS; identity, stigma and health 77–8; see also films
cinematography 126, 178
cisgender 32–3, 35–6, 128
cisnormativity 24, 42, 119
citizens 43, 64, 68, 95, 137, 180, 201
citizenship 42, 51, 54
Clarke, V. 62
Class Media (Netherlands) 195
clicktivism 19, 22
clitoris/clitoral representations 46, 91
'cloak of invisibility' of ageing women on TV 142
close-up shots 147, 194
Cochrane, K. 11, 19, 20
Coco de Mer 90
Cohen, W. A. 151
Coleman, R. 161
comedy 136, 138, 140
Comella, L. 8, 90
comics 155
'coming-out' experiences 37, 53, 127
commercials 137
commodification 17, 88, 90, 163
communist countries 162, 167
comorbidities 75, 76
condoms 45, 79, 87
conglomerations: media 105, 106
Connell, R. W. 162, 164
constructionism 24
consumerism 90, 94, 137, 181
contraceptives 48, 51, 87
Convention on the Elimination of All Forms of Discrimination against Women (CEDAW) 101
Cookney, R. 91
Cooper, R. 141
Coppola, Sofia 178
Corcoran, F. 26
Cormier, R. 165
coronavirus 66, 67; see also COVID-19 pandemic
corporate pornography 191–2, 194–5, 197–9
Cosmopolitan 90
costume design 178
'cougar' discourse 139, 179, 197
Coulmont, B. 93–4
counselling support 29
counterculture 165
counter-hegemony 123–4, 126, 130–1
'countersexual' society 123–4

Coupland, J. 142
COVID-19 pandemic: childhood sexuality in digital spaces 58–70; fear of the predator 63–6; regulatory context of public discourse about sexuality in digital spaces 63; sexuality performed and consumed online 59–60; sexuality, digital culture and leisure 60–2
Cradock, G. 65
crafts 28
Crawford Monde, G. 182
'cream pies' 150
Crenshaw, K. 2
Crewe, L. 90
criminalisation 162, 166
criminality 30, 163
criminology 172
critical discourse analysis (CDA) 121
Croatia 178
cross-cultural research 5
cross-dressing 89, 199
Cuddy, A. 137
cultural trauma 75–83; see also HIV/AIDS
'cumshots' 147
'cunnilingus' 197
Curoe, K. A. 82
cyberporn 202
cybersex 202
Czech Republic 91, 167; Czechoslovakia, former 167
CzechHunter 161, 167

Dalí, S. 165
dance 121, 127, 162
Dancyger, L. 95
Daneback, K. 93, 98
dating apps 59, 62, 161–2, 168, 180; singles dating apps 180
Davis, Bette 183
Dawson, K. 155
De Vijver Media 31
De Vries, D. A. 59
De Vuyst, S. 1
death 58, 108, 137, 181, 183, 195
decolonial perspective 130
defamation 116
defecation 154
Democratic Party 116
demonisation of pornography 66
demonstrations 11, 82
Dench, Judi 186
Denmark 25
Dennis, J. P. 24, 25, 31, 38
depression see mental health
derogatory terms 115, 123

Derrida, J. 192
desexualisation of women 46
Dhaenens, F. 2, 13, 24, 138, 142
Dhoest, A. 26–9, 38
dialectic practice 13, 54, 191, 192
didactic devices 14, 119, 120, 124–6, 130
Dieffenbach, C. W. 82
digital culture: COVID-19 pandemic and childhood sexuality 58–70; see also COVID-19 pandemic
digital revolution 177, 190–1
dildos 90, 96; see also sex toys
disability 86, 89, 96–7, 105, 176, 182, 195, 199
discrimination 77, 80, 82–3, 96, 100, 101, 103–4, 108, 138, 163
discriminatory language: in Albania see Albania
diseases: cardiovascular 75; sexually transmitted 45, 47, 51; see also COVID-19 pandemic; HIV/AIDS
disgust: ambivalent 158–9; disgusting behaviour 151–3; see also age
dispositif: definitions of 42, 122–3
DIY tutorials 58, 192
Dizdari, D. 104, 117
Dobson, A. 12
doctors 6, 79, 119, 124, 128–30; role of 129–30
documentary film 14, 26, 78, 135, 163
Dolan, J. 2, 137, 141, 178, 179, 186, 198
dolls: Barbie 199
domestication of media 66, 68
domesticity 66
Donati, S. 48
Donnelly, Don 29
Döring, N. 12, 20, 41, 90
Douglas, Kirk 165
Douglas, Lord Alfred 165
Dove 143
Dovidio, J. 78
DPG Media 31
drama series 30, 35, 37, 137, 140
dreams: sexual 157–8
drugs 70, 110; prescription 75
Drummond, M. 95
Ducastel, Oliver 79–80
Dworkin, A. 87
Dyer, R. 30, 78, 161, 165, 191

Edström, M. 1, 137, 141, 176–7
Egan, R. 42, 60–1
eHarmony 180
Eisinger, R. W. 82
El Tornillo 18–19

elderly people 4, 6–7, 80, 133, 136, 140, 161, 169–70, 193 *see also* age
electronic music 170
Ellerson, B. 166
emojis 148
emotions 46, 49, 78, 121, 124, 127, 131
En Daarmee Basta 31–2
endocrinology 129
'enfreakment' 194, 195, 200; 'enfreaked' women 193–6
epistemology 1, 3, 50, 53, 59, 63, 123
equality 4, 12, 37, 87, 103, 124, 148
equity 82, 123, 130
erectile dysfunction 155
erections 197
Erjavec, K. 101
erotic-affective relationships 130
eroticisation 194–6, 199; of power 195–6
essentialism 19, 182
Ethical Journalism Networks (EJN) 104
ethics 94, 147, 202
ethnic minorities 105, 168
ethnicity 2, 100, 103, 123, 163, 170; ethnic-racial bias 123, 130
ethnocentrism 100, 166
European Women's Audiovisual Network 178
Evans-Lacko, S. 75
exhibitionism 199
exotic 166, 168, 194
exoticisation 194, 196, 199
extremism: political 108

Facebook 102, 147, 183, 185
fact-based media 176, 177, 180
Fahs, B. 42, 90, 94
Fairclough, N. 121
Fairclough-Isaacs, K. 138
fairy tales 157
Faktoria Lila 14
fallacies: sexist 15
family 45–6
Fanning, Elle 121
Farrell, K. P. 77
fashion industry 90, 136, 140–2, 164, 180–1
Fauci, A. S. 82
Featherstone, M. 137, 191, 194–5
Fejes, F. 24
fellatio 169, 197
'feminazi': concept of 16, 18
femininities 6, 135–43
feminism 1, 2, 4, 7, 11–20, 67, 90, 94–5, 97, 120, 146, 148, 154, 156–7, 177, 194; fourth wave 11, 19–21; new luminosity

of 12–13; Spanish 11–12; YouTube 13–14; YouTubers in Spain 11–21
Ferdy, Will 29, 38
Fernández, E. 11
fetish 67, 93, 138, 149, 153–4, 195
Figueroa, M. G. 151
film festivals 120, 121
films: as queer didactic devices 124–7; as queer pedagogical devices 121–4; *see also* cinema
Finland 3, 6, 138, 146–8, 165
Fiske, S. 137
'fisting' 48, 150, 156
fitness 7, 58, 138, 161
flaccidity 193–5
Flanders 4, 25–7, 30, 37–8
Flemish television 4, 24–32, 34, 38; LGBT+ representation 24–39; *see also* LGBT+ representation
Flick, U. 44
folklore 29
Fonda, Jane 135, 141, 180–1, 183–4
Ford, A. 120
Foucault, M. 42, 53, 121–3, 129, 193
France 29, 63, 66, 79–80, 93–4, 167, 178
Frankenberg, R. 169
'freaks': sexual 194, 196, 199–200
Freud, S. 62
'fucking' 150, 152, 155, 157

Gabhainn, S. N. 155
Gaddam, S. 41, 56
Gagliardone, I. 100–1, 106, 110
Gailienė, D. 80
Galland, O. 43
Gamma Entertainment 192–3
'gangbang' scenes 150, 155
gangs 46, 165, 169–70
Gao, X. 75
gatekeeping content 27, 51
gay community 29, 161–71
'gaze': concept of the male 124–7, 129, 164
'geeking out' online 62
gendertrolling 20
genitalia 147, 168
Genz, S. 13
George, J. J. 19
Gerbner, G. 176, 187
Germany 25, 110, 178
Ghost Rockers 32, 34
GILF ('grandma I'd like to fuck') 146
Gill, R. 12, 13
Gilleard, C. 138, 142, 195, 200
Gilligan, P. 26–8, 37, 39
'girlification': practice of 138, 140, 142

Givskov, C. 136–7, 142
GLAAD 120, 132
globalisation 4, 27, 66, 137, 166
Goffman, E. 53, 77
Goldsmith, J. 184
Google 49, 62
Gough, B. 77
governmentality 42, 66
grandpa porn 195–8, 200
granny porn 193–5, 200
grassroots practice 12, 191–2, 198
Graziano, F. 48
Grazzani Gavazzi, I. 46
Greece 3, 108, 164
Griffin, C. 66
Grist, H. 177
grooming online 30, 63
Gross, L. 30
grotesque, the 125, 194, 196, 200
gruesomeness 150
Grunert, C. 95
Guardian, The 62, 64, 66, 68
Guasch, O. 161
Guerra Palmero, M. J. 13
Gullette, M. M. 196
Gunderson, J. 195
Gurley Brown, Helen 140
Gwynne, J. 136–7, 139, 140, 197

Haarr, R. 101, 108, 114
Haber, D. 163
Habermas, J. 15
hacking attacks 68
Haddon, L. 41
hairstyles 165, 193
Hant, M. 137–8, 141
harassment 17–18, 105, 125
hardcore pornography 151
Härmä, S. 190
Harris, P. 179
Harrison, K. 1
Hart, K.-P. 78
Hartley, Nina 198
Harwood, J. 138
Hasinoff, A. A. 60
Haslam, C. 77
Haslam, S. A. 77
Hastall, M. R. 78
hate speech 101: in Albania *see* Albania
'haters' on social media 20
Hathaway, Anne 184
hatred: online 101; queer films 124–6;
   racial 100
Hatzenbuehler, M. L. 78
Hawkes, G. 42, 60–1

Healey, T. 142
health-related information 45, 50
healthcare professionals (HCPs)
   76, 79
Healy, T. 175, 176
Hearn, J. 195
hedonism 81, 82
hegemony 12, 15, 20, 169; hegemonic
   constructions 19, 120, 124, 125, 128,
   151, 161, 162, 165, 166, 170
Helsper, E. J. 64
Hepp, A. 68
Hepworth, M. 137, 191, 194
Herbenick, D. 96
Herman, D. 34
hermeneutics 122, 163
Herreman, R. 29
Herrero-Jiménez, B. 162
Herrmann, L. K. 78
heterocentricism 123
heterogeneity 27, 122, 126, 131, 146, 163
hetero-happiness 181
heteronormality 24, 81
hetero-normative 161, 166, 181
heteronormativity 3, 5, 25, 42, 47, 81, 86,
   88, 89, 95, 97, 122, 124, 179, 186;
   heteronormative sexualities 88–9; sex toys
   and 86–97
heteropatriarchy 125, 164
heterosexual 28, 42–3, 48–9, 51, 81, 87–9,
   95, 122, 153, 155–6, 162–5, 169, 182,
   192, 200
Higgs, P. 138, 142, 195, 200
Hilton-Morrow, W. 24, 34
Hinchliff, S. 197, 198
Hispanic boys 161
HIV/AIDS 5, 75–87, 164; *Bohemian
   Rhapsody* (2018) and Pride (2014) 80–2;
   conflictive representations of a cultural
   trauma 75–83; HIV-positive population
   75, 80; HIV-related stigma in European
   cinema 5, 75–85; identity, stigma and
   health 77–8; people living with HIV
   (PLWH) 75–7, 82; *Theo et Hugo dans le
   même bateau* (2016) and *Drole de Félix*
   (2000) 78–80; undetectability, era of
   82–3
Hoffman, Dustin 179
Hollywood 120, 121, 178–9, 184–5
Holt, E. 27
homelessness 166, 169–70
homoeroticism 153
homophobia 19, 30, 37, 163–4, 166–7
homosexuality 28–9, 32–6, 88, 107, 154,
   162–4, 168, 170–1

homosocial males 155
hooks, b. 51
hormones 129, 157; blockers 121, 129–30;
   hormonal transition 6, 47, 119, 121, 127,
   129, 130; hormone replacement therapy
   (HRT) 127
hospitals 66, 79, 129
hostility 100, 108, 126
housewives 139–41, 176, 183
Howard, G. 138
Hubbard, P. 93–4
Hudnall Stamm, B. 80
Huemmer, J. 162
humiliation 152, 156, 199
Hummert, M. L. 137, 141
humour 14, 16–20, 46, 138, 142–3, 183
Hunt, T. A. 11
hustlers 7, 161, 163, 165–71
hyper-muscularity 7, 161, 165
hyperbole 149, 152, 155, 158–9, 165, 196
hysteria 87

immigration 100, 128, 163, 168
immorality 61, 129, 169
inclusivity 95, 97
Independent Press Standards Organisation
   (IPSO) 185
indie pornography 198
industrial society 64, 191
inequality: social 11, 12, 166
influencers: social media 18
informational categories 28, 47, 50
information-seeking 54
innuendos: sexual 46
institutionalisation of feminism 13
interdisciplinary approach 163
intergenerational relationships 119, 121,
   127, 150, 152; queering 127
inter-generational sex 154
International Covenant on Civil and
   Political Rights (ICCPR) 100
International Women's Day 11
internationalisation of television 37
intersectionality 2, 11, 89, 97, 182
intersubjectivity 54
intolerance 100
invisibility: theme of 7, 18, 24, 30, 37, 130,
   142, 161, 162, 164, 166, 168–70;
   invisible aged femininities 135–43
Iranian-American productions 121
Ireland 3, 4, 24–30, 34–5, 37, 38, 40;
   LGBT+ representation in Irish children's
   television 24, 39 see also LGBT+
   representation
irony 16, 18–20

Italy 3, 5, 41, 43–6, 48, 50–2, 63, 66, 178;
   sex information and the internet 41–54
   see also youth
Ito, M. 62
ITV (TV Channel) 27

Jablonski, R. A. 163, 172
Jackson, S. 61
Jacobs, K. 192, 198
James Bond 184
Japanese rape porn 150
Jenkins, J. 191
Jennings, R. 138, 142, 177
Jensen, H. S. 24, 25
Jeremy, Ron 152–3
Jermyn, D. 177, 179, 180
Jerslev, A. 14, 136, 140–1, 183
Johnson, J. 193
jokes 17, 46, 69
Jones, J. 165
Jönson, H. 162
Jouët, J. 12, 14, 16–19
journalism 11, 18, 102–5, 107, 113, 115,
   147–8, 185
Juffer, J. 87
juvenile deviance 61; see also youth
Jyrkinen, M. 168

Kansteiner, W. 80, 84
Kate Spade (brand) 180
Katsarova, I. 178
Katz, A. 95
Katz, S. 138, 140, 164, 195, 198
Kaziaj, E. 6, 100, 102, 104–8, 110, 112,
   114, 116, 118
Keaton, Diane 184
Keeler, L. 168
Keller, J. 13–14, 17–18
Kelly, D. 151
Kelly, J. J. 161, 164
Kelly, M. 78
Kelso, T. 24, 31
Kennedy-Hendricks, A. 78
Kerrigan, P. 4, 24, 26–8, 30, 32, 34, 36–8
Kessler, E. M. 177
KETNET (TV channel) 27, 29–34
Kidman, Nicole 178, 184, 186
Kies, B. 24
KiKa 25
Kimmel, M. S. 161
King, A. 64, 71
kink community 95
Kinkly 95
Kinsler, J. J. 76, 79
kissing 31, 37, 169, 196

Knauer, N. J. 163
Kochman, A. 79, 84
Koepnick, L. 126
Kolnai, A. 151, 159
Kovačič, M. P. 101
Krainitzki, E. 1
Krekula, C. 2
Krijnen, T. 1
Krippendorf, K. 106, 117
Krotz, F. 68
Kubey, R. 136, 141
Kuhar, R. 161
Kulick, D. 154

L'Oreal (brand) 135, 181
labour market 12
Lacy, S. 135, 136
Lancaster, R. N. 169
Lange, Jessica 184
Langman, L. 196
language: advertising 181; English-language
    programming 37; hate speech 102–16;
    medical 48; regional 27; sexist 101
Lapsi.al 105, 107–9, 111
Latvia 178
Lauzen, M. M. 178
Lawrence, E. 12, 14–16, 18–19
Lazarus, J. V. 76
Leccardi, C. 43
Lee, R. S. 79
legislation 11, 42, 93–4, 100, 103, 110, 113
Lehman, P. 190, 199
Leider, J. 76, 79
Leidner, D. E. 19
leisure 5, 60–2, 64, 69
Lekas, H.-M. 76, 79
Lemish, D. 1
lesbianism 32, 34–8, 81, 130, 156, 163, 165
Lesbians and Gays Support the Miners
    (LGSM) movement 81
Levi, J. 75, 84
Levinson, R. 176
Lewis, D. C. 33, 34, 141
LGB 44, 49
LGBT 4, 24–32, 34, 35, 37–9, 50, 90; rights
    activists 81
LGBT+ representation: Flemish and Irish
    children's television 24–39; LGBT+
    characters in Flemish domestic youth
    fiction programming since 1999 **32–3**;
    LGBT+ characters in youth fiction
    programming broadcast in Ireland since
    1992 **35–6**; LGBT+ portrayals in
    21st-century youth programming 30–7;
    LGBT+ televisibility in 20th-century

youth programming 28–30; youth
    programming in Flanders and Ireland
    26–8
LGBTI community 105, 113–14
LGBTQ community 53, 87, 95, 120, 171
LGMS 81–2
liberal attitudes 12, 87
liberalisation: sexual 87–8
libido: sexual 52, 92
Lieberman, H. 87
Lien, S. C. 137
lifestyle 5, 62, 81, 93, 137–8, 146, 148,
    166, 182
Lillian, D. 101, 115
Linehan, H. 27, 37
linguistics 27, 110, 121; see also language
Linneman, T. J. 161
literacy 19, 42–3, 48–9, 52, 70, 155, 159
Livingstone, S. 2, 59, 63–4, 68
Lizardo, E. 161
Lloyd, M. 89
Lobe, B. 44
lockdown: COVID-19 pandemic 5, 58, 61–9
logos 88
Londo, I. 103–5
loneliness 161, 163, 166
longitudinal analysis 176, 178
lookism 164
Lovascio, S. 95
love 34, 59, 76, 79, 93, 135, 151, 163, 179,
    180, 197
Love, Brandi 197, 198
Lovelock, M. 120, 128
Lövgren, K. 137, 144
Lozano, T. 16–17
Luketic, R. 135
'luminosity' of feminism 12–13
Lumley, Joanna 136
Lumme-Sandt, K. 182
Lupton, D. 76
luxury brands 94, 136, 141, 180
Lykke, N. 2
Lynch, Edmund 38

MacGregor, C. 177
machismo 19
macho discourse 17
MacKinnon, C. 115
MacNeela, P. 155
Madonna 179
magazines 14, 28, 139, 142, 180, 182
Maina, G. 191, 192
Maines, R. P. 87
male bodies: 'old gay' 163–6
Malek, Rami 81

manga 157
'man-haters' 19
Mantilla, K. 19
marginalisation 29, 89, 154, 165
Marinho, S. 43, 55
marital intercourse 88, 156
marketing 86–7, 89–90, 93–4, 96–7
Markovitz, J. C. 75
Markula, P. 95
Marmocchi, P. 43
marriage 37, 62, 109–10, 140, 153, 164, 169; equality referendum 37
Marshall, B. L. 138, 140, 164, 178, 181–2, 195, 198
Marshall, D. 24
Martin, A. 24, 88, 90, 94
Martin Hernández, R. 76
Martineau, J. 79, 80
Marttila, A. M. 168
Masanet, M. J. 60
masculinity 19, 45, 51, 95, 138, 150–1, 162, 165–6, 169, 196
masking of ageing discourse 139, 140, 142
masochism 199
masturbation 90–1, 93, 150, 154, 158, 199
materiality of bodies 121, 124, 151
Matsuda, M. 101
McCleerey, M. 81
McGinty, E. E. 78
McIntosh, M. 67
McKee, A. 147, 158
McLean, J. 11
McRobbie, A. 12, 15, 17
Meanley, S. 82
'mediaworld': realworld versus 176
medication 75, 79–80, 155
Medvedev, K. 141
Mehta, Deepa 178
melodrama genre 76
memes 18, 20
memetic communication 20
memory 29, 80
Mendes, K. 13–14, 17
Méndez, Z. 16–17
Mendieta-Izquierdo, G. 168
menopause 140–2, 179
menstrual cycles 128
mental health 75
Mercer, J. 166
merchandise: sex 93–5, 169; *see also* sex toys
Mercury, Freddy 81–2
Messina, S. 199
Mestre-Bach, G. 66
#MeToo campaign 4, 14, 184
Metro 62, 65, 68

Michelangelo: *David* 164
micro-celebrities 13–14
micro-porn spaces 198
middle classes 37, 44, 94, 165, 200
middle-aged cohort 192, 197, 199
midlife women 197–8, 200
migrants 100, 105, 166, 168–9, 171
Mihajllova, E. 104–5
MILF ('mother I'd like to fuck') 146, 190, 197
Miller, D. J. 59
Miller, K. 184
Miller, W. I. 151
Millward, L. 78
Milner, J. 137
Miltner, K. M. 13, 17
Mindgeek 66, 192
minorities 1, 42, 100, 105, 117, 162, 171
Mirren, Helen 136, 175, 181, 184, 186
misinformation 101
misogyny 13, 15–17, 19–20, 22, 101, 118
Mocarski, R. 120
mocking 46, 53, 143, 196
modernisation of sexuality 86, 97
Mohseni, M. R. 12, 20
montage: video 16
Montemurro, B. 2
Montiel, A. V. 1
Moore, Demi 179
morality 69, 87, 123, 151
Moran, K. 26
Moran, M. 101
Morina, F. 107, 109
Morrison, M. A. 52
Morrison, T. G. 52
mortality of human bodies 151
motherhood 140
Motörhead (rock band) 88
Mountz, A. 168
Mourinho 109
Mowlabocus, S. 41
MSM ('men who have sex with men') 76
Mulholland, M. 88, 89, 94
multidisciplinary approach 75
Munt, S. R. 24
murder (domestic) 114
muscle-building 164–5
muscular bodies 95, 149, 151–2, 164–5, 167
music 29, 30, 170, 178
myths 17, 179

Nachescu, V. 162, 167
nakedness 79, 95, 125, 139, 199
naming practices 108–9
Nash, J. C. 89

Nash, M. 140
nastiness 152
nationalism 100
nationality 101, 113–14, 123, 149, 166–7
necrophilia 153
Needham, G. 79
Neefs, Louis 29
neoconservatism 13, 19–20
neoliberalism 12–14, 18–19, 65, 66, 68–70,
    138, 142, 181; neoliberal
    responsibilisation 65, 68, 70
Netflix 120, 136, 177
Netherlands 3, 27, 137
Neville, L. 158
Newcomb, R. 167
newsgroups 200
newspapers 58, 62, 196
Nichols, B. 78
Nickelodeon 31
Nicols, Mike 179
Nikanda, P. 2
Nikunen, K. 71
NIR 38
Nixon, P. G. 5, 86, 88, 90, 92, 94,
    96, 98
Nogueira, C. 43
Nolen-Hoeksema, S. 78
non-binary gender identification 38, 127
non-Christian 168
non-cisgender 25, 120, 123
non-commercial films 130, 153
non-conforming gender identity 120,
    130–1, 138
non-consensual sexual content 66–7
non-consent 157
non-discriminatory reporting 103
non-fiction programming 25, 29
non-gendered couples 95
non-hegemonic sexuality 53
non-heteronormative sexuality 5
non-heterosexual people/characters 25, 29,
    31, 34, 50, 81, 95, 120, 123, 168
non-normative bodies and identities 42, 59,
    89, 148–9, 194, 200
non-scripted television shows 120
normalcy: concept of 81, 129, 159
normalisation of sexual consumption 88,
    90, 120
normativity 45, 124–5, 169, 194
Norton, M. 137
Norway 25, 31
NSPCC (National Society for the
    Protection of Cruelty to Children) 64
Nubiles Porn Network 197
nuclear family 124

nurseries 64

O'Neil, M. 68
objectification 67, 115, 164
Odello, L. 192
offensive behaviour and language 68, 69,
    104, 110, 152
Ogas, O. 41
Ólafsson, K. 52
Olshansky, J. 143
omnipresent discourse 139, 140, 142
Ondigital 175
opera-singing 29
orgasms 48, 87, 90, 92, 152, 154, 157
orgies 154
Ornaghi, V. 46
Oró-Piqueras, M. 138, 142
Oscar award ceremonies 81, 135, 184
osteoporosis 75
'otherness' 67, 137, 158, 192–3

Paasonen, S. 6, 7, 41, 59, 146, 148–52,
    154–6, 158, 191, 195
Padovani, C. 1
paedophilia 30
Pais, J. M. 44
Palmero, G. 13
pandemics see COVID-19 pandemic; HIV/
    AIDS
paraphilia 48
Parekh, B. 109
parents, role of 127–9; parental mediation
    64, 65
parody 20, 140, 143
parsing online information 48–9
Parsons, J. T. 82
Pascoe, C. J. 46
Pascoe, J. 61
Pastor-Ruiz, Y. 13
Patel, R. R. 82
paternalism 27
Paterson, R. 66
patriarchy 14, 16, 95
Pauwels, C. 30
PCmag.com 69
pedagogy 6, 43, 119–31; films as queer
    pedagogical devices 121–4
peers 45–7, 68, 125, 127, 151, 161
penises 51, 87, 91, 96, 125, 129, 199
Pérez Riedel, M. 6, 119, 120, 122, 124,
    126, 128, 130
Pérez-Torres, V. 13
performativity 123
Perkins, C. 138
perverse amateurs 196–200; see also age

'perverts' 149, 163, 166
Petersen, L. N. 136–7, 142
Peterson, M. 1, 176
Petrich, K. 24
Peyrefitte, M. 95
phallic: hysterics 165; instruments 87, 91, 96; power 196, 200; see also sex toys
phallocentric sexuality 169
phallogocentric hegemonic medical model 124
phallus 165, 192
Piha, S. 89, 93
Pilcher, J. 62
pimps 170
Pinto, D. 101
plagiarism 104, 106–7
Platero, L. 19
Plummer, K. 42, 51
Pocius, J. 77
podcasts 146, 147
police 37, 81, 82, 108–10, 122
policymaking 61, 68
populist movements 20
Pornhub 5, 58, 62–3, 66–9, 155, 190–2, 197
pornification of culture 66, 89
pornography 190–201: addition to 62; ageing body in contemporary pornography 191–3; amateur 166, 190–3, 196, 199; anti-porn arguments 67; corporate 191–2, 194–5, 197–9; cyber- 202; demonisation of 66; fantasies 146–59; grandpa 195–8, 200; granny 193–5, 200; hardcore 151; indie 198; Japanese rape 150; micro-porn spaces 198; prosumers of 192; revenge 66–7; social media and 146; taxonomies 155–8
Porras Sánchez, M. 7, 161, 162, 164, 166, 168, 170, 172
Porrovecchio, A. 44, 46
Portmann, J. 69
Portugal 3, 5, 41, 43–50, 52; sex information and the internet 41–54; see also youth
Pöschl, S. 90
post-communist societies 167
post-feminism 12–13, 15, 18, 138–40, 142, 180
post-Soviet Europe 162
post-structuralism 4
Potter, J. 63, 164
poverty 166, 182
power relations: asymmetry of 156
pranking 69
predators: fear of 63–6

pregnancy 43, 47, 51, 53, 116
prejudice 49, 194
prime-time television 66, 137
privacy: protection of 45, 65, 68
productivity: value of 137
produsage practices 12–13
professional-amateurs (pro-am) 192
propaganda 101
prosocial discourses 25, 28–30, 38
prosthetics 48, 150
prostitution 7, 161–3, 166–71; male scene 168–70
prosumers of porn 192
protests 16, 19, 108–9, 111
Provencher, D. M. 80
Pruchniewska, U. M. 16, 18
pseudoscience 181
psychoanalysis 1, 7
psychology 77, 129–30, 153, 163–4
Pua, P. 186
puberty 121, 130
public service broadcasting (PSB) 4, 5, 25–6, 28, 29, 31, 34, 38
Pugh, S. 165, 172
puritanism: moral 43
purity reform movement (19th century) 61

Quadara, A. 59
quantitative data analysis 5, 6, 97, 102, 105–6, 148, 178, 192
quarantine 5, 58, 62–3, 66; see also COVID-19 pandemic; lockdown
queer community 4, 24–5, 31, 38, 49, 120–1, 123–5, 154, 158, 165, 193
queering 24, 95, 127; intergenerational relationships 127
queerness 28–9, 38
questionnaires 91, 147–8

Raats, T. 30
Rabelaisian character 182, 188
race 80, 89, 97, 100, 101, 103, 123, 149, 163, 166, 170, 182, 190, 200
racial: ageing bodies 200; bias 123, 130; epithets 69; hatred 100; stereotypes 168, 182
racism 101, 108, 111, 116, 117, 149, 168, 182
radical feminism 16, 67
radio 38, 105
Rahman, M. 138, 178, 182
raids see 'zoombombing'
Rama, Edi 107, 109, 116
rape: culture 14; porn scenes 150, 156–7; taboo fantasies 153

Raphael, A. 195
Rappler 64, 65
Raun, T. 1
'realcore' 199
'realworld': mediaworld vs 176
Reeve, P. 170
referenda: on marriage equality 37
refugees 169
Reik, T. 199
religion 101, 103, 163; beliefs 103;
    communities 105; hatred 100;
    organisations 163; settings 83;
    symbolism 154
Renaissance period 164
Rendina, H. J. 82
Rentschler, C. 18, 19
reproductive system 45
repulsiveness 7, 146, 156, 157, 171; *see also*
    disgust
responsibilisation: neoliberal 65, 68, 70
Retallack, H. 14–15
revanchist scenarios 196, 200
revenge porn 66–7
Richardson, J. E. 105, 108
Ricoeur, P. 163
Riedel, M. P. 6, 119–20, 122, 124, 126,
    128, 130
right-wing political parties 13, 20
Ringrose, J. 12–19
risk-averse online culture 64, 68
Ritterfeld, U. 78
Robards, B. 158
Robinson, J. D. 176
Robinson, K.-H. 42
robotic-partnered sex 91
rock bands 81, 88
Rodriguez, N. S. 161
Röhm, A. 78
Roma community 105
romance: discourses of 79, 170, 179;
    romantic storylines 31, 34, 140, 180, 184
Romania 162, 167, 169
Romany 163
Rooke, A. 151
Rose, N. 61, 64, 72
Rosenberger, J. G. 86
Rosón, M. 19
Rosow, I. 190
Ross, K. 1, 3, 7, 142, 175–6
Rothmann, J. 166
Rottenberg, C. 18
Rotter, A. J. 126
Royal Society for Public Health 185
Rozanova, J. 137

RTÉ (Raidió Teilisfis Eireann) 25–30, 35,
    37–9
Rubin, G. 88, 152–4
rule-breaking behaviour 140
Russia 162, 167
Russo, V. 30
Ryan, B. 165

sadomasochism 166
safeguarding 65, 68
safety: online 53, 64, 68
same-sex desire 25, 29, 31, 34, 38, 81
Sandberg, L. 2
Sanders-McDonagh, E. 95
Sandfort, T. 167
sarcasm 17–19, 20
satire 143
saunas 168
Scarcelli, C. M. 1, 5, 41–2, 47, 60
Scharagrodsky, P. 6, 119–20, 122, 124, 126,
    128, 130
Schatzberg, E. 87
Schatzki, T. 64–5, 70
Schilt, K. 88–9
school 45–6
Screen Actors Guild Awards 178, 184
Screenshot magazine 58
Segal, L. 67
self-esteem 82, 170
self-expression 199–200
self-identity 62, 177
selfies 13
self-regulation 5, 58, 61–2, 67, 70, 102
Sellars, A. F. 101, 118
Selmer, A. 5, 86, 88, 90, 92, 94, 96
semiotics: visual 163
Seponski, D. M. 141
serials: historical 29
sex boutiques 94
sex industry 87
sex information: young people in Italy and
    Portugal 41–54
sex retailing 90, 93–4, 97
sex shops 90, 93–5; as 'oases of ugliness'
    93–4; 'upscale' 94; women-focused 90, 94
sex toys 5–6, 86–98, 147, 153–4;
    consumption, upscaling of 94; designs
    90–1; distribution and consumption,
    patterns of 90; embracing sexual and bodily
    diversity 95–7; feminine sexualities 94;
    heteronormativity and age 86–97;
    integration into sexual practice 92; origins
    of 87; sex toy market 92–4
sex wars (1980s) 67

sexism 14, 15, 17–20, 90, 101, 114–15, 141, 149, 151, 184–5, 194
sexology 199
'sexperts' 200
sexting 59, 60
sexual orientation 3, 44, 52, 103
sexualization of infancy 42
Shapiro, T. 48
Shea, H. 80
Sheehan, H. 27
Shelton, E. 152–3
shopping online 93
Shove, E. 60, 65–6, 70
showbiz 114, 116
Shqiptarja.com 105, 107–11
Siegel, K. 76, 79
Signorile, M. 164–5
Sikes, A. W. 167
Sikkema, K. J. 79
'silver' generation 175, 179, 180; see also age
'silver tsunami' 136
Simbayi, L. 79
Simona, F. 101, 115
Singh, V. 101
singing 115
sitcoms 29, 31–2, 34, 37, 138, 179, 183
Siverskog, A. 162
Sky 35, 37
slacktivism 19
Slater, D. 61, 70
Slevin, K. F. 161
Slovenia 101
Smahel, D. 48
Smith, C. 1, 91, 93–5, 158, 194–5
Smith, S. L. 177–8
soap operas 25, 32–5, 37, 138, 186–7
social hygiene movement 164
social justice 148
social media: celebrity platforms 107, 112, 115; humour, types of 20; online sexual abuse and 58–9, 68; pornography 146; sexual liberalisation and 87; as a space of awareness and self-reflection 14–16; as a space for youth interaction 61; see also Facebook; Twitter; YouTube
socialisation 14, 41, 65
Socialist Party 116
socio-historical approach 6–7, 76
sociocultural trends 5, 38, 59, 86, 142
socioeconomic approaches 7, 163, 191, 197
sociological studies 4, 43, 59, 77
sodomy 166
Sorrentino, P. 135
Sosa Valcárcel, A. 11
sovereignty 192–3

Soviet Union 162, 166
Spain 3, 4, 11–21, 40, 63, 66, 84; feminist YouTubers 11–21
spanking 90
speeches 183
spirituality 163
SPSS software 106
Stald, G. 41
state interventions 64, 66
Steenburgen, Mary 184
Stella, R. 199
Stenvoll, D. 168
stepmom videos 146, 197–8
stepsons 197
stereotyping 77, 120, 138, 176
stigmatization 5, 11, 75–83, 89, 125, 163–4, 167–9, 195, 197; HIV/AIDS related see HIV/AIDS
STIs (sexually transmitted infections) 53
Stolpe, J. 190
stranger danger 63–5, 70, 99, 159, 182; strangers online 59, 63
Štulhofer, A. 167
subcultures 199
subjecthood: sexual 89, 97
subjectivity 53, 120, 122, 126, 128, 177, 192–3
Suen, Y. T. 164–5
superfoods 181
surgery 128, 180; gender confirmation 121, 128; plastic 135, 139
surveillance society 64
Swank, E. 90, 94
Sweden 176–8
'swiping left' see singles dating apps
symbolism 154
Symes, K. 120
Szostak, N. 14, 16
Sztompka, P. 80

taboo 7, 88–9, 93, 150, 152–5, 157–8, 162, 198; age differences and porn 153–5
Taggart, T. 77
tags 155
Taiwan 137
Takács, J. 161
tattoos 95
technology: online discursive strategies 11; of the self 44, 52–3, 60, 63, 69; sexual see sex
toys; technologization of sex 87
Tel-A-Friend 29
teledildonics 86, 91
Telegraph, The 62, 65, 184
televisibility 4, 25–31, 34, 38

teleworking 58
testicles: surgical removal of 48
testimonies 53, 122
testosterone 48, 127–9, 150
Thatcher, Margaret 81
theatres 121, 168
third-age discourse 141, 177, 182
third-wave feminism 12
Thompson, M. 41
Thompson, N. L. 165
Thorfinnsdottir, D. 24–5
'threesomes' 197
Thrift, S. 18–19
Ticknell, E. 2
TikTok 69
TimesUp 14
Tincknell, E. 137, 141, 182
Tinder 88, 180
titillation 149, 153–4, 157–8
Tomkins, S. S. 151–2, 154
Tomlin, Lily 136
Tortajada, I. 2, 4, 11–16, 18, 20, 22, 138
Towanda Rebels 12, 14–19
toxic youth and sexuality 63, 66, 68–70; see
    also COVID-19 pandemic
trans folks 6, 13, 34, 37, 119–31
transfeminists: radical 16
transgender people 6, 119–21, 125, 127–31,
    155, 168
trans-Hispanic community 130
transnationality 11
transnormativity 120
transsexuality 107
transvestites 169
trauma: cultural 5, 75, 76, 78, 80–3, 157
Treas, J. 167
Trentmann, F. 65
trolling: internet 20, 101
Trump, Donald 107
trust: relationships of 13, 46–7,
    78, 82
truth 42, 53, 122–3, 129, 183
Tsaliki, L. 42, 46, 52, 59–61, 63–4,
    66, 69, 151
Tulloch, J. 76
Tumblr 182
Turan, J. M. 79
TV Gaga 28, 38
Twigg, J. 136, 142, 164, 181, 189
Twitch 69
Twitter 20, 101

ugliness 8, 125, 129, 150–2, 196
Ukraine 165, 167, 169
uncle figure 149, 156

underage transgender characters 6,
    119–21, 128
Undetectable = Untransmittable (U = U)
    initiative 82–3, 85
unfair treatment 79, 123, 125
United Kingdom (UK) 42, 62, 175–8
United States (US) 24–5, 31, 38, 41, 101,
    123, 131, 176–9, 183, 197–8, 200
unity among women 11
urination 154
users: engagement in different countries 67;
    premium accounts 66; producers and 13;
    profiling of 41; segmentation 92; user
    guides 50

Vaakakapina ('Scale Revolt') 146–7
Valcárcel, S. 11
Valkenburg, P. M. 41
Van Bauwel, S. 1, 6, 12–13, 24,
    135–42, 183
Van den Bulck, H. 190, 198
Van der Veur, D. 167
van Dijk, T. A. 106, 109
Van Selm, M. 137
Vance, D. E. 163
vanity 181
Vanlee, F. 4, 24–8, 30–2, 34, 36, 38
Varela, I. 12, 14, 18–20
Varjakoski, H. 138
Veliaj, E. 109, 110
Velvet Revolution (1989) 167
venereal illness 45
verbal aggression 20
Vermicelli, A. 29, 39
Vernon, J. A. 176
Viacom 31
vibrators 87–8, 90–91; see also sex toys
victims: of hate speech 105, 113, 114; of
    racial bias 130; of sexual abuse 58
Victorian period 61, 69
video-sharing platforms 67
video-teleconferencing (VTC) platforms 68
Vieira, P. 43
vignettes 197
VIJF 31
Villanueva Baselga, S. 5, 83
violence: in film-making 125; gender-based
    and sexual 4, 11, 18, 87; hate speech and
    100–2, 106–8; offline 18; online 12, 18;
    portrayals in youth programming 27;
    sexist 14, 19
viral messages 20
virginity 156, 197
virility discourse 138, 164
virtual spaces 162, 168

viruses 58, 75, 76, 81, 82; *see also* coronavirus; COVID-19 pandemic; HIV/AIDS
visual semiotics 163
vomiting 154
voyeurism 149, 153
VRT (Flemish PBS) 25–30, 34, 38
VTM Kids 31, **33**
vulnerability 104, 127, 150; vulnerable groups 131, 164, 166, 168; of women 101, 115

Wagner, M. 91
Walker, A. 177
Wallander, K. 137–8, 141
Walters, S. D. 34
Warchus, M. 81
Warner, M. 24, 154
Warwick University 68
water-sports 156
Waterston, Sam 135
webcam sex 59
Weeks, J. 169
welfare state 66, 136
wellbeing 58, 61, 64, 129, 141, 146, 185
Wernick, A. 195
Westbrook, L. 88, 89
Westerhof, G. 137
Wetherell, M. 63
Whelehan, I. 136, 137, 139–41, 194
Whitaker, H. 184
White, R. 138
whiteness 169–71
Whitford, G. S. 163
Widmer, E. D. 167
Wikipedia 18
Wilde, O. 165
Wilińska, M. 2, 8
Willem, C. 2, 4, 11–16, 18, 20, 138, 142
Williams, B. 177
Williams, L. 160, 190, 192
Wilson, A. 87
Wilson, S. 140
Wilson, W. C. 41
Winskell, K. 83
wisdom 136, 139, 141–2, 198
wives 110
Wohlmann, A. 138, 144

womanhood 6, 7, 127
Wood, M. J. 164
Woodward, C. 139
Woodward, K. 140, 164, 193–4
working-classes 30, 65, 200
workplace 1, 83, 87
World War II: post-war period 87
wrinkles 149, 152, 180–1, 183, 193–5, 198
'writings with such content, by any means or forms' 103
wrong body discourse 119–20, 128, 130
WtFOCK (web series) 31, 33–4
Wuhan region (China) 63

xenophilia 168
xenophobia 67, 100–1, 168
XFC INC 197
xHamster 155
Xvideos 155, 191–2, 199–200

Ylänne, V. 138, 177
YLE (Finnish broadcasting service) 146–7
Yoshida, E. 119, 128
Youngline 28
youth: curiosity 47; experiences versus information 50–1; gender and performance 51–2; internet potentials, affordances and challenges 47–52; self-knowledge 51–2; programming in Flanders and Ireland 24–39; sex information and the internet in Italy and Portugal 41–54; sex-related information, categories of 47–8; social groups 45–6; toxic 66–9 *see also* age; childhood sexuality; COVID-19 pandemic; LGBT+ representation; youthfulness 96, 165, 190, 194, 198
YouTube 4, 11–21, 69: Spanish feminist YouTubers 11–21; *see also* social media
Yves St Laurent 180

Zafra, R. 18
Zecca, F. 7, 190–2, 194, 196, 198–200, 202
Zeilig, H. 181, 188
Zhang, Y. B. 137, 141
'zoombombing' 5, 68–9
zoophilia 153